THE
POLITICAL SCANDALS

ACKNOWLEDGEMENTS

Corbis UK Ltd 43
Owen Franken 143 left
Hulton-Deutsch Collection 34, 88, 101, 123
Katherine Kamow 129
Corbis-Bettmann 23, 61, 68, 93, 106, 109, 143 right
Hulton Getty Picture Collection 83, 112, 138
Rex Features 103, 115
N. Jorgensen 27

THE WORLD'S GREATEST
POLITICAL SCANDALS

Nigel Cawthorne

CHANCELLOR
PRESS

This 1999 edition published by Chancellor Press,
an imprint of Bounty Books, a division of
Octopus Publishing Group Ltd.,
2–4 Heron Quays, London E14 4JP

Reprinted 2002

ISBN 0 75370 086 7

A CIP catalogue record for this book is available from
the British Library

Printed in England by Mackays of Chatham

Contents

Introduction

New Labour came into power in Britain in 1997 with a squeaky clean image. Within months, Foreign Secretary Robin Cook, while pursuing an ethical foreign policy, was found to be shacked up at home with his secretary. Under instructions from the Prime Minister's press secretary, Alistair Campbell, he dumped his long-standing wife, Margaret, and married his lovely mistress Gaynor.

Eighteen months in, the government had its first casualty. Welsh Secretary Ron Davis resigned after an incident on Clapham Common that had nothing to do with a homosexual pick-up. It was merely an error of judgement.

Next, the Agriculture Secretary Nick Brown was outed, as was the Trade Secretary Peter Mandelson – although the BBC was not allowed to say so. Everyone held their breath, expecting another outing not a million miles away from Number 10.

Wronged wife and woman scorned, Margaret Cook then savaged the errant Foreign Secretary with a scandalous autobiography, but she failed to damage him politically. In fact, Cook benefited from what has become known as the 'Clinton effect'. Suddenly the cheating Foreign Secretary's approval rating shot up in the polls. Before Margaret Cook's blistering attack he had been dismissed as a ginger-bearded gnome. Afterwards, people suddenly saw the mischievous twinkle in his eye. *Sun* readers said they wanted to go to bed with him. He was Lothario who could down a bottle of brandy in one go and still bed 12 mistresses.

There was a minor 'cash-for-access' scandal, then along came the big sleaze. Peter Mandelson, the spin doctor responsible more than anyone for the election of New Labour, had borrowed £375,000 from Paymaster-General, Geoffrey Robinson, the very man his department was investigating for irregularities over off-shore funds. They both resigned, soon to be followed by Treasury spin doctor, Charlie Whelan, who was thought to have leaked the story on the orders of Chancellor of the Exchequer, Gordon Brown, as part of a vendetta against Mandelson. The Blair government seemed to be living up to the dizzying standards of its predecessors. Meanwhile, the Tories were trying to clean up their act when Conservative MEP Tom Spencer was caught smuggling drugs and gay porn into the country.

At least Tony Blair can stand tall though. His international reputation for integrity was bolstered by his close relationship with... President Clinton.

But then, politics and scandal have always gone hand in hand. Even before he came to power Hitler covered up an incestuous affair with his niece, who was murdered when she tried to finish with him. Five of his lovers committed suicide in revulsion at his perverted sexual demands.

Karl Marx escaped scandal by a hair's-breadth, when his collaborator Friedrick Engels claimed the son Marx had fathered by his wife's maid as his own, confessing the truth only on his deathbed. And when Lenin was returned to Russia in the famous closed train to start on the revolution, with him were his wife and two of his lovers – one of whom went on to become the mistress of Mussolini.

The most prolific lover of the political world was Mao Tse-tung. Into his 80s, he would fill the swimming pool in the Forbidden City with naked 18-year-old girls and go for a dip.

Scandalous though this behaviour may seem, these were not proper scandals because the stories did not come out during the protagonists' lifetimes. This book contains the stories of a few characters who got found out.

1 ❖ Zippergate

The story of President Clinton and his peccadilloes was the political scandal of the 20th century. Although President Nixon would have been impeached if he had not resigned following the Watergate scandal, Bill Clinton continued to tough it out – even after finding himself the first president to be impeached since Andrew Johnson, who was tried by the Senate in 1868.

Interestingly, like Clinton, Johnson was accused of adultery. But the substantive charge that brought him to an unprecedented two-month trial was violation of the Tenure of Office Act, which was designed to stop the President sacking Northern carpetbaggers who had seized Federal posts in the South under the authority of Congress after the Civil War. Johnson, a Southerner, sought reconciliation between the states and refused to accept the act. He caused a scandal by defying Congress and sacking the Secretary of War, Edwin Stanton.

When Stanton refused to stand down, Congress rallied around him and Johnson found himself the first president to be impeached. Although Johnson was a Republican, it was the Republicans who were out to get him. Abraham Lincoln had been a Republican and the Republicans on Capitol Hill were vehemently opposed to Johnson's kid-glove treatment of the defeated Confederacy.

The newspapers vilified Johnson as 'the Great Criminal' and accused him of everything up to, and including, being one of the conspirators in the plot to assassinate Lincoln – and, of course, adultery. Illinois senators were warned that if they voted for acquittal, they would be hanged when they returned home. And the mistress of Kansas Senator Robert Ream was told that if she had any influence on him, she had better use it to get him to vote to convict.

Johnson acted with great decorum throughout the Senate trial. He held himself above the fray, refusing to dignify the proceedings with his presence. The final vote was 35 to 19, just one vote short of the two-thirds majority required by the Constitution.

However, 1868 was an election year and Johnson lost any chance of a second term in the White House. He returned to his home state of Tennessee where he stood for election to Congress in 1870. He lost. He lost again in 1872, but was returned to the Senate in 1874, where he was warmly greeted by a number of senators who had voted for his conviction six years before.

Bill Clinton's impeachment also began with something more substantive than adultery. The investigation began with the appointment of a Special Prosecutor to look into a land deal, known as Whitewater. In August 1979, while Clinton was an Arkansas state attorney and campaigning for his first term as governor, Bill and Hillary Clinton bought 230 acres of river front land in the Ozark Mountains of northern Arkansas, which seemed prime for development. They paid no money. The deposit was provided by the couple's friends, Jim and Susan McDougal.

The land was never developed and the Clintons made no money out of the deal. However, some time later the McDougals' mortgage company ran into difficulties and the McDougals ended up in jail. It was discovered that the land had originally been sold at a very favourable price by a major logging company, which seemed to get an easy ride from Bill Clinton, who was in the governor's mansion. There were also allegations that Whitewater accounts were used to funnel money to Clinton's campaign funds.

Hillary Clinton's extraordinary success at commodities trading also came under investigation. Her activities at the Arkansas law firm of Rose Law, where she had worked on some of the McDougals' other dealings, came under scrutiny when her colleague there, Vince Foster, who had gone on to become a White House attorney, was found shot in the head in a park in Washington. The coroner's verdict was suicide, but many suspected that there was more to it. One persistent rumour was that Vince Foster and Hillary Clinton had been having an affair.

Hillary was also accused of illegally firing seven members of staff working in the White House travel office, replacing them with cronies from Arkansas. And the White House was accused of making illegal use of FBI files.

However, these cases were extraordinarily arcane and convoluted. They failed to catch the public's imagination and the investigation was getting nowhere until the Special Prosecutor got lucky. A young woman named Paula Jones sued Bill Clinton for sexual harassment. She alleged that while he was Governor of Arkansas, a state trooper had told her that the Governor wanted to see her and had taken her up to Clinton's hotel room. There, she said, Clinton had pulled out his penis and asked her to kiss it. She had declined. However, when the magazine *American Spectator* said that she had slept with Clinton, she brought suit against him for 'severe emotional distress' in an effort, she claimed, to clear her name.

Paula Jones had been a state employee at the time, so Clinton was her boss. If he had made any unwanted overture – particularly such a gross one – she had an open-and-shut case. But Clinton denied that any such incident had ever taken place.

The Special Prosecutor asked the Attorney General to extend his remit to investigate the Paula Jones case, on the grounds that he might be able to prove a pattern of lying that would be pertinent to the Whitewater affair. That Special Prosecutor was Ken Starr and he had been involved in the preparation of Paula Jones's suit.

It was no secret that Clinton was a womanizer. Born in Hope, Arkansas, in 1946, he had wanted to be a politician in the Kennedy mould, especially after meeting his hero in the White House when he was 13. While a Rhodes scholar at Oxford, he was such a fearless stud that he had propositioned arch-feminist Germaine Greer.

At Yale Law School, he met Hillary Rodham who shared his political ambitions. She went with him to Arkansas as his campaign manager in the 1974 congressional race. He lost.

While Hillary was running his campaign, Bill was having an affair with one of his other campaign workers. Nevertheless, Bill and Hillary were married in 1975 and she stood by him throughout six terms as Governor of Arkansas, although his extramarital affairs during that period are now the stuff of legend.

When Clinton decided to run for the presidency in 1992, his good looks and Kennedyesque charisma soon put him ahead of the field. And the rumours of his marital infidelity did him no harm. During the New Hampshire primary in February 1992, supermarket check-out scandal sheet *The Star* ran the banner headline, 'DEMS FRONT-RUNNER BILL CLINTON CHEATED WITH MISS AMERICA'.

It then went on to name five women whom Clinton was alleged to have slept with, including former Miss America and *Playboy* centrefold, Elizabeth Ward Gracen. Bill denied everything and the major newspapers dismissed the allegations as the 'unverified reports of supermarket tabloids'.

The Star hit back with 'MY 12-YEAR AFFAIR WITH BILL CLINTON'. This time it wheeled out former Little Rock night-club singer Gennifer Flowers. She was, in newspaper terms, the 'smoking bimbo'.

In an interview, she said: 'We made love everywhere, on the floor, in bed, in the kitchen, on the cabinet, the sink… I called his testicles "the boys" and he called my breasts "the girls".'

She also said that he once tried to have sex with her in the men's room in the governor's mansion while Hillary was entertaining on the lawn outside. He even used his jogging as cover – he jogged over to her apartment, made love to her and jogged home. That way, his being sweaty did not arouse Hillary's suspicions.

'I admired his stamina,' Flowers said, 'being able to make love with such enthusiasm after running. I used to tease him about running back much slower.'

Naturally the media loved such tales. In a press conference in 1992, one reporter brought the house down by asking Flowers: 'Did the Governor use a condom?'

Such salacious details were much more interesting to the general public than the political issues at stake in the election, and after a few queasy moments Clinton bounced back in the polls.

Soon his campaign team managed to turn his womanizing into an advantage. With consummate skill, they called the CBS and demanded the right to reply to Flowers' accusations on the network's prestigious *60 Minutes* programme. Their timing was perfect. Clinton got on the show directly after the Superbowl, guaranteeing a massive audience of slightly inebriated males. With Hillary beside him, Clinton admitted that there had been problems in their marriage. When asked whether that meant that he had committed adultery, Hillary answered coolly: 'People who have been married a long time know what it means.'

It was a riveting performance. In one fell swoop, the two of them blew every other candidate out of the water. Hillary made only one slight slip when she said that she was not there just to 'stand by my man like Tammy Wynette'. She later apologized to Tammy when the spin doctors realized they were in danger of losing the Country and Western vote.

Later, Clinton admitted to having smoked marijuana but 'he did not inhale'. Besides, he had done it while he was a student in England, so he had broken no American law. Not even his admission that he had dodged the draft during the Vietnam War prevented him from winning the 1992 presidential election. Committing adultery, smoking dope and dodging the draft actually endeared him to the baby boomers who now made up the bulk of the voters. However, these things alienated him from the old-fashioned religious right. This sector hated him with a passion and would do anything to bring him down.

Once Clinton was in the White House, the state troopers from Arkansas who had guarded him when he was governor, revealed that Clinton had had hundreds of women.

'There was hardly an opportunity he would let slip to have sex,' one said. This included being given oral sex by a woman in the back of a limousine in the parking lot of his daughter's school, while he was waiting to pick up his daughter, Chelsea.

Alleged lovers included the wife of a prominent judge, a local newspaper reporter, a former state employee, a sales clerk from the cosmetics counter at a Little Rock department store and a black prostitute named Bobbie Ann Williams. She claimed that Clinton had fathered her mixed-race child in one of their 13 sex sessions.

Sally Perduc, a former Miss Arkansas, claimed to have had an affair with Clinton in 1983, when she was a radio-show host in Little Rock. After the affair was over, she claimed a Democratic Party official had promised her a $40,000 job if she 'behaved like a good girl'. The implication was, she said, that otherwise she might get her legs broken.

Rock'n'roll groupie Connie Hamzy had a brush with Clinton. She told *Penthouse* magazine that a Clinton aide had approached her as she lay sunbathing by a swimming pool in a scanty bikini. She boasted that she had fondled the future president.

Blonde power-company executive Jo Jenkins denied having an affair with Clinton, but his phone record revealed that he telephoned her 11 times in one day. One of the calls, late at night, lasted 94 minutes. According to Gennifer Flowers' book, *Passion and Betrayal*, Clinton liked to indulge in mutual masturbation sessions while talking to his lover over the phone. Flowers said she had to fake it as telephone sex did not turn her on.

All these allegations did Clinton no harm. They merely enhanced his reputation as a stud. There has long been talk inside the Beltway that Bill and Hillary had made a pre-presidential pact long ago. She would stand by him and cover up for his womanizing, if he gave her a big job in government. When they got into the White House, she was put in charge of a revolutionary health-care plan that would give Americans a health service along the lines of Britain's NHS. However, right-wing Republicans characterized the Clinton health-care plan as a Communist plot and the insurance companies stumped up millions to run a series of TV commercials to protect the private system that brought them in a vast fortune each year. The health-care programme was soon in tatters and Hillary was out of a job.

The only real danger to Bill Clinton came from Paula Jones. She now had powerful backers, wealthy right-wing Republicans, and threatened to take him to court. The White House responded to her allegations by trying to trash her. Clinton's spin doctor, James Carville, called her 'trailer park trash'. The Republicans gave her a make-over and she pressed on.

She did not want money, she said. All she wanted was an apology. But for Clinton an apology would mean an admission. That was not a chance he was prepared to take. Jones upped the ante by promising the press certain salacious details that would make her case stand up in court. She could, she said, describe in detail some 'distinguishing characteristics' of Clinton's genitals. The media went wild with speculation about what these 'distinguishing characteristics' might be.

The White House tried to keep the lid on things by claiming that, as President, Clinton could not be taken to court while in office. That was a matter that had to be decided by the Supreme Court and, while waiting for their ruling, Clinton squeezed through the 1996 election. His Republican opponent, Bob Dole, could not make political capital out of Paula Jones's allegations. He could hardly play Mister Clean. He was a twice-married divorcé, who was guilty of a little intramarital shenanigans himself. Besides, he was as old as Father Time and dared not risk playing the sex card against a younger, demonstrably more virile man. Clinton may not have been able to keep it in his pants, but at least he could get it up.

In November 1996, the American people went to the polls and gave an overwhelming endorsement to adultery. The economy was booming and presidential peccadilloes did not hit the voters in the pocket. Besides, when Clinton turned on the charm, the country – like Hillary – would forgive him anything.

It did not work on the Supreme Court though. Even in the Paula Jones case, the justices argued that 'justice delayed is justice denied'. In America, they insisted, no one, not even the President, is above the law. A hearing in the Paula Jones case was set for May 1998.

The President's lawyer came close to stopping the lawsuit with an 11th hour comprise. Slick Willie, it seemed, was about to slide again. But, in hubris, a White House aide told CNN that Paula Jones was pulling out because she knew her case was hopeless.

Paula put her foot back on the gas and, for the first time, spoke of the President's genital peculiarity. When he had dropped his trousers and asked her to kiss his dick back in Little Rock, she said, it was erect – but bent. And she demanded $2 million for 'emotional distress'.

To limit the damage, Bill and Hillary took a romantic holiday for two in the Virgin Islands, of all places, along with half the world's press. The happy, if slightly overweight, couple were pictured dancing on the beach in their swimming costumes. This seemingly spontaneous act of affection was a carefully rehearsed photo opportunity.

Some commentators were taken in by the Caribbean idyll. It was said that Hillary was no longer faking it. She had actually fallen in love with the big lug again. But fate was closing in.

First, President Clinton was called to testify under oath in a six-hour closed-door hearing as part of the discovery phase of the Paula Jones case. Paula sat only feet away. Under tough cross-questioning by Jones's lawyer, Clinton was asked whether he had ever been in 'close proximity' to Paula. Clinton said he could not recall meeting her. He denied dropping his trousers and asking her to 'kiss it'. His attorney added: 'In terms of size, shape, and direction the President is a normal man,' although the attorney did not say how he knew this. The President was then cross-examined generally about his sex life.

Also called to give a deposition was a young woman named Monica Lewinsky. She had been an intern in the White House. She was asked whether she had had sexual relations with the President. This was relevant because, if Clinton had asked her for sex, it would show that he made a practice of importuning employees. Monica stoutly denied any such sexual relations had taken place.

One person who knew that this was not true was 48-year old Linda Tripp. She had been an aide in the Bush White House and had stayed on as one of the transitional team that smoothed the hand-over of power when Clinton entered the Oval Office. Her other claim to fame was that she had served Hillary's law partner, Vince Foster, his last hamburger before he committed suicide – or was ruthlessly gunned down by the Clintons' hired assassins, as right-wing conspiracy theorists were now saying.

A committed Republican, Tripp was no Clinton fan. She had already reported that she had seen another White House staffer, Kathleen Willey, leaving the Oval Office after an interview with Clinton 'flustered, happy and joyful... dishevelled, her face was red, her lipstick was off'. Willey refused to comment publicly and Tripp was denounced as a liar by the President's lawyers. Reluctantly, Willey was forced to make a deposition in the Paula Jones case. She later told all on TV. The President, she said, had placed her hand on his member. She was asked whether the Chief Executive had been aroused. 'Yes,' she said.

Linda Tripp did not like being called a liar and she was determined to get her own back. She already had another card up her sleeve. After she had left the White House, she had gone to work at the Pentagon. There, she befriended a young graduate named Monica Lewinsky, who had also transferred from the White House. In the powder room, Lewinsky revealed that she had pleasured the President in a small room off the Oval Office. This was the same room where a former president, Warren Harding, was caught *in flagrante* with young mistress Nan Britton by his wife.

Tripp consulted New York literary agent and long-time Clinton-baiter,

Lucienne Goldberg. Goldberg had been a $1,000-a-week Republican spy in the McGovern camp in the 1972 Nixon 'dirty tricks' campaign. She went on to represent Mark Fuhrman, the racist cop caught lying in the O.J. Simpson case.

Goldberg lapped up Tripp's tale, but to make anything of it they would need evidence. Lewinsky had turned to Tripp as a shoulder to cry on and Tripp began taping Lewinsky's phone calls, pumping her for erotic detail. Everything she said directly contradicted what both Clinton and Lewinsky had said in their depositions.

Lewinsky said that her affair with the President had begun not long after she arrived in the White House. She was just 21. The daughter of a wealthy Californian physician, she had been to school in Beverley Hills. The video of her High School prom shows her in clinches with a string of boys. At college in Portland, Oregon, she was considered 'a bit flash' at the raucous barbecues the students held. There were even rumours of an affair with the professor. Monica was apparently a young woman with a taste for older men.

After graduating in 1995, her mother arranged for her to be an unpaid intern, or trainee, in the White House.

'There goes trouble,' said the White House staffer who interviewed her for the job.

She was given a desk that lay between the Oval Office and the President's private apartment. Every time the President walked by, it was plain that he noticed her. She wore low-cut blouses with the top three buttons undone. Under the desk, her short skirts reveal lacy stocking tops. The President even commented on the thong she was wearing that rose above the top of her skirt.

At first, White House wags put his attentions down to innocent flirtation. No one suspected that there was anything going on between them. But tongues started wagging when she turned up one night with a private visit pass. These are rarely issued to staff. She said she was visiting a close personal friend in the Chief of Staff's office, but the person whose name she wrote in the security log had already gone home.

Gifts were exchanged. Monica bought Clinton the tie that he wore when he gave his State of the Union address in 1997. He sent her flowers, and gave her a book of erotic verse and a dress, which she kept, unwashed, as a *memento amori* because, she boasted, it was stained with presidential semen.

Secret Service men were overheard saying that she should not be visiting the President's apartment so often – especially not when Hillary and Chelsea were away. She also appeared on the guest list at Camp David.

When gossip spread throughout the White House, Monica was transferred to a paid job in the Pentagon. There she developed a crush on another older man. But she continued to see the President, arriving late at night in figure-hugging dresses.

She began to get disillusioned, however, when she discovered that she was not the only filly in Bill's stable. She began to record her own phone calls with the President. Some of the conversations were very explicit indeed. There were hot telephone sex sessions. Memorably, the President expressed his desire to 'coat you with my baby gravy' – not an appetizing image, perhaps, but hardly a federal offence.

Tripp went to Kenneth Starr, the Special Prosecutor on the Whitewater scandal. She convinced him that Clinton had lied under oath in his deposition in the Paula Jones case, and that Clinton, via his attorney and close friend Vernon Jordan, had also asked Monica to lie under oath.

Starr got the FBI to wire Tripp's capacious cleavage. She invited Lewinsky for cocktails at the Ritz Carlton in Crystal City and the G-men taped their girl talk. Lewinsky began complaining to Tripp that the President was cheating on her with four other women – three of whom worked in the White House. It seemed he was running a state-sponsored seraglio. She called him 'The Creep' and 'El Sicko' and admitted giving Clinton oral sex, which the FBI gleefully taped.

Monica said she had asked Bill Clinton why he did not settle the Paula Jones case out of court. He apparently replied: 'I can't – because then they would all come out of the woodwork.'

'Were there that many?' Lewinsky had asked.

'Hundreds,' Clinton had replied.

The Federal agents moved in. They seized from Lewinsky's Watergate flat a copy of Walt Whitman's *Leaves of Grass* – which contains the line 'Copulation is no more rank to me than death' – inscribed by the President's own fair hand. They also seized jewellery that Clinton had bought for her while on holiday in Martha's Vineyard with Hillary. Meanwhile, Starr gave 24-year-old Monica an eight-hour grilling.

The media were fascinated by just who these 'hundreds' of other women could be. Soon the bimbo hunt was in full cry. Forty-eight-year-old Dolly Kyle Browning claimed that she had begun an affair with Clinton in high school that had lasted into his White House days. She claimed to have made love to the President three times in a senator's hotel room. And, while he was governor, they had had sex in the basement of the gubernatorial mansion, frolicked in houses borrowed from friends and made love in a neighbour's back yard.

Then there was leggy Susan McDougal, who went down for 18 months for refusing to testify against Clinton over Whitewater. Her husband, Jim, said that he had intercepted an 'intimate' phone call between his wife and the President, and that she had later admitted the affair. Again she stuck up for the President.

'I'm a small town girl,' she told the press, 'a Southern Baptist, I wouldn't do that.'

Sheila Lawrence was then accused of making love to President Clinton while her millionaire husband turned a blind eye. In return, he was made US ambassador to Switzerland. When he died, Clinton rewarded Sheila's discretion by having her husband's remains interred in Arlington National Cemetery, where John F. Kennedy is buried. His remains were later moved when it was discovered that Lawrence had lied about his military service.

Fearing she was being upstaged, Gennifer Flowers went on CNN with more details of her affair with Clinton. She told chat-show host Larry King: 'He's a chance taker and he will make you take chances. He wanted to make love with Hillary nearby.'

Clinton, she said, had made her pregnant and she had had an abortion. Meanwhile, Bill was caught on tape saying Flowers could 'suck a tennis ball through a garden hose'.

Back in Little Rock, Sally Perdue told the nation that Clinton liked nothing than better to cavort around her bedroom dressed in her black nightie. And 33-year-old Bobbie Ann Williams took a lie detector test in an attempt to get child support for her seven-year-old son and Clinton lookalike, Danny. Strapped to the polygraph, she claimed that her first paid encounter with the Governor took place behind a hedge in Little Rock. Later, she said, she had organized three-in-a-bed sessions for him with another prostitute. The polygraph operator was sweating. She was not. The needles remained as steady as her accusations.

Former Miss America and *Playboy* centrefold Elizabeth Ward Gracen, who was by then a prominent TV actress, left the country rather than be subpoenaed in the Paula Jones case. She later admitted to having sex with Clinton when she was 21, but insisted that the sex was consensual.

The spin doctors were maintaining that any sexual contact Clinton had with these women was oral. This was vital. Under the Constitution, a president can only be impeached for 'high crimes and misdemeanours'. Technically, adultery is a misdemeanour in the District of Columbia. However, Clinton and others maintain that oral sex does not constitute adultery because it is not mentioned, or condemned, by the Bible. This was the key to Clinton's defence, because none other than Newt Gingrich, Republican speaker of the House of Representatives at that time and Clinton's bitterest enemy, had used that very argument in his bitterly contended divorce case.

Clinton famously appeared on television, wagging his finger at the press and saying: 'I did not have sex with that woman, Miss Lewinsky.'

But slowly, he confessed to being 'emotionally close' to Monica. Hillary went on the chat shows and said she still loved and trusted her husband – only to be dubbed 'the world's most powerful doormat'. There was a right-wing conspiracy to bring her husband down, she said.

And, in a way, it was true. Special prosecutor Ken Starr was a committed Republican. He had spent $25 million and three years getting nowhere with the Whitewater investigation. But now, at last, he had something.

In the midst of the crisis, Clinton delivered a barnstorming State of the Union address. He held his nerve and things began to turn in his favour. The federal judge in charge of the Paula Jones case quashed her suit. Even if the incident in the hotel room she described had occurred, she had no civil case because she could not prove that she had been materially damaged by Clinton's behaviour. Indeed, after the incident, she had been promoted. And she could not show any emotional damage since she had gone on to get married.

Even so, Starr maintained that if Clinton had lied under oath in his deposition in the case, he was guilty of perjury. If he had put pressure on Monica Lewinsky to lie, then he was guilty of suborning a witness. And, if he had had some gifts he had given Monica Lewinsky removed from her flat – as was now being alleged – he was guilty of obstructing the course of justice. As President, Clinton was the chief law officer of the United States, so these were serious – impeachable – offences.

Starr managed to make a deal with Monica Lewinsky. If she testified in graphic detail to the Grand Jury, holding nothing back, he would guarantee her immunity from prosecution. If she did not testify, he would charge her with perjury over her testimony in the Paula Jones case. At her trial, Clinton would be called as a witness, so he would be exposed anyway.

Monica had no choice. She took the deal. She told the Grand Jury that she had both given and received oral sex with the President on numerous occasions. She said that she had entertained him by dancing around naked and performing sexual acts with a cigar. She also said that he had penetrated her, but he had not 'finished off' inside her. This was enough of a loophole for Clinton to continue to argue that he had not had sex with her. Within the narrowest Biblical definition, a sexual act means one that could result in reproduction. This was a whisper away.

She also handed over the semen-stained dress that she had kept. The semen proved to match a sample of DNA provided by the President.

President Clinton then consented to testify to the Grand Jury. But he would do so, not in person, but by a closed circuit TV from the White House. Again, he stuck to his guns. Although he admitted an 'inappropriate relationship' with Monica Lewinsky, he denied having sex with her under the definition provided in the Paula Jones case. He denied lying under oath and he denied asking anyone else to do so.

He went on television and admitted that he had deceived the country and brought pain to his family, and he asked for forgiveness. The press screamed that if he had only admitted that he had had sex with Monica Lewinsky in the first place, he would have been forgiven and the whole thing could have been forgotten. But that was the one thing he could not do. If he admitted that he had had sex with Monica Lewinsky, he would be admitting that he had committed perjury, both in his deposition in the Paula Jones case and in his testimony to the Grand Jury, and that he had lied to the American people. Besides, he was rising in popularity in the polls.

Although almost every detail of the evidence presented to the Grand Jury had already been leaked, the House of Representatives voted to publish the Starr report both as hard copy and on the internet. Clinton's televised testimony was also released. The Republicans in the House hoped that this would do the maximum damage to the Democrats before the congressional elections in November 1998.

It did the Republicans no good. The tide of gains in the House of Representatives that been flowing with them since Bill Clinton had first entered the White House now ebbed, although they retained a majority. And in the Senate, they failed to gain the two-thirds majority they would need to remove him from office. Despite this, the House of Representatives voted to impeach him anyway.

According to the *National Enquirer*, the impeachment rattled Hillary and she lashed out at Bill. His Secret Service guards had to fend her off. Courtesy of *The Star*, Bobbie Ann Williams had her son's DNA compared with that provided to the Starr Committee by Bill Clinton, and it was found that the President was not the father.

Meanwhile, the Senate duly sat and tried the President, with the Republicans dragging out the proceedings in the forlorn hope that some new and even more scandalous evidence against the President would be unearthed. Meanwhile, Bill Clinton continued to soar in the polls.

2 ❖ The Profumo Scandal

The biggest scandal in British public life took place, ironically, in the Swinging Sixties, when everyone was supposed to be having a lot of sex and having a good time – apart from government ministers that is. When it was discovered that Minister of War, John Profumo, had been sharing a prostitute with the naval attaché at the Russian embassy and had lied to the House of Commons about it, he was forced to resign. But that was not the end of the matter. Soon after, the Prime Minister, who had been fatally damaged by the affair, resigned and the following year the Conservative government was swept from power.

The scandal centred around Christine Keeler who, at the age of 15, quit her home in the Buckinghamshire village of Wraysbury for the bright lights of London. Within months, her self-confidence and good looks had taken her from being a waitress in a Greek restaurant to being a part-time model and a topless dancer in Murray's Cabaret Club in Soho, where she earned £8.50 a week. There, fellow show-girl Mandy Rice-Davis, a perky 17-year-old from Birmingham, introduced her to her friend Stephen Ward.

Ward was a thin and elegant man in his late 40s. He was a talented artist but earned his living as an osteopath. He numbered among his clients several high-ranking members of the establishment. These included Lord Astor, who let him a cottage in the grounds of his Cliveden estate for the peppercorn rent of £1 a year, and Sir Colin Coote, Editor of *The Daily Telegraph*, who associated with the head of MI5, Sir Roger Hollis – whom Peter Wright later named as the fifth man in the Cambridge spy ring.

Ward liked doing favours for people. He also liked drugs and the company of pretty women, including prostitutes. Christine Keeler and Mandy Rice-Davis moved in with him in his London flat in Wimpole Mews and would go with him to Cliveden at weekends for parties in his cottage.

In June 1961, over lunch at The Garrick, Coote introduced Ward to the Soviet naval attaché, Yevgeny Ivanov. MI5 had singled out Ivanov as a man who might easily succumb to the temptations of the West. They thought that a weekend party with some of Ward's attractive young female friends might be just the thing to turn him. The defection of such a high-ranking Russian official would be quite a prize. Specifically, MI5 wanted Ward to 'honeytrap' Ivanov with Keeler.

Ward invited Ivanov down to Cliveden on Sunday 9 July 1951. He took Keeler down there the night before when the Astors were holding a dinner party in the house. Keeler wanted to go swimming and Ward dared her to go in the nude. When she did, he stole her swimming costume.

Lord Astor and John Profumo were out in the gardens for an after-dinner stroll when they spotted the beautiful, naked 19-year-old in the swimming pool. Christine realized that they were coming and struck out for the edge of the pool. She emerged nude and grabbed a small towel to cover herself, moments before the two men caught up with her.

The two middle-aged men were fooling around with the near-naked girl when suddenly the floodlights were turned on. The rest of the guests – including Profumo's wife – came out into the garden, too. Christine was introduced. Later, Profumo managed to give her a guided tour of the bedrooms at Cliveden.

At 46, Profumo was a rising Tory politician. The son of a successful barrister, he was independently wealthy and lived the life of a Tory squire. Educated at Harrow and Oxford, he served on the staff of General Alexander during World War II, rising to the rank of lieutenant-colonel. He was elected to Parliament for Stratford-upon-Avon in 1950 and joined the government in 1952, rising to the position of Secretary for War in 1960. In 1954, he had married the actress Valerie Hobson.

The day after Christine met Profumo, Ivanov turned up at Cliveden. Ward laid on a swimming party as a way of introducing him to Christine. She fancied Ivanov immediately. She told the *News of the World*: 'He was MAN. He was rugged with a hairy chest, strong and agile.'

However, when they decided to have a piggy-back fight in the pool, it was Jack Profumo's shoulders she clambered on to, not Ivanov's. That evening, Christine left with Ivanov, but not before Profumo had asked her for her phone number. Christine was flattered and told him to contact Ward.

Back at Ward's Wimpole Mews flat, Christine and Ivanov demolished a bottle of vodka. Then he kissed her.

'Before I knew what was happening, I was in his arms,' she said. 'We left serious discussion and I yielded to this wonderful huggy bear of a man... He was a wonderful lover.'

Two days later, Profumo phoned and came round. On his third visit, he began to kiss her and soon, 'I was returning his kisses with everything that I suddenly felt for him,' she said.

Profumo would always call first before he came round for what Keeler called a 'screw of convenience'. They had to be discreet. With Ivanov, she

The beautiful Christine Keeler - mistress of John Perfumo

went out on the town, but Profumo could not risk being seen out with her in a pub or restaurant. Occasionally though they went for a drive. As well as having sex at Ward's flat, they had it in Profumo's red mini and a black car he borrowed from the Minister of Labour, John Hare. And once, when his wife was away in Ireland, Profumo took Christine back to their house in Nash Terrace near Regent's Park. It was late and the butler and staff were asleep. Profumo took her directly to the bedroom.

Profumo had no idea that he was sharing his mistress with Ivanov. He was deeply attached to her. But she did not share his feelings. For her, sex 'had no more meaning than a handshake or a look across a crowded room,' she said. Meanwhile, Profumo showered her with expensive gifts and money – ostensibly to buy her mother a birthday present.

After a month, MI5 learnt about Profumo's affair with Keeler. Fearing that it compromised their entrapment of Ivanov, Hollis asked the Cabinet Secretary, Sir Norman Brook, to warn Profumo. On 9 August 1961, in panic, John Profumo wrote a note to Christine Keeler:

Darling,
In great haste & because I can get no reply from your phone –

Alas something's blown up tomorrow night & I can't therefore make it. I'm terribly sorry especially as I leave the next day for various trips & then a holiday so won't be able to see you again until some time in September. Blast it.

Please take care of yourself & don't run away.

Love J

I'm writing this cos I know you're off the day after tomorrow & I want you to know before you go if I still can't reach you by phone.

It was this note that sealed his fate.

Despite the warning, Profumo continued seeing Christine Keeler for another four months. During that time, he took amazing risks. One evening an army officer turned up at the flat looking for Ward.

'I had to introduce him to the War Minister,' said Keeler. 'The colonel couldn't believe it. Jack nearly died.'

Profumo only broke it off in December because Keeler refused to move out of Ward's flat and into a discreet love nest that he was going to buy for her.

MI5 began to lose interest in the plan to honeytrap Ivanov. They were finding Ward increasingly unreliable. Keeler had moved on, too. While scoring marijuana for Ward, she had met West Indian jazz singer, Lucky Gordon, and, through him, another West Indian named Johnny Edgecombe.

She had begun sleeping with both of them. This had led to a fight at an all-night club in Soho in October 1962, where Gordon got his face slashed. Keeler moved in with Edgecombe briefly. When things did not work out, she moved back into Ward's flat. One night, Edgecombe came round to try and win her back. It was late and she would not let him in. He pulled a gun and blasted the front door. The police were called and Edgecombe was arrested and charged with attempted murder.

After this incident, Ward asked Keeler to leave the flat. She turned to one of his patients, solicitor Michael Eddowes, for help. She told him that she and Ward had actually been spying for the Russians and that Ward had asked her to find out from Profumo about British plans to arm West Germany with nuclear weapons.

She told the same story to former Labour MP, John Lewis, who had a personal dislike of Ward. He passed the information on to George Wigg, a Labour MP who disliked Profumo after he had bested him in the House. In January 1963, Paul Mann, a journalist, took Keeler to the *Sunday Pictorial*. Keeler showed the *Pictorial* the note that Profumo had written and the paper offered her £1,000 for her story.

However, the newspapers were exceedingly cautious at the time. The previous year, the exposure of the spy John Vassall, an admiralty clerk who had been passing secrets to the Soviets, had led to a Tribunal of Inquiry that had investigated the role of the press in the affair. In the course of it, two journalists had been sent to prison for refusing to name their sources.

The *Pictorial* contacted Ward, who managed to convince the paper that Keeler's story was a pack of lies and publication was dropped. This annoyed Keeler so she went to the police and told them that Ward procured call girls for his rich clients. A few days later, Profumo found himself being questioned by the Attorney General Sir John Hobson, the Solicitor General Peter Rawlinson and the Chief Whip Martin Redmayne. He denied any impropriety with Keeler. Although sceptical, they chose to accept what he was saying.

Prime Minister Harold Macmillan was briefed. A man of the world, he said that if Profumo had had an affair with Keeler he had been foolish, but sleeping with a pretty young woman, even if she was alleged to be prostitute, was hardly a sackable offence. Everyone hoped that that was the end of it. But on 8 March 1963, a small-circulation newsletter called *Westminster Confidential* ran a piece about the story that the *Pictorial* had dropped. It repeated the allegation that both the War Secretary and a Soviet military attaché, one Colonel Ivanov, were the clients of the same call girl.

On 10 March, George Wigg, who by this time had a bulging dossier on the relationship between Profumo and Keeler, took it to the Labour leader, Harold Wilson. Wilson urged caution, but events now had a momentum of their own.

On 14 March, Johnny Edgecombe came up for trial at the Old Bailey. The key witness, Christine Keeler, was on holiday and it was rumoured that she had been whisked out of the country to keep a lid on the scandal.

The next day, the *Daily Express* ran the headline, 'WAR MINISTER SHOCK'. It claimed that John Profumo had tendered his resignation for 'personal reasons'. Down the page was a picture of Christine Keeler under the headline, 'VANISHED'.

The *Express* later claimed that the juxtaposition of the two stories was purely coincidental. But everyone put two and two together.

On 19 March, during a debate on the Vassall case, George Wigg, under the protection of parliamentary privilege, raised the rumours circulating about the War Minister. He was supported by Barbara Castle and the Labour frontbencher Dick Crossman. The government was flustered. The Home Secretary, Henry Brooke, told the Labour critics that if they wanted to substantiate their accusations, they should use a different forum, one that was not shielded from the laws of libel by the cloak of privilege.

Profumo had one supporter though – backbench Labour MP, Reginald Paget.

'What do these rumours amount to?' Paget asked rhetorically. 'They amount to the fact that a minister is said to be acquainted with an extremely pretty girl. As far as I am concerned, I should have thought that was matter for congratulation rather than an inquiry.'

Profumo was then grilled again by the Chief Whip, the Leader of the House Iain Macleod and Bill Deedes, Minister without Portfolio and future editor of *The Daily Telegraph*. Profumo again insisted that he was innocent. He then made a parliamentary statement. In it he admitted knowing Christine Keeler, but said he had not seen her since December 1961. He also said that he had met Stephen Ward and Yevgeny Ivanov. He denied that he was in any way responsible for her absence from the trial and stated categorically: 'There was no impropriety whatsoever in my acquaintanceship with Miss Keeler.' He threatened anyone who repeated the allegations outside the House with a writ.

A few days later, the newspapers caught up with Christine Keeler in Madrid. She confirmed what Profumo had said, but George Wigg would not leave it at that. He went on the *Panorama* TV programme and said that Ward and Ivanov were security risks. The next day, Ward met Wigg and tried to convince him that it was not true. He failed. More than ever, Wigg

Tory politician John Perfumo

believed that Profumo had lied. He wrote a report of his meeting with Ward and gave it to Harold Wilson, who passed it on to Macmillan.

Although the Vassall case was keeping the British press subdued, there was no such reticence in the foreign papers. Profumo issued writs against *Paris Match* and *Il Tempo Illustrato*, which both said that he had been bonking Christine Keeler.

In an attempt to salvage the situation, the Home Secretary told the Metropolitan Police to try and find something on Ward. This was highly irregular. The police are supposed to investigate crimes and find out who committed them, not investigate people on the off chance they have committed a crime.

It soon became clear to Ward's friends and clients that he was in serious trouble. They deserted him in droves. Mandy Rice-Davis was arrested on trumped-up charges and held in prison until she agreed to testify against Ward.

Ward desperately wrote to everyone he could think of, protesting his innocence. Harold Wilson received a letter. He showed it to the Prime Minister, who agreed to set up a committee of inquiry under Lord Dilhorne. Profumo was on holiday at the time. When he returned, he realized that the game was up. He could not face a committee of inquiry and lie again, so he went to see the Chief Whip and Macmillan's Parliamentary Private Secretary, told them that he had lied and resigned.

His letter of resignation and Macmillan's reply were published the next day.

'I misled you, and my colleagues, and the House,' Profumo wrote, but, he explained, 'I did this to protect my wife and family.'

Macmillan's terse reply said: 'I am sure you will understand that in the circumstances I have no alternative but to advise the Queen to accept your resignation.'

The very day this exchange appeared in the papers, 5 June 1963, there was more drama. Christine Keeler's other West Indian boyfriend, Lucky Gordon, came to court on the charge of assaulting her outside a friend's flat. Keeler turned up in court in a Rolls Royce.

From the dock, Gordon accused her of giving him VD. She responded with an outburst from the public gallery. The newspapers lapped it up. Gordon was sent down for three years, which was overturned on appeal.

Ward appeared on TV on 9 June and denied that he had encouraged Christine Keeler to have an affair with John Profumo because he had a friend in the Soviet Embassy. The following day he was arrested and charged with living on immoral earnings.

By this time, newspapers world-wide were running the scandal on the front page. Mandy Rice-Davis told the *Washington Star* about society orgies in London. She mentioned that at one dinner party, a naked man wearing only a mask waited on table. The hunt for the masked man was on. Was it a senior judge, a cabinet minister or a member of the royal family?

Under the headline, 'PRINCE PHILIP AND THE PROFUMO SCAN-DAL', the *Daily Mirror* vehemently dismissed the 'foul rumour' that Prince Philip was involved. The Queen's Consort was a member of a gentleman's association called the Thursday Club, which also boasted Stephen Ward among its membership.

Allegations flew thick and fast. Everyone in any position in society was now a target. The Bishop of Southwark, Mervyn Stockwood, appealed for calm.

Politically the question came down to: how had John Profumo managed to lie about his affair for so long? Macmillan, who had taken a lenient attitude to the matter back in January, was now in the firing line. Colleagues began to sense that his tenure of office was drawing to a close. Lord Hailsham quit his title to become a contender for the premiership. He threw his hat into the ring by appearing on television and condemning

Profumo for lying. Again, Reginald Paget rallied to Profumo's defence.

'When self-indulgence has reduced a man to the shape of Lord Hailsham,' he said, 'sexual continence involves no more than a sense of the ridiculous.'

Milking the situation for all it was worth, Mandy Rice-Davis told the *Sunday Mirror* that the Soviet military attaché and the War Minister had missed bumping into each other at Ward's flat by a matter of minutes on a number of occasions.

Michael Eddowes issued a press statement, saying that he had warned the Prime Minister of the security risk as early as 29 March. Meanwhile, Christine Keeler sold her 'confessions' to the *News of the World*, which began serializing them.

The Times attacked the Conservative government for its lack of moral leadership. To this, Lord Hailsham responded petulantly: '*The Times* is an anti-Conservative newspaper with an anti-Conservative editor.'

Even the *Washington Post* got in on the act, saying that 'a picture of widespread decadence beneath the glitter of a large segment of stiff-lipped society is emerging'.

Labour went on the offensive. In a debate in the House of Commons on 19 June, Harold Wilson said that the Profumo scandal had 'shocked the moral conscience of the nation'. Pointing the finger at the Prime Minister, he said that for political reasons he was gambling with national security.

Macmillan could not even count on the support of his own back-benchers. Conservative MP, Nigel Birch, stated the simple facts of the case.

'I must say that [Profumo] never struck me as a man at all like a cloister monk,' he told the House. 'And Miss Keeler is a professional prostitute. There seems to me to be a basic improbability that their relationship was purely platonic. What are whores about?'

Addressing the Prime Minister directly, he said: 'I myself feel that the time will come very soon when my Right Honourable Friend ought to make way for a much younger colleague.'

Macmillan survived the debate but was badly wounded. Four days later, he announced an official inquiry under Lord Denning. It did not save him. Macmillan resigned in the early autumn, shortly before the party conference. He was replaced by Sir Alec Douglas Home, but the Conservative government was tainted by the scandal and was swept from office the following year.

Although Lord Denning was supposed to look into possible breaches of security caused by the Profumo scandal, like Ken Starr, he concentrated on the salacious aspects – so much so that when he cross-questioned witnesses, he often sent the official stenographer out of the room to save her, or perhaps his own, blushes.

When Ward went on trial at the Old Bailey, the world's media were there in force. Again, the salacious details were played up. One newspaper in New Zealand was prosecuted for indecency for merely reporting the case.

The star of the show was undoubtedly Mandy Rice-Davis, whom the judge mistakenly addressed as Marilyn Monroe. When it was put to her that Lord Astor had denied that he had met her at his house parties at Cliveden, she said: 'Well, he would, wouldn't he?' That remark is now in the *Oxford Dictionary of Quotations*.

In his summing up, the judge pointed out that none of Ward's high-born friends had come to testify on his behalf.

'One would have thought from the newspapers that this country has become a sink of iniquity,' he told the jury. 'But you and I know that the even tenor of family life over the overwhelming majority of the population goes quietly and decently on.'

He might as well have been putting the noose around the defendant's neck. The judge was implying that Ward was not just guilty of introducing rich and powerful people to a couple of attractive and available girls, but that he was responsible for the general loosening of moral standards that many people felt was engulfing the country. Ward knew that he was being made a scapegoat.

'This is a political trial,' he told a friend. 'Someone had to be sacrificed and that someone is me.'

On the night of 3 July 1963, Ward took an overdose of sleeping tablets. He left a suicide note saying that, after the judge's summing up, he had given up all hope. He asked that resuscitation be delayed as long as possible, adding, bizarrely, that 'the car needs oil in the gearbox'.

With Ward unconscious in St Stephen's Hospital, the jury found him guilty on two counts of living on immoral earnings. He died on 3 August, without regaining consciousness. Even after he was dead, the newspapers kept vilifying him.

There were only six mourners at Stephan Ward's funeral and only two wreaths. One came from his family. The other was from Kenneth Tynan, John Osbourne, Arnold Wesker, Joe Orton, Annie Ross, Dominick Elwes and Penelope Gilliatt. The card on it read: 'To Stephen Ward, victim of hypocrisy'.

When the Denning report was published in October 1963, it was an instant best-seller, selling over 4,000 copies in the first hour. It, too, laid the blame squarely at the door of Stephen Ward, who was in no position to answer back.

Profumo left political life and threw himself into charity work, for which he was awarded the CBE in 1975. He remained married to Valerie Hobson. Christine Keeler was jailed for six months for contempt of court for failing to appear at the trial of Johnny Edgecombe. Her autobiography *Scandal* was published in 1989 and was made into a successful movie.

Mandy Rice-Davis wrote a series of novels, became a film actress, opened two clubs in Israel and married a millionaire. George Wigg became chairman of the Horse Race Betting Levy Board and later pleaded guilty to soliciting for prostitutes in Soho.

3 ❖ The War Bonds Scandal

Although nothing this century can rival Bill Clinton's peccadilloes or the Profumo affair as a sex scandal, there have been a number of financial scandals that have equalled them in terms of political fallout.

One concerned Horatio Bottomley. He was the Robert Maxwell of his day, but his swindles were even more pernicious. Under the guise of supporting the war effort during World War I he cheated people out of hundreds of thousands of pounds in order to keep himself in a champagne life style.

Bottomley was a self-made man. Orphaned at the age of four, he suffered for five years in a harsh children's home in Birmingham. At the age of nine, his aunt took him in on the condition that he buckled down to hard work.

At 14, he moved to London where an uncle found him a job as a messenger. Later, he joined a firm of solicitors in Coleman Street as an office boy. There he got a grounding in the law that would later prove invaluable. He also learnt the delicate art of swindling from the managing clerk, who was pocketing the non-existent county tax he was charging city firms.

He moved on to a career in journalism, working for the *Freethinker* and the *Secularist*, which were published by Charles Bradlaugh, who was rumoured to be his real father, and his uncle George Holyoake. Bottomley was gifted at shorthand and, with the help of his wife Eliza Norton, began reproducing local government speeches in his *Battersea Hansard* and *Hackney Hansard*. When these publications folded, he began the *Financial Times*, although it was in no way connected to the newspaper currently published under that name.

These publishing ventures were merely a front for fraudulent property ventures. When the whole lot went belly up, Bottomley ended up in court. It was here that his legal knowledge came into play. It should have been an open-and-shut case. From the £1-million capital in his company, £600,000 was missing. But Bottomley defended himself, arguing so persuasively that the jury acquitted him on all charges. The judge, the notoriously harsh Mr Justice Hawkins, took him aside afterwards and recommended that he begin a new career in the law. But Bottomley was too busy cashing in on the Australian gold rush.

Instead of going Down Under and panning for gold, he made his mint out of greedy shareholders. He floated mining companies then wound them up again after he had pocketed the investors' money. He used his new-found wealth to indulge an expensive passion for racehorses and protected his financial interests by surrounding himself with a growing circle of lawyers, accountants and bodyguards.

To give himself a veneer of respectability, Bottomley thought it would be a good idea to be an MP. He stood as Liberal candidate for South Hackney. During his campaign he used every dirty trick in the book. His men defaced rivals' posters and disrupted the Tory challenger's meetings. A string of horses trotted down Hackney High Street, carrying saddlecloths that read 'Vote for my owner'. They were, of course, owned by Bottomley.

The popularist newspaper *John Bull*, a precursor of *The Sun*, reported such incidents. Although its slogan was 'Politics without Party – Criticism without Cant.' Bottomley's political aspirations – which was hardly surprising as he owned it. After he won the 1906 election, Bottomley used the newspaper to quell criticism over the fraud charges – this time over his gold-mining scams, which had him hauled into court again. Again, he walked.

Bottomley was re-elected in 1910, but his political career suffered a setback in 1912, when he was declared bankrupt with liabilities of nearly a quarter of a million pounds. As a bankrupt, he was forced to give up his seat in the House of Commons and he lost his flat in Pall Mall.

But there were plenty more tricks up Bottomley's sleeve. He began a lottery, the proceeds of which were routed via Switzerland to get around the UK gambling laws. But his greatest opportunity came with the outbreak of World War I. Naturally, *John Bull* backed 'our boys' all the way. So did Bottomley, ostensibly. A gifted orator, Bottomley was an invaluable recruiter. He went on a speaking tour, charging £200 a speech, plus a percentage of the door. This netted him up to £4,000 a week.

Through *John Bull*, Bottomley sold War Bonds off the back of a crooked sweepstake, where the non-existent prize was £20,000. Instead of using the money to support the war effort, Bottomley squandered £42,000 on failed publishing ventures. The rest went on maintaining his increasingly opulent life style.

With the end of the war, Bottomley was miraculously solvent again and was returned to Parliament as an Independent. However, rival publications began to smell a rat. *Truth* magazine began to investigate him. Then a former colleague, Reuben Bigland, issued a pamphlet condemning Bottomley's War Bond scam. Bottomley sued, only to find himself charged by the Director of Public Prosecutions.

Bottomley may well have been able to save himself again in court had the swindle not concerned War Bonds. Britain was still reeling under the huge slaughter of World War I and had little sympathy for anyone who had profited out of it. As it was, Bottomley managed to persuade the judge to call a recess every morning at 11.30 so that he could consume his first bottle of champagne of the day. And he managed to cut a deal so that the name of his favourite mistress, the actress Peggy Primrose, was kept out of the proceedings, even though she had benefited to the tune of £1,000.

He was sent down for seven years. In prison, the story goes, a visitor saw him hard at work making mail bags and said: 'Sewing, Bottomley?'

'No, reaping,' he replied.

When he was released after five years for good behaviour, Peggy Primrose was waiting for him. He made another attempt at a comeback with a lecture tour of the Empire. In 1932, he collapsed on the stage of the Windmill Theatre in London with a heart attack. A second one killed him a few months later.

4 ❖ Lloyd George Knew My Father

David Lloyd George was one of the greatest British political reformers of the 20th century. In 1909, he introduced the old age pension; in 1911 unemployment insurance. He solved the 'Irish question', which had plagued British governments throughout the 19th century, giving Ireland Home Rule in 1922; and many credit his energy and application for Allied victory in World War I. He was also a great political survivor, who was mired in scandal throughout his career, but somehow managed to emerge without a stain.

Elected to Parliament for Caernarfon in 1892, he was threatened with disgrace in 1897 when he was named in a divorce case. A friend and constituent of Lloyd George's, a Montgomeryshire doctor named Edwards was suing his wife, Catherine, for divorce on the grounds of adultery, naming as co-respondent a man called Wilson. However, Catherine also confessed to sleeping with Lloyd George. She said that it had happened on the night of 4 February 1896. Lloyd George had been staying the night at the Edwards' house. When her husband had been called out, 'criminal conversation' – as the divorce laws at the time so succinctly put it – took place. Six months later, she gave birth to a child. Catherine Edwards claimed that Lloyd George was the father.

David Lloyd George

Although Catherine Edwards mentioned that they had slept together on other occasions, Lloyd George could prove that he did not have sex with her on 4 February. On that night, he had voted in the House of Commons. Lloyd George claimed that Catherine Edwards was a fantasist, a would-be political groupie. That part of her evidence had to be withdrawn. As Dr Edwards had plenty of other evidence of his wife's adultery with other men it did not matter. He was granted his divorce anyway.

When Lloyd George became Chancellor in 1908, the political journal *The Bystander* made a veiled reference to his womanizing. Then, fearing a libel suit, it donated £300 to Caernarfon Cottage Hospital. But *The People* followed up, citing the Edwards case and forthcoming divorce suit in which, the paper said, Lloyd George was going to be named as co-respondent.

This time Lloyd George sued. He hired as his attorney his most outspoken political opponent, the Tory MP F.E. Smith, who was also a close personal friend. Against them was Edward Carson KC, the man whose shrewd cross-examination had destroyed Oscar Wilde.

Lloyd George clearly perjured himself when he told the court that *The People*'s allegations were 'an absolute invention, every line of them'. Everybody knew that Lloyd George was a ladies' man. So to add weight to his denials he brought his long-suffering wife, Margaret, with him to court. According to their son, Richard, this conversation took place between them before their court appearance:

'You must help me, Maggie. If get out of this I give my oath you shall never have to suffer this ordeal again.'

'And you will give your oath that this story is untrue?' she asked.

'I have to.'

Maggie then asked: 'And you give me your oath that I shall not have to suffer this sort of thing again. How can I rely on your "oath"?'

'One day,' said Lloyd George, 'I shall be Prime Minister. I shall be a force for the public good. If you help me you shall never forget your decision.'

As it happened, Edward Carson did not embarrass the future Prime Minister or his wife with any questions. On behalf of *The People* he offered a sincere and heartfelt apology and £1,000 was donated to another Welsh charity.

Of course, Lloyd George's oath to his wife was no better than his oath in court. His continued philandering earned him the nickname, 'The Goat'. In 1912, he took as his lover Frances Stevenson, his daughter Megan's tutor, sleeping with her at Number 10. Thirty years later, after his wife died, they married.

Although Lloyd George did manage to stay out of court in subsequent years, he did not stay out of the way of scandal. That same year, 1912, his involvement in the Marconi Scandal nearly brought the Liberal government down.

At the time, radio was still in its infancy. But in 1910, it hit the headlines when a radio message helped capture Dr Crippen and his mistress, who were fleeing to Canada on a transatlantic liner. The Marconi company had proposed to the British government that they set up six radio stations that would directly link the government in Whitehall to all quarters of the Empire. The contract was drawn at the end of 1911, but it could not be finalized until it had been approved by Parliament.

On 9 April 1912, the Managing Director of the Marconi company, Godfrey Isaacs, was having dinner at the Savoy with his brother Rufus Isaacs, who was the Attorney General in Asquith's Liberal government. Godfrey told his brother that Marconi's US subsidiary was planning to issue 1.4 million $1 shares and that if he bought now at pre-market prices he would make a killing.

Rufus Isaacs snapped up 10,000 shares. He told the Chief Whip Alexander Murray, who bought 1,000 on his own account and a further 2,500 with Liberal Party funds, and Lloyd George, who was then Chancellor of the Exchequer, and who bought 1,000.

The shares were given a further fillip on 15 April when the *Titanic* sank. It was estimated that the SOS signal it sent out on the wireless saved 700 lives. The three men had bought the shares at 40 shillings. Trading opened on 19 April at 65 shillings and climbed to 80 shillings by the end of the first day's trading.

In the summer, the government made an unsuccessful attempt to force through a bill approving the Marconi contract. Rumours were soon circulating in the City that Isaacs, who was responsible for the legal side of the contract, and Lloyd George, who was responsible for the financial side, were seeking to benefit from their insider knowledge by dealing in Marconi shares.

As it happened, the three government ministers were not very skilled at playing the stock market. By the time they got out, Lloyd George and Murray had each lost £213 and Isaacs £1,700.

On 8 August, a magazine called *Eye-Witness* broke the story, although Lloyd George's name was omitted. Another magazine, *Outlook*, followed up the story and made the connection with the Chancellor. Then the *Daily Mail*, in typical fashion, launched an attack on the 'Welsh solicitor and the Jew barrister'.

When Parliament reassembled on 11 October, Isaacs tried to quell the story by telling the House of Commons that neither he nor any member of the government had 'one single transaction with the shares of that company'. This was true. They had not been dealing in the British Marconi company involved in the contract. Naturally, he omitted to mention that he and his colleagues had staged an early raid on the shares of Marconi's American sister company. Even so, Parliament was far from satisfied and Asquith was forced to set up a Select Committee to investigate the affair.

Meanwhile, the French newspaper *Le Matin* called Isaacs a liar. Isaacs sued, using the court case to explain how he and his two colleagues had bought shares in the American Marconi company, not the British one. But this failed to end the affair. The Select Committee then went into action. Once Leo Maxse, Editor of the *National Review* and an acknowledged expert on the affair, had spelt out the details, Isaacs and Lloyd George had no choice but to come clean. Isaacs openly admitted that the three cabinet members had bought shares unavailable to the public and had attempted to profit by speculating in them. Lloyd George's performance was pitiful. He portrayed himself as an honest man trying to build up a little nest egg for his old age.

Both denied having misled the House of Commons, protesting that it would have been too complicated to explain the difference between the British and American companies. This was universally seen as feeble.

Alexander Murray did not bother to take part in this charade. He had retired from politics and was in business in Colombia at the time, some 14 days' mule ride from the nearest telegraph office and out of range of even the newfangled wireless.

Isaacs and Lloyd George had both tendered their resignations when the scandal first broke, but Asquith refused to accept them. Privately, he told King George V that their actions were 'lamentable' and 'difficult to defend'.

However, the Select Committee had a built-in government majority. It produced what was known as the Whitewash Report, although *Punch* called it the 'Won't Wash' report. Lord Robert Cecil produced a minority report, which condemned official corruption. Nevertheless, after two days' heated debate, the official report was accepted by the House.

Neither Isaacs nor Lloyd George resigned. The government had come through unscathed, although Asquith dropped his plans to hold an early election. A few months later, Isaacs was promoted to Lord Chief Justice. In 1916, Lloyd George went on to become Prime Minister.

After winning the war, Lloyd George promptly embroiled himself in fresh scandal. In 1918, the Liberal Party split. Asquith, who commanded the bulk of the party's funds, returned to the opposition benches. The radical wing, under Lloyd George, stayed in government, continuing the wartime coalition with the Tories. But it found itself short of funds.

Like other parties before it, Lloyd George's Liberals benefited from the sale of patronage. All governments had sold honours, but they had always done so with some decorum. Formerly, candidates had had to deserve an honour. Then, if they paid money into party funds, so much the better. But under Lloyd George, the niceties were stripped away and honours were dished out on a strictly cash basis.

The business was handled by the Chief Whip, Freddy Guest, who was succeeded by Charles McCurdy in 1921, and Lloyd George's press agent Sir William Sutherland. But these men could not be seen to be dealing directly in such a sordid trade and Maundy Gregory, publisher of *The Whitehall Gazette*, acted as a go-between with the clients.

Gregory was a shady character. He had failed as a teacher, actor, playwright and theatrical impresario and his war record was far from glorious. But from his offices in Parliament Square he was as powerful and well connected as anyone in the land. His connection with the *Gazette* was also useful since the paper could puff recipients of honours and make them sound like they really deserved it. For example, when Sir Joseph Robinson was elevated to the peerage in 1922, the *Gazette* said that he had rendered 'national and imperial service' as chairman of the Robinson South African Banking Company. However, that company had ceased to exist in 1905 and Robinson had in fact been fined £500,000 for defrauding the shareholders. His appeal to the Privy Council had been turned down the previous November. General Smuts, Prime Minister of the Union of South Africa, had not even been consulted about the honour. Neither had either of the recent governors. And nobody would say who had recommended Robinson for a baronetcy.

Doing away with the old makeshift system of buying honours, Gregory established a price list. A knighthood cost from £10,000 to £12,000. A baronetcy cost £30,000 and peerages started at £50,000.

From 1917 onwards, Lloyd George created peers at twice the rate of any previous government. Over 1,500 knighthoods were doled out between December 1916 and July 1922. He also introduced a new honour – the Order of the British Empire. Some 25,000 were awarded in just four years, netting Liberal Party funds £1 million. Music hall comics quickly dubbed the OBE, the Order of the Bad Egg.

Gregory would scrutinize the list of those proposed to receive honours in the usual way. Then he would approach them in the hope that they would pay handsomely for what they would have received free in the normal course of events. He would also seek out new customers, wealthy men who would not usually have considered themselves candidates for elevation. For example, Richard William, who received a CBE for 'untiring work for charity', was a Glasgow bookmaker with a criminal record.

The marketing was shameless. One of Gregory's touts sent out a letter saying:

'There are only five knighthoods left for the July list – if you decide on a baronetcy you may have to wait for the Retiring List. It is not likely that the next government will give so many honours, and this really is an exceptional opportunity, but there is no time to be lost if you wish to take it. It is unfortunate that governments must have money, but the party now in power will have to fight Labour and Socialism, which will be an expensive matter.'

To cover his tracks, Lloyd George also gave away honours – to the press barons. Between 1918 and 1922, the great and the good of Fleet Street were awarded 49 Privy Councillorships, peerages, baronetcies and knighthoods.

King George V began to object to the misuse of the honours system. Although he could not defy the government, the King began deferring honours, sometimes for up to a year or so.

The straw that broke the camel's back was the July 1922 Honours List. It contained the names of Sir William Vessey, a wartime tax dodger, and Sir John Drughorn, a shipowner who had been convicted for trading with the enemy in 1915. Both were awarded baronetcies. The press turned against the system, so did the House of Lords. Fury focused on the Robinson case, which was 'regarded as little less than an insult to the Crown and the House of Lords'.

Lloyd George was forced to defend the list to the House of Commons. He insisted that he had 'never departed from precedent' and that the only reason there had been an increase in honours was because of the war. The sale of honours to the highest bidder, he said, was 'a discreditable system. It ought never to have existed. If it does exist, it ought to be terminated, and if there is any doubt on that point every step should be taken to deal with it.'

In private, he defended the sale of honours as the 'cleanest way of raising money for a political party'. If political parties did not take money for awarding baubles, he argued, they had to take the money they needed from those who sought influence over their policies. After all, Lloyd

George had been the power behind the 1911 Act, which had effectively stripped the House of Lords of its powers, so what was wrong with taking money from people who wanted to sit there and pretend they had power? The worst thing about selling honours was, he conceded, 'you cannot defend it in public'.

The House of Commons wanted Lloyd George to set up a Select Committee to look into the matter, but Lloyd George only conceded a less powerful Royal Commission – on the spurious grounds that the awarding of honours involved the royal prerogative. He also insisted that it examine the future management of the honours system, not specific incidences of its misuse in the past. This way he escaped any blame for the scandal.

However, the sale-of-honours scandal undermined confidence in the government. Lloyd George was ousted and Bonar Law took over. Apart from a small presence in the coalition government formed during World War II, the Liberals have never returned to power.

Under Bonar Law's Conservative government, a Political Honours Scrutiny Committee, comprising three Privy Councillors, was set up and in 1925 the Honours (Prevention of Abuses) Act made it a criminal offence to trade in honours. However, those who bought their honours kept them. Where the honours purchased were hereditary, the heirs of the purchasers benefited, too.

However, Maundy Gregory did not have any other immediate career openings. Using his influential web of contacts, he continued to sell honours. In 1933, he was jailed for trying to sell a knighthood to a naval commander for £2,000. He was also suspected of murdering a lady friend for her inheritance and when he was released from prison he fled to France, where he committed suicide in 1941.

5 ❖ Charles Parnell and Kitty O'Shea

Ireland has always provided Britain with its most intractable political problems. In 1889 and after nearly a century of struggle, Home Rule at last seemed to be in sight, only to be blown off the political agenda for another 30 years by a scandalous divorce case involving the Home Rule Party's charismatic leader, Charles Stewart Parnell.

Born in County Wicklow, the son of a Protestant landowner, Parnell had swallowed anti-British sentiment with his mother's milk. She was the daughter of Commodore Charles Stewart, a US Navy hero of the war of 1812, whose parents had emigrated from Belfast before the War of Independence.

Parnell went to school in England, then on to Cambridge. But he was sent down after a drunken brawl with a local merchant. When he was arrested, Parnell tried to bribe the policeman, but mistakenly gave him a shilling instead of a sovereign. He was charged and sent down.

Returning home to Ireland, Parnell found it in the grip of the Fenians, who had taken up armed struggle against British rule. He allied himself with their cause and got himself elected to Parliament in 1875. The following year, he told the House of Commons that three Fenians executed in Manchester for murdering a policeman were Irish martyrs, a sentiment that won him a huge following at home.

In Parliament he began to adopt the filibuster techniques that had been effectively used in the United States Congress to hamper government business. However, although in Congress it was permissible for a politician to read at length from a newspaper, in the British Parliament a speaker was required to stick more or less to the point. Parnell managed to do this brilliantly, and with interminable speeches managed to talk government bills out. He believed that he could hinder the British Parliament to the point that setting up a separate government in Dublin would seem like a blessing.

In 1878, Ireland faced another famine and Parnell allied himself with the Irish Land League, who resisted evictions and used violence against rent collectors. In 1880, he was returned to Parliament with 85 other Home Rulers. Parnell was then voted party leader with the support of Captain William O'Shea, Member for County Clare.

A Dublin-born Catholic, O'Shea had served in the 18th Hussars before becoming interested in politics. He retired from the army at the age of 26, then married Kitty, the daughter of an English aristocrat. They had three children. Generous handouts from Kitty's aunt and the untiring entertaining of his wife allowed O'Shea to develop the connections needed to make a career in politics.

In 1880, the newly elected O'Shea sought to advance his career by holding a series of dinner parties at St Thomas's Hotel. Parnell was invited, but failed to show up and O'Shea sent his wife to Westminster to find out why.

'He came out, a tall, gaunt figure, thin and deathly pale,' Kitty recalled. 'He looked straight at me smiling and his curiously burning eyes looked into mine with a wondering intenseness that threw into my brain the sudden thought, "This man is wonderful – and different".'

But first Kitty chided him.

'I asked him why he had not answered my last invitation, and if nothing would induce him to come. He answered that he had not opened his letters for days but, that if I would let him, he would come to dinner directly he returned from Paris.'

The tryst made, there then came a truly romantic moment.

'In leaning forward in the cab to say goodbye,' Kitty wrote, 'a rose I was wearing in my bodice fell out on to my skirt. He picked it up and, touching it lightly to his lips, placed it in his buttonhole.'

Later he sealed it in an envelope with Kitty's name on it.

Kitty O'Shea pressed a number of buttons for Parnell. She was a short, stout woman with beautiful hair and her incessant chatter and quick wit reminded him of his mother. These maternal attributes helped him overcome the guilt he felt over the death of his first love, a beautiful farmer's daughter from County Wicklow. At the age of 19, when he had tried to break it off with her, she had committed suicide. He had been out in a boat on the river with his sister Fanny when he had seen a crowd pulling her body from the water. Ever since then, he had been dogged by dark depressions.

The O'Sheas' marriage had been only for show for some time. When O'Shea was not abroad, he spent most of his time in his *pied-à-terre* in Victoria. Kitty lived in Wornersh Lodge in Eltham, Kent. Soon after they had met, when Parnell was worn out by campaigning, O'Shea invited him to stay there. Kitty nursed him and often slipped into his sick-bed beside him. How much her husband knew about this is unclear.

A maid said that Parnell used the name Stewart when he visited. When she went to her mistress's room she would have to knock and wait 10 minutes before entering. And Parnell, she said, would escape down the fire escape if Captain O'Shea returned unexpectedly.

Certainly, their relationship was clandestine. When Parnell's support for the Land League led to charges of 'conspiracy to impoverish landlords', she hid him in a dressing room next to her bedroom, taking his meals to him there herself to avoid involving the servants.

They also met in rented houses and communicated by coded letters and sign language. If he twisted his handkerchief during a speech in the Commons, it meant he would see her later.

One day in 1881, O'Shea returned home to find Parnell's portmanteau in the house and challenged him to a duel. But Parnell talked him out of it, explaining that he had to work closely with Kitty as she was a vital conduit to Gladstone, who had gradually become convinced of the case for Home

Rule. O'Shea threatened Kitty with divorce, but she pointed out that he had been unfaithful to her on no less than 17 occasions. Although this was hardly an obstacle to divorce, O'Shea was dependent on Kitty's aunt's money so he backed down.

Politically, Parnell was still on the ascendancy. In 1881, Gladstone had

Charles Stewart Parnell, whose afffair with Kitty O'Shea caused massive uproar

conceded the Land Act, promising all Irish tenants rights of tenancy and fair rents. However, by supporting the passage of such a sensible piece of legislation, Parnell was seen to be colluding with the British. He therefore returned to Ireland to stir up sedition and got himself arrested.

While he was in Kilmainham jail, Kitty gave birth to their first daughter, whom O'Shea nobly acknowledged as his own. The child lived for only two months, dying before Parnell was released. Later, they had two more daughters, who took O'Shea's name.

Rural Ireland was in turmoil. The only person who could restore order was Parnell. Using O'Shea as an intermediary, Gladstone negotiated the Treaty of Kilmainham, which offered Parnell further concessions in return for an end to agitation.

Four days after Parnell was released, Lord Frederick Cavendish and his senior civil servant Thomas Burke, a Catholic, were gunned down in Phoenix Park, Dublin. The killings appalled even the nationalists. Parnell used the crisis to bring the growing nationalist movement under his control.

The killings also resulted in a tightening of security. Parnell was put under 24-hour surveillance. Soon the Home Office became aware of his irregular domestic arrangements and the Home Secretary, Lord Harcourt, warned that the Treaty of Kilmainham would be seen as tainted if it was known that Parnell had negotiated it with the husband of his mistress.

Parnell never acknowledged O'Shea's part in his release. O'Shea grew resentful and it became harder for him close his ears to the rumours about his wife's infidelity. While campaigning during the elections of 1885, Parnell was asked about his relationship with Kitty O'Shea in front of a boisterous crowd. He refused to answer.

While Parnell was a troublesome supporter of Gladstone, O'Shea began to side with Joseph Chamberlain, who was hostile to Parnell's Home Rule plans. Even though, at Kitty's behest, Parnell had found him a safe seat as a Home Ruler, O'Shea was the only Irish nationalist to follow Chamberlain and the Tories into the lobby to vote against the limited 1886 Home Rule Bill. The bill was defeated.

Things began to go badly wrong for Parnell. In May 1886, while Captain O'Shea was away in Europe, Parnell's carriage collided with a market gardener's cart while he was travelling home to Eltham. The *Pall Mall Gazette* ran the story and pointed out: 'During the sitting of Parliament the Hon. Member for Cork usually takes up his residence at Eltham, a suburban village in the south-east of London. From here he can often be seen taking riding exercise round by Chiselhurst and Sidcup.'

Later that year, the Sussex *Daily News* reported that he was staying with Mrs O'Shea in Eastbourne. In an effort to keep a lid on things, Parnell adopted the alias Fox and they became a little more careful about their movements.

In 1889, the Home Rule Bill came up again. Negotiations went on throughout the summer and the prospects looked better than they had for many years. However, on Christmas Eve 1889, Captain O'Shea filed for divorce, naming Parnell as co-respondent.

'I fear a thundercloud is about to burst over Parnell's head,' wrote Gladstone, 'and I suppose it will end the career of a man in many respects valuable.'

The divorce was a coup for O'Shea. The evidence against them was now so overwhelming that Parnell and Kitty did not show up in the court. Kitty's aunt had recently died, leaving Kitty her fortune. O'Shea won custody of the children, including Parnell's, and her money. Delivering his verdict, the judge condemned Parnell as 'a man who takes advantage of the hospitality offered him by the husband to debauch the wife'.

O'Shea's mentor, Chamberlain, was happy, too. Parnell had been wiped off the map. In Ireland, the Catholic Church turned against him.

'I cannot but look forward with dismay to our interest, religious as well as civil, being placed under the guidance of a convicted adulterer,' said the Archbishop of Armagh.

The nonconformist churches, which were the backbone of the Liberal Party, condemned him. Even the Irish newspapers turned against him. Parnell fought on, but only succeeded in splitting the nationalists. This ceded the field to the Conservatives and the increasingly militant Ulster Unions and delayed Home Rule for another 30 years. In his disappointment, Parnell grew more outspoken, losing the support of the mainstream while feeding the aspirations of the fanatical nationalists.

In 1891, Parnell and Kitty married in a registry office. A few months later, when he was canvassing for a candidate in Cregas, he gave one last barnstorming speech in a rain storm. He stayed up all night, chatting in his wet clothes. The following day he left Ireland. Seven days later he died in Brighton of 'rheumatism of the heart'.

As Parnell's coffin was being closed, ready to be shipped back to Ireland, Kitty slipped inside the rose that he had kept from their first meeting 11 years earlier. She was advised not to accompany the coffin to Dublin, where Parnell was given a magnificent funeral.

Ruined by the divorce and blamed for the downfall of Parnell, Kitty had a nervous breakdown and withdrew from public life. She published her memoirs in 1914 and died in 1921, at the age of 76. She never remarried.

6 ❖ The Disappearing MP

A t 4.05 p.m. on 20 November 1974, John Stonehouse, a Labour MP and former government minister, walked out of the Fountainbleu Hotel in Miami. He asked the beach attendant, Helen Fleming, to look after his clothes while he went for a swim. He did not return for them. The following day he was reported missing, presumed drowned.

However, at the very moment that the BBC was announcing the death of the MP, Stonehouse was sipping a cocktail in a topless go-go bar in Honolulu. He was on his way to make a new life for himself in Australia. And he was not planning to do so alone. While his wife and 25-year-old daughter were grieving, 27-year-old Sheila Buckley, his former House of Commons secretary, was packing her bags.

John Stonehouse had always fancied himself a high-flyer. His father had been a leading trade unionist, his mother President of Southampton Co-operative Society. Although he left school at 16, after wartime service in the RAF, he studied at the London School of Economics on an ex-serviceman's grant.

In 1957, he was elected to Parliament as a Labour MP. When Labour came to power in 1964, he moved quickly up the ministerial tree, becoming Aviation Minister, Technology Minister, Postmaster General and a Privy Councillor.

When Labour lost the 1970 election, he turned his hand to business, aiming, as he said, to earn 'enough to live reasonably comfortably, to afford to travel and to have the peace of mind to devote myself to political work'. However, he was no businessman. Although he set up 20 companies, including one merchant bank, none was successful. He only managed to keep them afloat by juggling funds from one to another. By 1974, he was over £800,000 in debt. Evenworse, Czech defector Josef Frolik claimed that while Stonehouse had been a cabinet minister he had also been working as a Soviet spy.

Meanwhile, he had begun an affair with his secretary, who would meet him after work in his Westminster flat. She soon became sucked into his fraudulent business dealings. Together they plotted his disappearance. By this time, he had £100,000 salted away in a Swiss bank – more than enough to start a new life together Down Under.

Using a trick borrowed from Frederick Forsyth's *Day of the Jackal*, he went to a local hospital and obtained information on two constituents, Joseph Markham and Donald Mildoon, who had recently died. Then, as their constituency MP, Stonehouse visited their grieving widows. They filled in enough details for Stonehouse to assume the identities of the dead men.

Stonehouse disguised himself with a pair of spectacles and a wide grin for a passport photograph. The application was made in the name of Joseph Markham and he countersigned it with the name of fellow MP Neil McBride, who was dying of cancer at the time. Joseph Markham's passport was processed without question.

Stonehouse then began opening bank accounts in the names of Markham and Mildoon. He established himself as 'J.A. Markham, export-import consultant', using a business forwarding service and took out several credit cards in Markham's name, using a London hotel as his address.

On 6 November 1974, he made a dry run. He bought a return ticket to Miami on Markham's credit card and flew there and back using Markham's passport. When he returned, he announced to his girlfriend Sheila Buckley that his plan was foolproof. But it wasn't. On 7 November, something unforeseen happened. Lord Lucan attacked his wife and killed his children's nanny with a piece of lead piping. Then he disappeared. Soon a world-wide hunt was on for the missing peer.

On 19 November, Stonehouse flew back to Miami, this time as himself. He was accompanied by James Charlton, deputy chairman of one of his companies. The following day, Stonehouse nonchalantly announced that he was going for a swim. But he didn't.

Once he had deposited his clothes with Helen Fleming, making sure that he had given her his name, he went to a disused building where he had hidden a suitcase containing clothes, his fake passport, money, travellers' cheques and the credit cards in the name of Markham. As Markham, he took a cab to the airport and flew to San Francisco. From there he picked up a flight to Hawaii. Confident that his plan was working, he phoned Sheila Buckley in England and told her to get ready.

However, when Stonehouse arrived in Melbourne, everyone was on the lookout for Englishmen behaving strangely. They were looking for Lord Lucan, but Stonehouse fitted the bill. He began transferring large amounts of money out of an account in the name of Mildoon into one in the name of Markham. Suspicions were aroused. An eagle-eyed bank employee called the police.

Convinced that they had found Lord Lucan, the police put Stonehouse under surveillance. And on Christmas Eve, he was arrested.

However, one of the detectives had read about Stonehouse's

disappearance from the Fountainbleu Hotel in Miami and spotted a book of matches from that hotel in his room. When the Melbourne police requested a picture of Lord Lucan from Scotland Yard, they asked for one of Stonehouse, too.

As soon as his true identity was revealed, Stonehouse contacted his wife and asked her to fly out to him. She did. But when she discovered that he had been planning to start a new life with Sheila Buckley, she flew back to England and started divorce proceedings. However, Sheila Buckley stood by Stonehouse in Australia until they were both extradited in July 1975.

In the meantime, Prime Minister Harold Wilson had been forced to set up a Select Committee to investigate the missing MP's position. Stonehouse was invited to return to England voluntarily to appear before it. He refused on the grounds that 'it would be exceptionally dangerous to my psychiatric health'. Instead, he sought asylum in Sweden, courtesy of his old friend, Prime Minister Olof Palme. Palme refused, as did the authorities in Canada, Bangladesh, Tanzania, Mauritius, Kenya and Botswana.

Even when he was returned to England, the disgraced MP refused to resign his seat. He claimed that he was an idealist, forced to escape Britain's corruption, and he quit the Labour Party to join the newly formed English National Party.

At his 68-day trial – which cost the taxpayer an estimated £750,000 – he wore the ENP's symbol, a red rose, in his buttonhole and clutched a St George's flag in his hand. He claimed that the charges against him had been 'politically rigged' and that he was fighting against the national sickness of 'cant, hypocrisy and humbug'.

In his summing up, Mr Justice Eveleigh pointed out that Stonehouse was guilty of all three.

'You did not simply decide to disappear because you were oppressed by business burdens,' he said. 'You decided to do so in comfort, and it is clear to me that self-interest is well to the fore. You aimed to get rich quickly.'

Stonehouse was found guilty of 18 offences and sentenced to seven years' imprisonment. Sheila Buckley – who claimed she did not realize what was happening – was given a two-year suspended sentence for helping him.

Stonehouse suffered two heart attacks in jail and was released after three years. Sheila Buckley was waiting for him. They married secretly in 1981. He eked out a living as a writer and died in poverty in 1988.

'I have never met a man like John,' the ever-loyal Sheila said after his death. 'He was gentle with everybody, and in particular with me. I shall miss him forever.'

7 ❖ A Sick Dog

The charismatic Liberal leader, Jeremy Thorpe, revived the party's fortunes in the 1960s and brought the Liberals, for the first time since the fall of Lloyd George, within striking distance of power. But he was brought down by a scandal involving the shooting of a dog and allegations of homosexuality. Throughout, he maintained his innocence and he was acquitted at trial. It made no difference.

Both Thorpe's father and grandfather were Tory MPs, but when the 26-year-old barrister ran for election in the Tory stronghold of North Devon in 1955, he ran as a Liberal. He lost, but in 1959 he won the seat that he was to hold for 20 years.

Educated at Eton and Oxford, where he was President of the Union, Thorpe was well connected and seemed set for a brilliant career. But early in his career as an MP he made one small slip that would result in disaster. Visiting a friend's riding stables in Oxfordshire in the autumn of 1961, he befriended a good-looking young groom named Norman Scott.

Scott was mentally unstable and latched on to Thorpe. Later he turned up to see Thorpe at the House of Commons, asking for his help as he was now penniless and unemployed after being sacked over the theft of a horse. According to Scott, Thorpe drove him to his mother's home in Oxted, Surrey. That night, Thorpe appeared in his bedroom. There, Scott said, Thorpe had anal sex with him while he bit the pillow to stifle his cries.

The following morning, Thorpe was the perfect gentleman, preparing his guest's breakfast, then driving him back to London. Scott said that Thorpe gave him money to rent a flat in Westminster and letters authorizing him to purchase clothes on his account. Thorpe denied this.

However, Thorpe did make an effort to find his young friend a job, putting ads in *Country Life*. Scott had lost his national insurance card at the stables. Thorpe got him another, stamping it for a few months as his employer.

He arranged for him to spend Christmas in the Devon home of May and James Collier, who was prospective Liberal candidate for Tiverton. Scott was highly unstable and neurotic, and after a few weeks they asked him to leave.

Then in February 1962, Scott was accused of stealing a suede coat from Ann Gray, a woman he had met at a psychiatric clinic. Thorpe told the police that he was 'more or less' Scott's guardian and insisted that the interview take place in his room in the House of Commons. Impressed, the police dropped the case.

Scott wanted to go to France to study dressage. To raise the money, Thorpe fixed him up with a job tending horses in Somerset. He wrote to him there, enclosing more job offers from *Country Life* and saying: 'Bunnies can and will go to France.' Thorpe called Scott 'Bunnies', Scott said, because that night when he approached him in the bedroom of his mother's house he looked like a frightened rabbit.

Scott had told Thorpe that his mother had inexplicably disappeared and that his father had recently died in a plane crash in South America. Thorpe thought that he might be due some compensation and had a solicitor look into the matter for him, only to discover that Scott's father was alive and well, and that his mother continued to live in the family home. She blamed Thorpe for the estrangement of her son.

Thorpe was livid that Scott had lied to him. Scott, in turn, went to Chelsea police station and made a statement alleging that he had had homosexual relations with Jeremy Thorpe. Homosexuality was still against the law. A medical examination indicated that Scott had indulged in anal sex and, to substantiate his story, he handed over two letters from Thorpe – one of which was the letter where Thorpe had addressed him as 'Bunnies'.

In 1964, Thorpe was returned to Parliament with an enlarged majority. Scott contacted him again, saying that he had been offered a job in Switzerland. Thorpe paid for him to go. Scott hated it and returned, losing his luggage along the way. Thorpe tried to retrieve it, but told Scott that he wanted nothing further to do with him.

In retaliation, Scott wrote to Thorpe's mother, saying that he had had a homosexual relationship with her son. It had begun that night he had brought him to her house, Scott said.

'With Jeremy that day, I gave birth to the vice that lies latent in every man,' he wrote.

Thorpe's mother forwarded the letter to him. Thorpe was worried. He showed it to his closest friend in Parliament, Peter Bessell, Liberal MP for the neighbouring constituency of Bodmin.

Bessell was a Congregationalist lay preacher who amazed his Cornish constituents by campaigning in a Cadillac. He was also a slick businessman who let Thorpe in on a number of get-rich-quick schemes. Thorpe became a non-executive director of a number of Bessell's shady companies and sat on the board of London and County Securities, a merchant bank. It went bust in 1976, earning Thorpe a slap on the wrist from the Department of Trade and Industry that only added to his woes.

Like a number of MPs, Bessell was bedding his secretary although, apparently to hold Thorpe's interest, he pretended that he swung both ways. Scott was in Dublin at the time. Bessell went to see him. He told Scott disingenuously that his letter to Thorpe's mother constituted blackmail and said that he had an extradition order in his briefcase. Scott promised to be a good boy and Bessell put him on a retainer. This kept him quiet for the next three years.

In 1967, Jeremy Thorpe was elected leader of the Liberal Party. The following year, he married his first wife, Caroline Allpass, who gave birth to a son. However, by then, Bessell's companies were beginning to come apart at the seams. Scott's latest career venture – as a male model – had come to nothing, and Scott ended up on Thorpe's plate again.

This time Thorpe tried to ship him off to the USA, but the American embassy refused Scott a visa. It was then, Bessell claimed, that Thorpe snapped. Thorpe called him up at the Commons and said: 'Peter, we have got to get rid of him... It's no worse than shooting a sick dog.'

It was also alleged that Thorpe had asked his friend, the merchant banker David Holmes, to organize Scott's murder. However, they suddenly got news that Scott had married and his wife was pregnant. That, everyone hoped, would be the end of the matter.

But the following year, the marriage broke up. Scott left his wife and child and moved to Wales, expecting Thorpe to pick up the tab. He contacted Thorpe and got no joy. So he called Bessell and threatened to take his allegations to the newspapers. Meanwhile, Scott poured out his heart to an elderly postmistress. She, in turn, wrote to her Liberal MP, Emlyn Hooson, warning of the dangers. Hooson passed the letter on to the Liberal Chief Whip, David Steel.

A secret inquiry was set up under the Liberal peer, Lord Byers. Before Scott flounced from the committee room 'like a jilted girl', he had told Byers that he had been stopped by the police while carrying a gun in the House of Commons in 1965. This was easily disproved. Thorpe presented himself as the victim of an obsessed and deluded young man.

That seemed to be the end of it. But, on his way out of the Palace of Westminster, Scott claims that he was threatened with death by a mysterious stranger. Frightened for his life, Scott told his story to freelance journalist Gordon Winters. Winters touted it around Fleet Street but it was generally considered too hot to handle. However, the Mirror Group, which was run by Thorpe's friend Lord Jacobsen, bought the story and locked it in their safe. It would have gone no further, but Gordon Winters was also a spy for the apartheid regime in South Africa and he sent a copy to Pretoria.

Meanwhile, Scott moved into Thorpe's North Devon constituency and started telling his story to anyone who would listen. This brought Scott to the attention of MI5. The Devon and Cornwall police arrested Scott, ostensibly on the charge of stealing £28 from a hotel nine months before, but they questioned him about any documents he might hold that would incriminate Thorpe, on the hope of bringing a charge of blackmail against him.

Thorpe was riding high at the time. Although his first wife, Caroline, was killed in a car crash in 1973, he quickly remarried. His second wife was Marion, Countess of Harewood.

Peter Bessell was now out of Parliament and had absconded to America to escape his creditors. In 1974, builders were working on Bessell's London office when they came across some photographs and papers – one of which was Scott's letter to Thorpe's mother. But Thorpe was lucky. The builders took them to the *Sunday Mirror* and they joined Scott's confession in the Mirror's safe.

The Conservatives, under Ted Heath, had narrowly lost the February 1974 election. Thorpe was summoned to Number 10 for preliminary talks. There were rumours that he might be offered the position of Foreign Secretary in a coalition government, but the party vetoed any such arrangement.

In 1975, it was alleged, the murder plot was revived. At the subsequent trial at the Old Bailey, it was said that David Holmes, along with George Deakin and John Le Mesurier, used a political donation to hire a hit man. The contract was worth £5,000, with another £5,000 on completion. The bungling assassin they chose was an airline pilot named Andrew Newton.

Newton was so incompetent that, when he was told that Norman Scott was in North Devon, he went to Dunstable, not Barnstaple. But in October 1975, he caught up with his quarry. Instead of fleeing, Scott greeted Newton as his saviour. He believed that a hitman was on his way from Canada to murder him and, perversely, assumed that Newton had been sent to protect him.

Scott and his Great Dane, Rinka, got into Newton's car. Newton drove to a deserted part of Exmoor. When they got out, Newton pulled a 1910 Mauser and shot the Great Dane.

'It's your turn next,' he said to Scott. But the gun either jammed or

Newton pretended it had. He drove away, leaving Scott sobbing over the body of his dead dog.

Newton was arrested and a small item about the shooting of Scott's dog appeared in the *News of the World*. But then, on 14 November 1975, *Private Eye* ran this intriguing item:

'A Mr Norman Scott has sent me some very curious material concerning his close friend, the Liberal leader Jeremy Thorpe. If Mr Thorpe would send me my usual fee of £5, I will send him the dossier and say no more.'

In January 1976, things began to come unravelled. Scott answered a summons in Barnstaple on charges of defrauding the DHSS. The magistrate was shocked to find the courtroom packed with journalists. Scott then announced that he was being hounded because he had once had a sexual affair with Jeremy Thorpe. Since the allegation was given as testimony in a courtroom, it could be reported without danger of a libel writ.

The Prime Minister Harold Wilson defended Thorpe in the Commons, saying that the regime in Pretoria was trying to discredit his government by attacking Thorpe. Thorpe himself stoutly denied that he was a homosexual.

In March 1976, Newton was found guilty and sentenced to two years for a firearms offence. Newton claimed that it was he, not Thorpe, who had been the victim of Scott's blackmail. But Scott stuck to his story.

When David Steel discovered that David Holmes had been given £20,000 that was intended for the Liberal Party, he asked Thorpe to step down. Thorpe refused, but the tide was running against him. The newspapers found out about the retainers Bessell had paid Scott. When they tracked down Bessell in America, Bessell denied that he had given Scott cash for Thorpe's benefit. But now that his creditors knew where to find him, he needed money. He sold his story to the *Daily Mail*. It appeared on 6 May. Under the headline, 'I TOLD LIES TO PROTECT THORPE', he said he had paid Scott to protect Thorpe. Worse, he said that Thorpe had wanted Scott dead and that the botched assassination attempt had resulted in the death of the dog Rinka.

At the same time, Scott's solicitor issued a summons for the return of the letters Scott had handed over to the police in 1962. Thorpe followed suit. The court ruled in favour of Scott, who was given the originals. Thorpe received copies. In a bold move, he published them in *The Sunday Times* on 9 May 1976 with a protracted explanation. The paper agreed to make no comment. On the Monday morning, T-shirts appeared in Oxford Street, bearing the slogan: 'Bunnies can and will go to France'. By the end of the day, Thorpe had resigned.

Thorpe blamed a press witch-hunt and the public backbiting of ambitious colleagues. The speaker, George Thomas, agreed and condemned the Liberal members' 'disloyalty just when their leader needed them the most'. But the third act had not yet started.

First, however, there was an 18-month interval with Thorpe sitting quietly on the back benches. Then in April 1977, Newton was released from prison. He sold his story to the London *Evening News* for £3,000. It appeared under the headline, 'I WAS HIRED TO KILL SCOTT'. In October, *The Sunday People* paid him a further £8,000 to photograph Holmes's business associate, John Le Mesurier, pay off the £5,000 owed on the murder attempt.

Thorpe held a press conference and denied everything once again. He denied that he had had a homosexual relationship with Scott, although their friendship had been 'close, even affectionate'. Then came the $64,000 question. A BBC correspondent asked if he had ever had a homosexual relationship.

It was then that Thorpe lost it.

'If you do not know why it is improper and indecent to put such a question to a public man you ought not to be here,' he said.

But he did not say 'no'. Although homosexual acts between consenting adults in private had been legalized by the 1967 Sexual Offences Act homosexuality, especially among MPs, was still frowned on.

The police were busy putting a case together. Although Newton had admitted, at the very least, conspiracy and perjury in his last trial, he was granted immunity from prosecution if he turned queen's evidence. Detectives also travelled to California to interview Bessell and offered him immunity, too. Eager to profit from the situation, Bessell began touting a book. The *Sunday Telegraph* offered a massive £50,000 for the serial rights. One-third of this would be paid upfront. The rest would be paid if Thorpe was convicted. If Thorpe walked, Bessell would receive only another £8,000.

When charges were drawn up, Thorpe, along with Holmes, Deakin and Le Mesurier, surrendered themselves to the police. Thorpe had already delivered a long written statement to the police denying everything. He said he had tried to help Scott who was 'suicidal and unbalanced', but 'my compassion and kindness towards him was in due course repaid with malevolence and resentment'. He knew no more than that, he said.

On his formal arrest, Thorpe refused to answer any further questions on the grounds that the answers might be leaked and prejudice the case.

Even after being charged, Thorpe made a dramatic appearance at the Liberal Party conference. It was beholden on the new leader, David Steel, to greet him. His appearance was a great embarrassment. It overshadowed coverage of the policy issues and, with an election only months away, it was the worst sort of publicity for the party.

Thorpe was still on bail when he fought the 1979 election. At campaign meetings, his once-loyal followers stayed away in droves. The satirist Auberon Waugh stood against him as candidate for the Dog Lovers' Party. Only one Liberal MP, John Pardoe, from a neighbouring seat, turned out to lend his support. Thorpe was resoundingly trounced by the Tories. Pardoe lost his seat, too.

Five days later, Thorpe was in the dock of the Old Bailey, charged with conspiring to murder Norman Scott and inciting David Holmes to commit murder. He pleaded not guilty.

Although the case against him looked strong, Thorpe's barrister George Carmen QC made mincemeat of the prosecution witnesses. Bessell's statement that Thorpe had said in 1968 'we have got to get rid of' Scott was the only evidence of the involvement of Thorpe in any plot. Carmen demonstrated that Bessell had given several different versions on different occasions of how Thorpe had told him this. He also pointed out to the jury that Bessell stood to profit considerably from the contract with the *Sunday Telegraph* if Thorpe was convicted. He similarly savaged Scott who was, admittedly, an easier target.

These points were not lost on the judge who, in his summing up, described Bessell as a 'humbug' and Scott as 'a crook, an accomplished liar, a fraud, a sponger, a whiner, a parasite and a spineless neurotic character addicted to hysteria and self-advertisement, although the judge conceded, 'he could still be telling the truth'.

The jury did not think so. They also thought that Bessell's evidence was tainted by the £25,000 he stood to gain if Thorpe went down. After two days' deliberation, they returned a verdict of not guilty.

There was some criticism of Thorpe for not appearing on the witness stand to tell his side of the story. But the people of North Devon were delighted. Even though he had been defeated in the election, 23,000 of them had still voted for him. A thanksgiving service was held for him and he was elected President of the North Devon Liberal Association, in due course becoming President of the Liberal Democrat Association.

Thorpe has stuck by his story of complete innocence ever since. However, two years after his acquittal, David Holmes spilt the beans in the *News of World*, in exchange for the donation of a 'substantial fee' to charity.

He said that Thorpe was the inspiration behind various attempts to silence Scott because of the threat he posed to Thorpe's political career. The plan had been to frighten Scott, not kill him, and certain actions had taken place 'after discussion with Jeremy and with his authorization'.

8 ❖ Watergate

Until the presidential follies of Bill Clinton, it was a safe bet that Watergate was going to be the political scandal of the 20th century. It involved break-ins, cover-ups, slush funds, dirty tricks, black lists, presidential paranoia, illegal taping and deleted expletives. As a result, Richard Nixon became the first – and, so far, only – US President to be forced to resign from office.

The causes of the Watergate scandal lay deep in the character of Richard Nixon. Born in small-town California, he saw himself as the perpetual outsider. Even when he was President, he thought that the Eastern Establishment and the liberal big city press would stop at nothing to get him. He may have been right. Few politicians have been more hated and feared than Richard Nixon.

Nixon started off on the wrong foot. As a young congressman, he sat on the House Un-American Activities Committee and was pivotal in the downfall of Alger Hiss, an official with the State Department revealed, falsely, many believe – to be a Soviet spy.

Being conspicuously on the right of the party, he was picked as running mate to the liberal-leaning Dwight Eisenhower in 1952 to balance the ticket. This provoked an immediate scandal when it was alleged that he controlled a secret slush fund set up by wealthy Californian businessmen. Nixon responded by going on television – still a relatively untried medium – and made his famous 'Checkers' speech. In it he protested his innocence. He claimed that instead of going around in fur coats, his wife Pat wore a good old-fashioned cloth coat. The only gift his family had ever received, he assured viewers, was a puppy dog called Checkers – and he was darned if he was going to give that back. It was a bravura performance and earned him the sobriquet, among opponents at least, of 'Tricky-Dicky'.

After two terms as vice-president, Nixon was nominated to be Eisenhower's successor, although with little enthusiasm from Eisenhower himself. However, he narrowly lost the 1960 election to John F. Kennedy, possibly as a result of Democratic ballot-stuffing in key districts. Although Kennedy was an Irish Catholic, in Nixon's eyes he was everything he hated – moneyed, an Easterner, a writer, an intellectual and a Harvard man.

In 1962, he was decisively defeated when he ran for the governorship of California. At a press conference the following day, he told reporters: 'For 16 years, you have had a lot of fun. Now you won't have Nixon to kick around any more because, gentlemen, this is my last press conference.'

But he was wrong. He got a further kicking when he and his campaign manager, H.R. 'Bob' Haldeman were fined for using unfair campaign practices. Even so, his appetite for power was unsated.

After the Republican Barry Goldwater was routed by the incumbent Lyndon Johnson, Nixon set about re-establishing himself as a leading figure in the party. In 1968, he won the Republican nomination once again. This time he had luck on his side. Johnson's popular domestic policies were completely swamped by the nation's catastrophic involvement in the Vietnam War and Johnson refused to run again. The assassination of Robert Kennedy robbed the Democrats of their natural leader, and the assassination of Martin Luther King that year sparked race riots. The Democratic convention in Chicago degenerated into a running battle between Mayor Daley's brutal police and the peace protesters and civil rights activists. Nixon claimed to speak for the 'silent majority' and promised to bring back law and order. He also stole what was left of the Democrats' clothes. The Democratic nominee, Hubert Humphrey, although a man of impeccable liberal credentials, had been vice-president in the Johnson administration and was thus tainted by the war. Nixon, however, promised to end the war, bringing 'peace with honour'. He won by a landslide.

But Nixon was not a peacemaker by instinct. He stepped up the war, extending into neighbouring Laos and Cambodia. This was illegal. War could only be declared by Congress. But Nixon figured that even if this did not bring the victory the Pentagon promised him, it would help bomb the Vietnamese to the bargaining table.

To conduct such a clandestine policy under the very eyes of the Eastern Establishment required the utmost secrecy. There were few people in Washington he could trust. Nixon surrounded himself with other outsiders, men who had not held public office and had no political ideas above the acquisition of power for its own sake.

Haldeman, a former public relations man, became the White House Chief of Staff, who controlled access to the President. Nixon's former law partner and 1968 campaign manager, John Mitchell, became Attorney

General. Another PR man and a friend of Haldeman, John Ehrlichman, became the Assistant for Domestic Affairs.

Nixon felt the danger of domestic sedition most keenly due to the growing opposition to the Vietnam War. But he also mistrusted such a natural ally as the FBI Director, J. Edgar Hoover, and tried to sack him more than once. Hoover had been head of the Bureau since its inception in the 1920s. He had a power base of his own and was not to be shifted. Nixon saw him as a rival and a threat.

Even more, Nixon mistrusted the CIA for what he saw as its Ivy League pedigree and its history of accommodation with America's enemies. He set up his own private intelligence capability, responsible only to the White House.

Then there were the Democrats. In 1970–71, he set up a number of projects to bug political opponents and harrass the press. The operations were overseen by Nixon's appointment secretary Dwight Chapin, press secretary Ron Ziegler, Haldeman's aide Gordon Strachan and White House attorney Don Segretti – all of whom had been members of a student club at the University of South California called the Trojan Knights, which specialized in stuffing ballot boxes and other election tricks.

Opposition to the war entered the mainstream when, in June 1971, the *New York Times* began publishing the 'Pentagon Papers'. These were a secret history of the war in Vietnam and contained damaging information about America's involvement, particularly Nixon's illegal incursions into Laos and Cambodia. The source was Daniel Ellsberg, a former intelligence analyst at the Pentagon.

Nixon's response was to set up a 'special investigations unit' to collect information on Ellsberg and his links to the Democrats, especially to Ted Kennedy, who threatened to run for president in 1972. Wrapped in the mantle of his two dead brothers, he would have made a formidable opponent.

The unit was quickly dubbed the 'plumbers'. Ehrlichman was in charge and his aide Egil Krogh Jr ran the unit from Room 216 in the Executive Office building next door to the White House. It had a staff of about 50 in all. The senior men included National Security Council staff lawyer, David Young, and Nixon's own special counsel and action man, Charles Colson.

Colson recruited E. Howard Hunt, an ex-CIA man who had been involved in the abortive CIA invasion of Cuba that was thwarted at the Bay of Pigs. He was joined by former FBI agent and assistant district attorney, G. Gordon Liddy.

Their first object was to smear Ellsberg. On 3 September 1971, Hunt and Liddy stood guard as three of Hunt's Cuban contacts burgled the office of Ellsberg's psychiatrist.

Liddy was plainly a man who could be relied on so in December 1971, White House counsel John Dean picked him to work under John Mitchell and Jed Magruder at the Committee to Re-Elect the President, known by the wonderful acronym CREEP. Liddy's job title was General Counsel, but his job was 'political intelligence-gathering'. On 27 January 1972, he outlined a plan called Operation Gemstone to Mitchell, Magruder and Dean. In the forthcoming election, he aimed to wage a campaign of sabotage, blackmail, kidnapping, break-ins and electronic surveillance. It would cost a cool $1 million.

Although Mitchell rejected the plan as too expensive, Liddy was authorized to put a scaled-down version of Gemstone into effect, with a budget of just $250,000. The first operation was to be a break-in at the campaign headquarters of Senator George McGovern, who had emerged as the front-runner for the Democratic nomination that year. It was a failure. But that same night, 26 March 1972, Liddy, Hunt and their team of Cubans broke into the Democratic National Committee offices in the Watergate building. James W. McCord, CREEP's 'security co-ordinator', installed two wiretaps. In the nature of things, only one of the wiretaps worked and it produced little more than secretarial chitchat.

The 'plumbers' decided to have another go on the night of 16 June 1972. It ended in disaster. An alert night-watchman called the police who arrested five intruders on the sixth floor of the Watergate building. They were carrying bugging devices, walkie-talkies and substantial sums of money. They gave false names, but on interrogation quickly admitted their true identities. The five men were James McCord, which tied the break-in to CREEP; former CIA agent Bernard Baker; Frank Sturgis, a US-born mercenary who had fought both for and against Castro; and two Cubans, Virgilio Gonzalez and Eugenio Martinez, a locksmith. Liddy, Hunt and Alfred C. Baldwin, a former FBI agent, were nearby supervising the operation and got away.

These men may well have staged this break-in on their own authority. But the chain of command ran back via Strachan and Krogh to Haldeman and Ehrlichman, the President's closest advisers, and via Mitchell to the President himself.

Nixon claimed that news of the break-in came to him while he was on holiday in Key Biscayne, Florida. His reaction was that bugging the headquarters of the Democratic National Committee was stupid – 'anyone who knew anything about politics would know that the national committee headquarters was a useless place to go for inside information on a presidential campaign,' he wrote in his memoirs.

When the five burglars were arraigned in court on 17 June, they identified themselves as 'anti-Communists' and McCord whispered 'CIA' to the judge. Press reports identified McCord as the security co-ordinator of CREEP, but Mitchell issued a statement saying that McCord had been hired merely as a temporary security consultant who had been let go a month before.

The story would have ended there, but for two young reporters at the *Washington Post* – 29-year-old Bob Woodward and 28-year-old Carl Berstein – who discovered that address books found on two of the burglars contained the name of E. Howard Hunt. On 20 June 1972, the *Washington Post* reported that Hunt worked as a consultant to Charles Colson, Nixon's own special counsel. This linked the break-in dangerously close to the President.

The White House was rattled. The internal phone directories were recalled and amended to disguise the fact that Hunt had an office there. John Dean told Hunt to get out of the country, which he did – briefly. Liddy melodramatically offered to stand on a street corner where he could be gunned down.

Dean devised complex cover stories to prevent the operation being traced beyond Liddy and up the chain of command. Hush money was paid to the burglars. The cover-up was in full swing.

But there was another wild card. Baldwin, who had probably been an FBI plant, told the FBI that Hunt and Liddy had been involved. Nixon had to be informed. Fatefully, on 23 June 1972, Nixon and Haldeman discussed the possibility of using the CIA to block the FBI's enquiries.

Hunt and Liddy had to be sacrificed, but the trial of the 'Watergate Seven' was scheduled for January 1973, conveniently after the November election. As it was, Nixon romped home. The Democrats were in disarray. In July they had to drop their vice-presidential candidate, Thomas Eagleton, when it was revealed that he had been hospitalized three times for 'nervous exhaustion and fatigue'. Their presidential nominee, George McGovern, was an anti-war candidate. But, since Nixon was only months away from a negotiated end to the American involvement in the Vietnam War, it seemed sensible to let him finish the job.

At the trial, McCord and Liddy both pleaded not guilty, but at the last minute Hunt changed his plea to guilty. Throughout the hearings, the judge, John Sirica, was irritated by the government prosecutors who

Richard Nixon. The Watergate Affair was one of the most notorious political scandals of the Twentieth Century

seemed to be handling the defendants with kid gloves. The trial passed off without anyone, outside the seven conspirators, being implicated and all seven were convicted of conspiracy, burglary and illegal wiretapping. However, press stories, largely in the *Washington Post*, continued to link the conspirators to the White House and it was beginning to become clear that the Watergate break-in was only part of a wide programme of electoral dirty tricks. On February 1973 the Senate voted to set up a committee under Senator Sam Ervin to investigate irregularities during the presidential campaign.

FBI director J. Edgar Hoover had died in May 1972. Nixon wanted the acting director, L. Patrick Gray, to be confirmed as his replacement. So while the Ervin committee sat, Gray went before the Senate Judiciary Committee. There he revealed that the FBI had failed to interview key witnesses in the Watergate case and that he had allowed the President's counsel, John Dean, to sit in on interviews of White House personnel.

This put the spotlight on Dean, the man who had co-ordinated the cover-up. He was called to testify to the Ervin committee, but refused. Nixon had already made it clear that he would not let White House staff testify on the grounds of executive privilege. Ervin warned that White House staff were not 'nobility or royalty'. If they failed to comply with subpoenas, he would recommend that the Senate issued warrants for their arrest.

On 23 March, Judge Sirica handed down savage sentences on the Watergate conspirators – 20 years for Liddy, 35 for Hunt and 40 years for Barker, Gonzalez, Martinez and Sturgis – more than they would have expected for murder in the District of Columbia. However, Sirica made it clear that these sentences were provisional and would be reviewed in the light of how much they co-operated with Ervin's committee.

McCord was not sentenced at that time. Instead, Sirica read a statement from McCord, admitting that political pressure had been applied for him to plead guilty and keep quiet. The defendants had perjured themselves, he said. They knew that others involved in the Watergate operation had not been identified at the trial. He was released and given immunity to subsequent prosecution.

On 26 March, McCord told the *Los Angeles Times* that both Magruder and Dean knew of the Watergate break-in in advance. Dean was beginning to get rattled. He warned Nixon that there was 'a cancer close to the presidency, and it's growing'. Hunt was now demanding more money, otherwise he would tell what he knew about the Ellsberg break-in and bring Ehrlichman down.

By 8 April, Dean was talking to the prosecutors via his lawyer. Haldeman and Ehrlichman were pressuring him to persuade Mitchell to take the rap for the break-in, hoping the buck would stop there. Meanwhile, Magruder was talking to the prosecutors, telling them that Mitchell and Dean had coached him to commit perjury as part of the cover-up. He also outlined Liddy's Gemstone plan and confirmed that hush money had been paid to the burglars.

Under pressure from the prosecutors, Dean gave way, implicating Haldeman in the hush-money payments and Ehrlichman in the destruction of incriminating documents removed from Hunt's safe.

Nixon summoned Dean to the Oval Office. Dean expected to be hauled over the coals, but Nixon was surprisingly cautious in his choice of words. For the first time, Dean began to suspect that conversations in the Oval Office were being taped.

Nixon wanted Dean to resign, citing his 'involvement in the Watergate affair'. When Dean refused, Nixon removed executive privilege from White House staff, hoping to force Dean's hand. If his testimony to the Senate committee resulted in his prosecution, only the President could offer him executive clemency. However, this move had the opposite effect on Dean. He now sought to make a deal with the prosecutors, telling what he knew in exchange for immunity from prosecution. He told the press that he was not willing to be 'a scapegoat in the Watergate case' and spent the rest of his time in the White House, gathering all the incriminating material he could put his hands on.

But a scapegoat is exactly what Nixon intended Dean to be. On 26 April, the White House leaked a story to the columnist Jack Anderson, saying that Mitchell and Dean had known about the break-in from the outset. They had orchestrated the cover-up and the payment of hush money. Dean had misled Nixon over the matter and Ehrlichman and Colson had laboured to discover the truth. This would not wash. The following day, Patrick Gray resigned as acting head of the FBI, after newspaper reports revealed that he had burnt documents from Hunt's safe, given to him by Ehrlichman and Dean.

On 30 April 1973, Nixon went on TV and admitted there had been a cover-up – 'an effort to conceal the facts from the public, from you and from me'. The break-in, he said, had been a 'senseless, illegal action'.

'The easiest course would be for me to blame those to whom I delegated the responsibility to run the campaign,' he told the American people unblinkingly. 'But that would be a cowardly thing to do. In any organization, the man at the top must bear the responsibility. I accept it.'

As to the cover-up, he had received 'continuing assurances' from those investigating the matter that no one in the White House was involved, up until 21 March. Now he was going to have to accept the resignations of Haldeman and Ehrlichman – 'two of the finest public servants it has been my privilege to know'. There was, he said, 'no implication whatsoever of personal wrongdoing on their part'. He pointedly did not give the same assurance when he announced the resignation of John Dean.

'I will do everything in my power to ensure that the guilty are brought to justice,' he said solemnly. 'There can be no whitewash at the White House.'

No one believed him.

In an effort to draw a line under the scandal, Nixon was fulsome in his praise for everyone in sight, including the 'vigorous free press'. Woodward and Bernstein were singled out for an apology by White House press spokesman, Ron Ziegler, for the vilification he had previously heaped upon them.

But the scent of blood was now in the air. If Haldeman and Ehrlichman knew about the cover-up, surely Nixon must have known, too. And if he was willing to sacrifice two of his closest advisors, he must be fighting for his very survival.

The following day, the Senate passed a unanimous vote calling on the

President to appoint a Special Prosecutor. This was to be Archibald Cox. He was professor of law at Harvard. Worse, he was a Kennedy man.

By now it was clear that the Watergate 'plumbers' had also been behind the break-in at Ellsberg's psychiatrist's. Charges against Ellsberg of theft, conspiracy and espionage for the leaking of the 'Pentagon Papers' were dismissed on the grounds of 'government misconduct'.

The task in hand now was to tie the Watergate break-in and the subsequent cover-up to Nixon himself. The Ervin committee, now staging televised hearings, were asking one central question. As Senator Howard Baker put it: 'What did the President know, and when did he know it?'

McCord told the committee that a Treasury Department official, John J. Caulfield, had brought him an offer of clemency 'from the very highest levels of the White House' in exchange for his silence at the Watergate trial. Caulfield testified that the offer had come from Dean, not Nixon.

Haldeman and Ehrlichman also blamed Dean. Along with the President, they had scarcely given Watergate a thought during the summer of 1972. It was up to Dean to keep them informed.

Dean came out with guns blazing. He told the committee that Nixon kept an enemies list. People on it were to be targeted for harassment by the FBI and the Internal Revenue Service. Dean denied that he had been employed by Nixon to investigate who was responsible for the Watergate break-in. Rather, he was to find out what the FBI and the Justice Department had discovered and to come up with 'plausible scenarios' to obscure White House involvement. He testified that as early as September 1972, Nixon had known of his cover-up activities. And, most damning of all, at a meeting on 21 March with Haldeman present, he said that Nixon had assured him that there was 'no problem' raising a further $1 million to buy the continuing silence of the Watergate burglars.

Dean was then asked whether he was 'fully aware of the charges you have made under oath against the highest official of our land'. He replied: 'I realize it's an almost impossible task, it's one man against another. And it's not a very pleasant situation.'

But Dean was lucky. It was not just one man's word against another's. On 16 July 1973, one of Haldeman's aides told the committee that Nixon had a system for taping the conversations in his private offices. Both the Senate Investigating Committee and Special Prosecutor then issued subpoenas demanding access to those tapes.

At this point, Nixon considered destroying the tapes. But that, he concluded, would look like an admission of guilt. He also thought that the tapes could still be of some use to him. They gave him a hold over others who, like Dean, might turn against him. He also thought that he still had some degree of control over the tapes and their release.

On 29 August 1973, Judge Sirica ordered Nixon to hand over the tapes of eight specified conversations. He refused, although he eventually conceded that he would hand over a summary of the specified tapes. These would be authenticated by John C. Stennis, a partially deaf senator from Mississippi. In exchange, Archibald Cox was to make no further attempts to gain access to the tapes. Cox refused. In response, Nixon abolished the office of Special Prosecutor and ordered the Attorney General, Elliot Richardson, to sack Cox. Both Richardson and his deputy resigned. Cox had to be sacked by the third in line in the Justice Department, Solicitor General Robert Bork.

The reaction to this high-handed action was overwhelming. Millions of letters and telegrams of protest poured into Washington. Congress considered impeachment for the first time. This became a genuine possibility on 10 October when the demagogic vice-president, Spiro Agnew, resigned after pleading *nolo contendre* – no contest – to charges that he had accepted millions of dollars in bribes from engineering contractors when he had been Chief Executive of Baltimore in the early 1960s. In his place, Nixon appointed the dull but safe Gerald Ford.

This move sealed Nixon's fate. No one would have removed him if Agnew was going to take over. But Ford seemed a decent alternative.

On 23 October, Nixon surrendered the tapes that Sirica had asked for. He was now isolated. He had lost all his top advisers and dared speak to no one. Even his new White House Chief of Staff, General Alexander Haig, was seen as a man loyal to the all-powerful Secretary of State, Henry Kissinger, rather than to Nixon. Kissinger was one of the few top men in the Nixon administration to come through with his reputation more or less unsullied.

Although Nixon had taken to brooding alone in the White House, on 17 November he gave a press conference. It was another mistake. Emotionally, he told the assembled journalists: 'I am not a crook.' It was a phrase that would become the derisive chant of the demonstrators who came to taunt him.

Things went from bad to worse. On 21 November, White House counsel J. Fred Buzhardt had to deliver the embarrassing news that the first 181/2 minutes of the first tape Sirica had subpoenaed had been wiped. It was from 20 June 1972, Nixon's first day back in the White House following the Watergate break-in. The story was that Nixon's long-serving secretary, Rose Mary Woods, had accidentally erased it. This was later shown to be impossible, but no one believed it anyway.

This was the straw that broke the camel's back. The House of Representatives then voted 401 to 4 for the House Judicial Committee to begin drawing up a bill of impeachment. Haldeman, Ehrlichman, Strachan, Mitchell and Colson were all indicted by a Grand Jury for conspiracy, perjury and obstruction of justice.

Nixon made one last bid to hold on to office. He offered to release to the Judiciary Committee all the tapes that the Special Prosecutor had demanded. And he admitted the broad outline of the conversation he had had with John Dean on 21 March. But this only whetted their appetite. They demanded more tapes. Instead, he offered to release transcripts of the tapes they asked for and others that, he assured the nation on television, would prove that he had no prior knowledge of the break-in and no knowledge of the cover-up, until the conversation with Dean on 21 March. The transcripts would be edited for relevance and national security considerations, and senior members of the Judiciary Committee would be able to check the tapes to ensure their accuracy.

On 30 April 1974, a 200,000-word transcript was released to the public. It did him no good. They clearly showed that Nixon had discussed misleading scenarios and hush money – though he claimed he was simply thinking out loud. Prudish supporters were shocked by the 146 gaps marked 'expletive deleted'. Others were appalled by the rambling nature of his thought processes which were sometimes reduced to a series of incoherent grunts.

And the transcripts, bad as they were, did not even tell the whole truth. The Judiciary Committee found a number of passages that had been incorrectly transcribed, and published its own version – transcribed, it said, using superior audio equipment. For example, the Judiciary Committee's version has Nixon telling Dean on 22 March to 'get on with the cover-up plan', whereas the White House version contains the rather less damning 'get off the cover-up line'. And in some places, key passages discussing the cover-up were missing from the White House version altogether.

Nixon was all but finished, when Judge Sirica revealed that when Haldeman *et al* had been indicted on 1 March, Nixon had been named as a co-conspirator, but an indictment had not been handed up because no one was sure if you could bring a criminal indictment against a sitting president. Despite the now familiar misgivings about the impeachment process, the House Judiciary Committee's hand was now forced. Three articles of impeachment were passed. Even so, Nixon still had his supporters in Congress, particularly in the Senate, and the outcome of the impeachment procedure was far from certain.

The killer blow came from the Supreme Court which, in a unanimous decision, ordered Nixon to hand over even more tapes to be used in the Haldeman conspiracy trial. On one of those tapes was a conversation from 23 June 1972, in which Nixon had ordered Haldeman to try to get the CIA to block the FBI's investigation into the origin of the money the Watergate burglars were carrying. Nixon had kept the existence of this conversation secret, even from his own attorney. It was what everyone had been looking for from the beginning – the 'smoking gun'. Here was the chief law officer of the United States using the machinery of government to block a criminal investigation. It was a clear case of obstruction of justice.

When Nixon told Buzhardt, Haig, Kissinger and his counsel James St Clair, they urged him to resign. Although Nixon admitted that portions of the tape were 'at variance with certain of my previous statements' he protested that 'the record, in its entirety, does not justify the extreme step of impeachment'. Congress did not agree. After a private briefing, Republican leaders told Nixon that 425 of the 435 members of Congress would vote for impeachment and that only a dozen senators would vote against his conviction.

The following day, 8 August 1974, Nixon made a speech trumpeting his foreign policy achievements, but announcing that he was going to stand down because 'it has become evident to me that I no longer have a strong enough political base in the Congress'. The day after that, he formally resigned and Gerald Ford became the first US president not to have been elected either as president or vice-president.

After only a month in office, Ford granted Nixon a 'full, free and absolute' pardon. This cooked his goose. Some of his staff resigned in protest and Ford was voted out of office in 1976.

9 ❖ The Prisoners Left Behind

The Watergate scandal covered up another, more serious, scandal created by the Nixon White House, that did not come to the attention of the American public until 1985 with the release of the film, *Rambo: First Blood Part Two*. In the movie, Vietnam veteran John Rambo returns to South-east Asia to rescue American prisoners of war held there more than 10 years after the US ignominious withdrawal in 1973. But it is not only the Vietnamese he has to fight. He also faces the opposition of the CIA,

Department of Defense and even the US government itself, which had been covering up the fact that they had left American prisoners behind in Communist hands after the end of the war.

Rambo was not the first film to suggest this. There had been a series of them, including one called *Missing in Action*. The missing prisoners were known across America as MIAs, in the mistaken belief that they had been listed as 'missing in action' during the war.

In the 1980s, polls showed that between 73 and 85 per cent of Americans believed that their government had left prisoners behind in Vietnamese hands. But the government denied it. Indeed, in 1978, the Carter administration had officially declared dead any men listed as 'missing' or 'prisoner' during the war, who had not returned home. So what was the truth?

To discover that, you have to go back and look at the whole conduct of the war. America's war in Vietnam began with the Gulf of Tonkin incident, when the US government claimed that the US *Maddox* was attacked by three Vietnamese gunboats in the Gulf of Tonkin. It is debatable whether this incident ever happened, but Congress passed the Gulf of Tonkin Resolution, which funded the war.

President Nixon, another scandal for the US President, who was accused of leaving prisoners behind at the end of the Vietnam war

Officially, the war was contained to Vietnam itself, but secretly the Americans fought in neighbouring Laos and Cambodia, too. On the ground in Vietnam, America, with its overwhelming technological superiority, falsified enemy casualty figures to Congress who had to foot the bill. This falsification of intelligence was a key factor in America's defeat in the Vietnam War. It also cast doubt on the US's own casualty figures.

Although Vietnam veterans claimed that comrades who had been listed KIA – killed in action – were, in fact, prisoners, they could not prove their case. It was non-commissioned officers at America's National Security Agency, who first discovered what was happening. The NSA, one of America's most secret intelligence organizations, eavesdropped on Vietnamese military communications. They discovered that American airmen shot down over Communist-held territory were being segregated as soon as they were captured. Ordinary pilots were taken to the camps around Hanoi. Those who had special skills – back-seat electronic warfare officers, the crews of the brand new F-111, those who had been on space programmes, or men with special qualifications – were flown into the Soviet Union. No airman shot down over South-east Asia was ever returned from the USSR.

Men who were badly injured were sent to the medical facilities in Shanghai, in China. Others were used as slave labour on installations of strategic importance. Since the war between North and South Vietnam continued after the Americans withdrew, these men could not be handed back. They knew too much.

Throughout the Vietnam War, the people of the Communist North were told that prisoners of war were valuable. Leaflets explained that downed American pilots would be exchanged for factories, hospitals, schools and money.

This was no empty boast. The Vietnamese had already beaten the French in 1954. US intelligence documents from the American war, 1965–73, show that large numbers of French prisoners were still being held then. But the French were prepared to deal. Year after year, they paid millions of dollars to get their prisoners back. The last French prisoner was returned from Vietnam in 1976.

After the Tet offensive in 1968, it became obvious that the war in Vietnam was unwinnable. President Lyndon Johnson announced that he would not stand again as president; he halted the bombing of the Communist North and began peace talks in Paris.

From the beginning of the talks, the Vietnamese asked for reparations. After all, they argued, they had not attacked America. America had attacked them and devastated their country.

Promising to end the war, Richard Nixon became president in 1969. Instead, he went on the offensive, upping the bombing of North Vietnam, Laos and Cambodia. More airmen were captured. Since action in Laos and Cambodia was illegal, it was not possible for the American administration to admit that prisoners had been taken there. The ground war was also extended into Laos and Cambodia. This was too much for the American people. Students and other demonstrators threatened to bring the country to a standstill and Congress repealed the Gulf of Tonkin Resolution, starving the American war effort of money.

The Nixon administration had to make what it dubbed 'peace with honour' quickly. In the Christmas offensive of 1972, the Nixon administration even tried massive new bombing strikes on Hanoi to force the Vietnamese to make a settlement.

The Paris Peace Accords, ending the US involvement in the war, were signed on 27 January 1973. They specified that there would be an 'exchange' of prisoners of war. The problem was that since no war had been declared (American involvement in South-east Asia was merely a 'police action'), the Geneva Conventions had not been observed and no prisoner of war lists had been exchanged during the hostilities.

When the North Vietnamese eventually produced a list, it contained less than half the number of names the Americans had expected. In fact, men whom the Americans knew the Vietnamese were holding – their names and pictures had appeared in Communist newspapers and propaganda films – were not on the list. The Americans could complain, but there was nothing they could do about this discrepancy. Public opinion was so against the war at this time that the US delegation in Paris had no leverage.

Even more glaringly, none of the more than 600 men the US knew had been captured in Laos appeared on the lists. When the Americans asked what had happened to them, the Vietnamese said to ask the Laotians. Since, officially, there had been no war in Laos, the Americans could not do this.

However, they did halt their troop withdrawals from Vietnam until the North Vietnamese cleared up the Laotian anomaly. Eventually, the North Vietnamese came up with nine men from Laos. But they were held throughout their captivity by the North Vietnamese. No one captured by the Lao Communist guerrillas, the Pathet Lao, was ever returned.

Men captured in Cambodia were simply written off. No one, it was assumed, could have survived Pol Pot's Khmer Rouge. However, there were more problems with the prisoner returns in South Vietnam.

The Paris Peace Accords had specified an exchange of prisoners. The Viet Cong, the communist guerrillas in South Vietnam, mustered the Americans they held in order to exchange them for men of theirs that the Americans held. But the Americans returned no one. They had either killed the Communists they had captured, or had given them to the anti-Communist South Vietnamese, who had killed them. So the Viet Cong simply held on to the Americans they had captured.

The Hanoi government also knew that the war had not been won on the battlefield. It had been won on the TV sets of America. Images of burning children and napalmed villages had changed the world's mind about the war.

Returnees were given a special nutritious diet so they looked good. The US authorities, expecting large numbers of burn cases and amputees among the downed airmen returned, put all the hospitals in the USA on alert. But the beds remained empty. Every American prisoner of war who stepped off the plane back into the USA in a whirlwind of publicity was fit and well.

A quick analysis of those returned showed that the highly trained back-seaters were missing. Returned prisoners also asked where their comrades in captivity were. The government asked them to be patient. The matter was in hand.

Indeed it was. The Nixon administration secretly promised the Vietnamese $3.25 billion for the return of the other prisoners. The problem was that such an expenditure had to be approved by Congress. By then, President Nixon was embroiled in the Watergate scandal. He had no clout with Congress and could not get the funds.

But the Nixon administration's one triumph was the end of the Vietnam War. It could not reveal that it had been short-changed at the peace talks. So the officials simply ignored the problem.

When President Carter came to power he wanted to heal the wounds left by the divisive Vietnam War. He tried to open diplomatic channels with Vietnam and declared the missing men dead.

However, boat people fleeing Vietnam brought news of Americans still being held. In 1981, within weeks of taking office, President Reagan received a telegram from the Vietnamese, asking for $4 billion for the return of American prisoners. Instead, President Reagan authorized a number of Rambo-style raids into Vietnam and Laos. They were unsuccessful.

After the fall of Communism in Russia, President Boris Yeltsin admitted that American prisoners captured in Vietnam had turned up in the former Soviet Union. America was still trying to reopen diplomatic relations with Vietnam. To clear the air, the US Senate set up a Select Committee to investigate.

In 1994, hidden in a thousand-page report, the committee found that American prisoners had indeed been left behind in Communist hands after the Vietnam War. But the committee concluded that they were all dead now – though it could produce no evidence showing how and when they had died. Nor could it explain the evidence that showed American prisoners were still being held by the Vietnamese in remote areas of Laos, which they occupy.

So what happened to the men? One of them, a US Marine named Bobby Garwood, returned in 1979, six years after the American withdrawal. He had been taken prisoner in 1965 and held in a number of PoW camps in North Vietnam.

In 1968, he was being moved when the truck carrying him stopped so that the driver could have a rest. Garwood saw tall, white men working in a field and approached them. They spoke French. Garwood knew that the French war in Indochina had ended in 1954. Fourteen years later, French prisoners were still there. The Vietnamese were serious when they told him: 'We can keep you forever.'

Garwood began to co-operate. He fixed jeeps and did other odd jobs. But he made himself a little too useful and, in 1973, he was not returned. Between 1973 and 1979 he often saw other American prisoners like himself.

In 1979, the Vietnamese economy was strained. Garwood persuaded his jailers to take him to Hanoi where, as a foreigner, he would be able to buy cigarettes that they could sell on the black market. On one of these trips he managed to slip a note to an official of the World Bank. He informed American authorities, who did nothing except complete the procedures, declaring Garwood dead. But Garwood's story broke on the BBC.

The US government was forced to ask for Garwood back. The Vietnamese denied having him, but eventually handed him over. The Americans immediately arrested him on four capital charges. His court-appointed lawyer advised him not to mention the other men he had seen at his court martial. He was found guilty on just one charge – collaborating with the enemy – fined the exact amount of his back pay and dishonourably discharged from the Marine Corps.

The fate of American prisoners after the end of the Vietnam War can have come as no surprise to the US authorities.

While investigating what had happened to American PoWs from the Vietnam War in 1990, the Senate Foreign Relations Committee looked into the fate of prisoners from previous wars. It was discovered that German prisoners from World War I had been taken into Siberia. Some remained there all their lives. During the Allied Intervention into Russia in 1919, British and American prisoners had been taken by the Communists and never returned.

During the Korean War, members of the UN forces fighting under US leadership were seen being transported under guard across the border from China into the Soviet Union. Others remained in China where there is evidence that they were used as guinea pigs in biological warfare experiments.

In 1953, when the Korean War ended, the American press was full of stories about the 954 US prisoners who had not been returned. One hundred and fifty-one British prisoners shared their fate. But since nothing could be done to put pressure on the Communists to return them, the matter had to be quietly forgotten about.

Even more shocking was the fate of British and American PoWs from World War II, when the Soviet Union was one of the Allied powers. As Russian troops swept across Eastern Europe, Allied prisoners of war 'liberated' from the camps were not repatriated. Some 20,000 American and 30,000 British servicemen found themselves in Soviet labour camps, along with large numbers of Frenchmen, Belgians and Dutchmen. Naturally, millions of Germans and Japanese shared their fate.

Since a Cold War existed between the Soviet Union and the West for the next 45 years, nothing could be done to get them out. During the occasional thaw – as in 1953, when Stalin died – some men were able to get out. They were initially held for 'debriefing' by the authorities and released on conditions of secrecy. Years later, when they have spoken out, no one has believed them.

10 ❖ Two Lords A'Leaping

In 1973, two ministers in the British government, both Lords, were forced to resigned when it became known that they enjoyed the company of prostitutes. Although they both did the right thing and tendered their resignations immediately, Lord Lambton, for one, was puzzled by the scandal his downfall provoked.

'Surely all men patronize whores,' he said.

Lord Lambton was a career politician. First elected to Parliament in 1951 as Conservative MP for Berwick-on-Tweed, he served as Parliamentary

Private Secretary to Selwyn Lloyd from 1955 to 1957, when he resigned over the Suez Crisis. He was a critic of Macmillan during the Profumo affair, but returned to the government in 1970 as parliamentary Under-Secretary for Defence, responsible for the RAF, on the recommendation of Lord Carrington.

The son of the Earl of Durham, Lambton was a wealthy landowner, with an income of £100,000 from his 25,000 acres of farmland in Durham and Northumberland alone. He owned racehorses and was reputedly one of the best shots in the country.

In 1942, he married Belinda Blew-Jones. They had six children. However, by 1972, he and his wife were living practically separate lives. Commander Bert Wickstead of the Metropolitan Police Serious Crime Squad, who investigated Lambton, remarked: 'The most remarkable feature of his London home was that it had been divided precisely into two halves. Lord Lambton's half was almost Spartan in appearance, more befitting a bachelor than a married man. Lady Lambton's half, by contrast, was beautifully furnished and full of female fripperies.'

Although Lambton was serious about politics and conscientious in his ministerial role, he lived the life of a man about town. He made frequent use of a high-class call girl service. His favourite playmate was 26-year-old Norma Russell, who would entertain Lambton alone – or with other prostitutes – in her Maida Vale flat. To put everyone in the mood, they smoked marijuana.

At first, Lambton used the *nom d'amour* 'Mr Lucas', but then became careless, even paying Norma for her services with a personal cheque. In November 1972, Norma married Colin Levy, an unemployed mini-cab driver with a drink problem and a criminal record. After five months of wedded bliss they had a row and Levy went abroad. While he was away, Norma went to the police and told them that he was on a drug smuggling trip. When he returned, the police pounced. They found no drugs on him, but he told the police that his wife was a prostitute and that one of her clients was Lord Lambton. He had seen his name on a cheque.

The information was passed to the Serious Crime Squad, which was investigating a ring of high-class prostitutes at the time. MI5 was also informed because of the security implications. The Home Secretary was also told. He informed the Prime Minister, Edward Heath, who was ever alert to ministerial misbehaviour in the wake of the Profumo scandal.

Meanwhile, Levy tried to sell his story to the newspapers. He and an accomplice hid a cine camera in his wife's bedroom. A microphone was hidden up her teddy bear's nose. They offered the resulting film to the

News of the World for £30,000. The film was not clear enough for publication, so the *News of the World* hid a photographer in Norma Levy's wardrobe, behind a two-way mirror. The resulting shots showed Lord Lambton with Norma Levy and a black night-club hostess cavorting on the bed. Nevertheless, the *News of the World* did not want to go ahead with the story and returned the material. Levy then tried to sell it to the German magazine, *Stern*. The deal fell through so he went to *The Sunday People*, who promptly turned the material over to the police.

When Lambton was confronted with the pictures, he said: 'She is a kind of prostitute. I liked her, but she played no important part in my life whatsoever.'

He immediately resigned, issuing a statement about 'this sordid story' of his 'casual acquaintance' with a call girl and one or two of her friends. He added: 'There has been no security risk and no blackmail and never at any time have I spoken of any aspect of my late job. All that has happened is that some sneak pimp has seen an opportunity of making money by the sale of the story and secret photographs at home and abroad. My own feelings may be imagined but I have no excuses whatever to make. I have behaved with incredible stupidity.'

Although he could simply shrug off his use of prostitutes, from the tapes it was quite clear that he was also using drugs. Later that day he was arrested for the possession of amphetamines and cannabis; charged, convicted and fined £300.

But Lord Lambton was not the only casualty of the scandal. The same day he resigned, Lord Jellicoe tendered his resignation, too. Son of the World War I naval commander, Admiral Earl Jellicoe, Lord Jellicoe was a war hero in his own right, having won the DSO, MC, *Légion d'Honneur*, *Croix de Guerre* and the Greek Military Cross in World War II. He rose to become Lord Privy Seal and Leader of the House of Lords. He also had a weakness.

'He is not flamboyant but he was a hedonist,' a colleague said.

His hedonism extended to hiring girls from two agencies advertised in the London *Evening Standard* in 1972 and 1973. He would take the women to dinner, then back to his London flat for sex.

Jellicoe was the soul of discretion. He dealt with the agencies under an assumed name and never revealed his true identity to his sexual partners. As a member of the cabinet, he had access to secret material, but never discussed his work with the girls. However, while the police were investigating the allegations against Lord Lambton, they came across rumours about Lord Jellicoe's liaisons in passing. Naturally, Ted Heath called Jellicoe in to ask him what he knew about the Lambton scandal and passed on the gossip.

'When you told me yesterday that my name was being linked with allegations about a ring of call girls,' Jellicoe wrote. 'I thought it right to tell you that, unhappily, there was justification for this because I had had some casual affairs which, if publicised, would be the subject of grave criticism. I also said that since this must be a grave embarrassment to you and to my colleagues I felt I must resign.'

Heath quickly accepted, remarking: 'Your decision accords with the best traditions of public life.'

When he heard of Jellicoe's resignation, Lambton said: 'The way things are going it will soon be clear that Heath is the only member of the government who doesn't do it.'

Ted Heath is a lifelong bachelor whose sexual proclivities – the libel laws being what they are – must remain unexplored. Heath was even criticized for being too quick to accept Lambton and Jellicoe's resignation.

'In the modern so-called permissive age,' the *Daily Express* commented, 'a splendid Member of Parliament and a junior minister have been cast into the wilderness... can we really afford to discard men of talent, wit and patriotism because their personal lives fall short of blameless perfect?'

However, it was Lord Lambton's use of drugs that were the real cause for concern. Interviewed on television by Robin Day, Lambton said that he had begun taking drugs in Singapore. But, he said: 'Taking opium in China is different to taking it in Berwick-on-Tweed.'

There were also rumours that other government ministers were involved with prostitutes. Edward Heath had to issue a statement saying that all his other ministers were as pure as the driven snow and the Security Commission, under Lord Diplock, was asked to investigate.

The Commission's report concluded that Jellicoe's affairs had been 'conducted with discretion. There was no abnormal sexual behaviour, no criminal offence nor any risk of compromising photographs.'

'Ordinary sexual intercourse' with a prostitute, the Commission found, did not pose a threat to security. However, Lambton had 'deviated from the normal' by having two girls at a time. This left him open to blackmail, although it was conceded that Lambton was not the sort of man to betray his country in those circumstances.

The *News of the World* attracted criticism for handing the 'instruments of blackmail' back to Levy, and Lambton's drug use was also a cause for concern.

'We do not suggest that Lord Lambton would consciously commit indiscretions when in his normal state of mind,' said the report, 'but we think that there would be a real risk that he might do so in a mood of irresponsibility induced by drugs.'

Lord Lambton withdrew from public life and went to live in Sienna, Italy, where he wrote a number of novels. Lord Jellicoe moved from the corridors of power into the boardroom, taking directorships in a number of large public companies.

11 ❖ Gladstone and Disraeli

William Ewart Gladstone was one of the greatest parliamentarians of the 19th century. Like Lloyd George, he diced with scandal all his life. On several occasions his addiction to prostitutes almost brought him down, but he somehow always emerged unscathed.

In the 19th century, the streets of London were awash with prostitutes. Despite the stifling strictures of Victorian values, it was not uncommon for gentlemen to seek the company of ladies of the night. Although he was married, Gladstone made no secret of his vice. He would even bring young prostitutes that he had picked up on the streets, back to 10 Downing Street, even though other members of the cabinet begged him not to.

Apologists pointed out that Gladstone was a fierce moralist and a lay preacher. Some contended that all he did with his 'erring sisters' was to read them an uplifting passage from the Bible. Indeed, he did manage to guide some of the young women he brought home into honest employment. However, Gladstone admitted in his own diaries that his motives were partly, at least, 'carnal'.

He began visiting prostitutes when he was a young man at Oxford in the 1820s. Tormented by guilt, he would scourge himself afterwards. But this did not seem to stem his appetite as he writes of returning to sin 'again and again'.

He married in 1839. It did not help. In 1843, when he joined Robert Peel's government as President of the Board of Trade, he wrote in his diary that he was 'fearful [of] the guilty sin of returning again and again in forms ever new but alike hideous'. Conscious of his position, he avoided prostitutes initially. Instead, like many another Victorian gentleman, he indulged in pornography. But by 1851, his diary shows that he was visiting a prostitute named Elizabeth Collins regularly – sometimes every other day. Afterwards, he notes, he always scourged himself. This continued when he became Chancellor in 1852.

And there were others. A man named William Wilson saw Gladstone picking up a prostitute near Leicester Square and tried to blackmail him. Gladstone handed over the blackmail demand to the police and Wilson went down for 12 months' hard labour.

There had been another brush with scandal with a courtesan named Laura Thistlethwayte. They exchanged passionate letters and he visited her regularly, both in her London town house and in her cottage in Hampstead. But Gladstone grew wary when she began showering him with gifts to the point that he feared her extravagance would ruin her husband, Colonel Thistlethwayte.

As prime minister, Gladstone had a close friendship with the Prince of Wales' mistress, the actress Lillie Langtry. And in the 1870s there were rumours that he was having an affair with Madame Olga Novikov, who advised him on Russian affairs.

However, he could not give up prostitutes. In 1880, when he was 70, he was still visiting brothels on what he called 'rescue work'. The situation became more ticklish in 1882, when the threat of assassination over the Home Rule Bill meant that he had to have a 24-hour police guard. Lord Rosebery, then a junior minister in the Home Office, warned him of the danger of some lowly paid policeman taking advantage of the situation and selling the story to the press. It did no good. Three months later the Tory MP, Colonel Tottenham, saw Gladstone talking to a lady of the night and decided to make some political hay in the House with it. Gladstone answered Colonel Tottenham's allegations with studied dignity.

'It may be true that the gentleman saw me in such conversation,' he said. 'But the object was not what he assumed or, as I am afraid, hoped.'

He survived. But even this close call did not stop him. In July 1886, his private secretary, Edward Hamilton, warned him that another blackmailer was at work. Gladstone promised Hamilton that he would stop, but his diaries record that he was still seeing prostitutes in 1892, although they may have accosted him rather than the other way around.

In 1896, two years before his death, Gladstone sought to set the record straight. He wrote a Clintonesque statement and sent it to one of his sons, Stephen, who had become a clergyman. In it, Gladstone said that he had 'not been guilty of the act which is known as that of infidelity to the marriage bed'.

As we know from President Clinton's case, that leaves an awful lot of room for misbehaviour. When one young prostitute came home with him for a second time, he wrote that he had 'certainly been wrong in some things and trod the path of danger'.

Maybe he just liked to watch. Some of the girls called him 'Glad-eyes'; others called him 'Daddy-do-nothing' – but he was 82 when he gave up visiting whores. His reputation, though, was far more formidable.

'Gladstone founded the great tradition,' ran one obituary, 'in public to speak the language of the highest and strictest principle, and in private to pursue and possess every sort of woman.'

GLADSTONE'S great political rival was, of course, Benjamin Disraeli who is reputed to have said to Gladstone: 'When you are out saving fallen women, save one for me.'

Disraeli, too, had his fair share of scandal. As a young man eager to make his way in the world, he borrowed heavily in order to buy into gold and silver mines in South America and to start up a newspaper with his friend, John Murray. However, a stockmarket crash in 1825, when Disraeli was just 21, wiped him out and the newspaper, which he could no longer afford to finance, collapsed after six months.

Left with massive debts, Disraeli wrote a novel about the collapse called *Vivian Grey*. It was so thinly fictionalized that it drew threats of a duel from Murray. The duel never took place, but it brought such notoriety to the book that Disraeli could pay off enough of his debts to keep going.

Disraeli then had a nervous breakdown and, to escape his remaining creditors, went off on a tour of the Middle East. He returned a changed man. Always a dandy, he was now positively effeminate, dressing in green velvet trousers and ruffles. He spoke openly at dinner parties of his passion for the East and, according to the painter Benjamin Haydon, 'seemed tinged with a disposition to palliate its infamous vices... sodomy'. Disraeli's biographer Jane Ridley concurred.

'Bisexuality came as naturally to Disraeli as did Tory Radicalism,' she said.

He then had a series of affairs with older women, some of whom were married. His affair with Henrietta Sykes became a public scandal. She was much older than him and had been married for 11 years to the ailing Sir Francis Sykes, who was the father of her four children. Her letters to Disraeli were signed 'your mother'.

Despite the gossip, they were seen out together at parties and the opera. Her husband turned a blind eye because he was having an affair with Clara Bolton at the time. Clara was another of Disraeli's former lovers.

She was jealous and encouraged Sir Francis to break up the affair. He did so, but soon after he found his wife in bed with Disraeli's successor. In a fit of pique, he kicked her out of the house and placed a notice in the newspapers, advertising her adultery and causing a scandal that tainted Disraeli along with everyone else involved.

How much the scandal harmed him it is hard to say as he seemed completely unelectable anyway. Voters did not appreciate his dandified dress, and his Jewishness counted against him. On the hustings he was greeted with cries of 'Shylock' and he was pelted with chunks of rotten pork and ham.

When he was elected for Maidstone on his fifth attempt, there were accusations that he had offered bribes to the electorate. This was a common enough practice, but Disraeli outraged the voters of Maidstone by not paying up.

He handled the resulting scandal by making even more scandalous allegations against his chief critic, a Maidstone lawyer called Charles Austin. Austin sued. Disraeli went to court where he apologized effusively. His court costs were paid by the latest woman in his life, Mary Anne Wyndham Lewis, the widow of his late rival for the Maidstone seat. It was a masterly stroke. This fresh scandal eclipsed the bribery allegations.

Mrs Wyndham Lewis was 12 years older than Disraeli. And she was rich. They married. But even his wife's fortune was not enough to discharge his debts. He left Maidstone and stood for Shrewsbury in 1841. It had a smaller electorate and consequently fewer voters to bribe.

Realizing his plight, his rivals for the seat plastered Shrewsbury with posters detailing his debts. They amounted to £21,000. Handbills pointed out that Disraeli needed to stay in Parliament, otherwise he would go to debtors' prison.

But the voters of Shrewsbury took no notice and soon found their MP making his way to the top of the greasy pole of the Conservative Party. However, the Conservatives were kept out of power by another scandal. At the age of 79, the Liberal leader Lord Palmerston was cited in the divorce case of the attractive 30-year-old Mrs O'Kane. Disraeli said that it was a pity that this had got out because Palmerston would sweep the country. With the unofficial party slogan 'she was Kane and he was able', Palmerston won by a landslide.

Disraeli had to compete with this. After his wife died in 1872, he began romantic liaison with two sisters, Lady Bradford and Lady Chesterfield, which he maintained until his death in 1881. In office, Disraeli bought the Suez Canal without the backing of Parliament. During a recess, he borrowed the money from the Rothschilds and bought the shares belonging to the ruler of Egypt, the Khedive Ismail Pasha. Fortunately, when Parliament reassembled they saw that it was a tangible asset to Britain and approved the purchase.

12 ❖ The Prime Minister Who Never Was

While the careers of Gladstone, Disraeli and Palmerston seemed to thrive on scandal, the new rising star of the Liberal Party, Sir Charles Wentworth Dilke, whom many saw as future prime minister, was destroyed by it – even though the allegations against him were never proved.

In July 1885, the youngest Cabinet Minister and Privy Councillor, Charles Dilke, then seen as Gladstone's heir apparent, was named in a divorce case of 22-year-old Virginia Crawford, a distant relative of Dilke's by marriage. She was the sister of his brother's widow.

Virginia was a bit of a girl. The daughter of a Tyneside shipowner, she had been forced to marry Donald Crawford, a Liberal MP who was twice her age. For years, she and her sister Helen entertained themselves with medical students from a nearby hospital. They also visited a brothel in Knightsbridge where they were both having an affair with a Captain Henry Forster.

Dilke and Virginia may well have been lovers. He visited her while her husband was away. But he was certainly the lover of her mother, Mrs Eustace Smith.

When Virginia's divorce was filed, Dilke feared that his political career was over.

'In the case of a public man, a charge is always believed by many, even though disproved, and I should be weighted by it throughout life,' he wrote.

However, he was determined to fight. He was engaged at the time to be married to Mrs Emilia Patterson, the widow of the rector of Lincoln College, whom he had been wooing for 10 years, even though for most of that time her husband had been alive.

Virginia's husband, Donald Crawford, knew nothing of his wife's affair with Captain Forster or her other dalliances. But he had received a series of anonymous letters telling him to 'beware of the Member from Chelsea' – Dilke.

Dilke and his fiancée Emilia had also being receiving anonymous letters, which sought to disrupt their marriage plans. A staunch Republican, Dilke had spoken out against the royal family and suspected his harassment was an establishment plot.

'In my belief the conspiracy comes from a woman who wanted me to marry her,' Dilke wrote to his fiancée. The suspect was a Mrs Rogerson, a friend of Virginia Crawford's, who may well have been another of Dilke's lovers.

When Crawford received a fourth letter naming Forster as his wife's lover, he confronted her. She denied that Forster was her lover but, seemingly eager for divorce, admitted to adultery with Dilke. She also alleged that Dilke had also had a string of other lovers, including her mother – which was true – and one of his maids called Sarah Gray.

Even though Dilke was being cited in a divorce case, Emilia went ahead and married him in Oxford, in October 1885. The following month, after writing to his constituents denying the charges of adultery, Dilke was re-elected as MP for Chelsea. However, as he had not yet cleared his name, Gladstone, a stickler for impropriety in others, dropped him from the government.

When the case opened in February 1886, Crawford told the divorce court that his wife admitted going to an 'assignation house' off Tottenham Court Road with Dilke. She had also visited him at his house in Sloane Street and entertained him in her own home when he, Crawford, had been away. But she was sketchy on the detail. What turned the trial from an ordinary divorce case into a huge Victorian scandal was one new and sensational allegation. Crawford said that Dilke had forced his wife into a threesome with a serving girl called Fanny Stock, and had taught her 'every French vice'. Asked who Fanny was, his wife had said that she was Dilke's mistress. She also said that Dilke had compared her to her mother.

All this was hearsay evidence. It was simply Crawford repeating what he alleged his wife – the defendant in this case – had said. He had no evidence, such as a love letter or a note arranging an assignation in Dilke's hand. The only witness he could produce was his wife's parlour maid, Ann Jameson. She said that when Mr Crawford was out of town, Mrs Crawford stayed out at night. Dilke had visited her at her house. Under cross-examination, however, it transpired that these were normal social visits. Captain Forster had also visited, and Ann had handled correspondence between Mrs Crawford and Captain Forster. There was none with Dilke.

After Crawford had finished presenting his case, Dilke's barrister, the

Attorney General Sir Charles Russell, insisted that there was no case to answer. The judge agreed.

As the redoubtable Fanny had disappeared, the only witness the defence could call was Dilke himself. He certainly did not want to take the stand and answer questions concerning his relationship with Mrs Eustace Smith, for example.

Explaining his client's reluctance to take the stand, Russell said: 'In the life of any man there may be found to have been possible indiscretions.' And he moved to have Dilke's name stricken from the petition. The judge agreed to do so and ordered that Dilke's costs be paid by Mr Crawford since he had accused Dilke of adultery without reasonable grounds for suspicion.

Legally, it had been found that Dilke had not committed adultery with Mrs Crawford. But Russell's decision not to put his client on the stand was a fatal error of judgement. Although Dilke had repeatedly denied sleeping with Mrs Crawford, verbally and in writing, it was not the same as swearing under oath in the witness box that he had not done so.

Sir Charles Wentworth Dilke. His career was ruined by a scandal, although allegations against him were never proven

The press naturally reported Russell's remark – that 'In the life of any man there may be found to have been possible indiscretions' – omitting the word 'possible'. In the puritan fervour of the time, this was tantamount to admitting that he had committed adultery with someone, if not the errant wife in the Crawford case.

But worse. Although the judge ruled that Virginia Crawford had not committed adultery with Dilke, it was clear to him that she had done it with someone. And he granted Crawford a *decree nisi*. The press had a field day. Even *The Times* commented: 'The nature of some of the judge's remarks must almost irresistibly raise in simple minds the question with whom was Mrs Crawford guilty.'

The *Manchester Guardian* condemned Dilke's behaviour at the trial and said: 'To ask us on the strength of this evasion to welcome him back as a leader of the Liberal Party is too strong a draft on our credulity and good nature.'

A Liberal Association in Scotland passed a resolution around the country, condemning any move to have Dilke back in a Liberal cabinet, saying it would condone things that were 'unrighteous and wrong'. But it was moralist W.T. Stead, campaigning editor of the *Pall Mall Gazette*, who pulled out all the stops.

'Grave imputations were stated publicly in open court, but there was no detailed reply,' he wrote. 'Far from having been disproved, they have not even been denied in the witness box.'

He was backed in his moral outrage by General Booth, founder of the Salvation Army, who condemned the Dilke business as 'a shameful combination of lust, fraud and falsehood'. With Booth's blessing, Stead called for the Member for Chelsea's resignation.

'We are willing to believe that the more terrible part of the charge brought against him is exaggerated,' Stead wrote, charitably. 'But if that charge in its entirety were true, we should not exaggerate the universal sentiment that the man against whom so frightful an accusation could lie is a worse criminal than most of the murderers who swing in Newgate.'

Dilke considered a libel suit, but was afraid that a courtroom would simply give Stead another soapbox. Stead was a man who enjoyed martyrdom. He had recently been to jail for three months for buying a 13-year-old girl from her parents for £5, to expose child prostitution.

In an effort to clear his name, Dilke went to the Queen's Proctor who had the power to annul a *decree nisi* before the *decree absolute* was granted. Dilke persuaded him to intervene, on the grounds that the divorce had been granted on the grounds of adultery, which the judge had admitted in court had not taken place.

The Proctor ordered a second hearing. Dilke was optimistic. Fanny Stock had been found and she was willing to deny the three-in-a-bed romp. He also had powerful new evidence about Mrs Crawford's affair with Captain Forster, which she still sought to deny.

But Dilke and his lawyers had made another mistake. Because the judge in the original case had stricken Dilke's name from the petition, he was no longer party to the action. His lawyers could not cross-examine Mrs Crawford, nor could they call any witnesses.

In the general election of 9 July 1886, Dilke lost his seat. Seven days later, the trial started. Dilke then found himself at another unforeseen disadvantage. Since Dilke was trying to overturn a *decree nisi* granted on the grounds of adultery, the prosecutor had to try and prove that there had been no adultery before Mrs Crawford, who now wanted her divorce, made the case that there had.

Dilke was the first witness to be called to the stand. In front of a packed courtroom, he denied sleeping with Mrs Crawford. He also denied sleeping with Fanny Stock and Sarah Gray. But when he was asked whether he had slept with Virginia Crawford's mother, Mrs Eustace Smith, he refused to answer. The judge ordered him to. Eventually, under cross-examination, he had to admit to the affair.

Then Mrs Crawford was called to the stand. This time she had her story together. The assignation house was in Warren Street, off Tottenham Court Road, she said. She even sketched a plan of the bedroom there. She also remembered the dates and places of other assignations. And she stuck to her story that she had had a threesome at Dilke's Sloane Street home with Fanny Stock.

This time, she also admitted adultery with Captain Forster, but denied that she had invented the story about having slept with Dilke to protect him. Forster was called and confirmed that they had had an affair, but denied that they hoped to marry. He was engaged to a Miss Smith Barry at the time. Mrs Crawford called three other witnesses who said that they had seen Dilke go into the assignation house at 65 Warren Street on other occasions with other women. Dilke had no opportunity to refute these fresh allegations, and no lawyer to shake them during cross-examination. His reputation was now irreparably damaged.

The trial lasted a week. It reached its climax in a summing up from Mrs Crawford's barrister, Henry Matthews QC. Dilke, he said, 'was charged (by Mrs Crawford's confession) not merely with adultery, but with having committed adultery with the child of one friend and the wife of another... he was charged with having done with an English lady what any man of proper feeling would shrink from doing with a prostitute in a French brothel, and yet he was silent.'

At this point Russell leapt to his feet to object, but the judge ordered him to sit down. Dilke was not a party to the case and had no right to legal representation.

'The burden of proof was on the Queen's Proctor who, in order to be successful, must show conclusively that Mrs Crawford had not committed adultery with Sir Charles Dilke,' Matthews continued. 'The jury could only give a verdict against my client if they believed that Mrs Crawford was a perjured witness and that a conspiracy existed to blast the life of a pure and innocent man.'

By this time, Dilke's character had been so irredeemably blackened that no one believed him to be a 'pure and innocent man'.

The prosecution was left with an impossible task. How could it prove that Dilke had not committed adultery with Mrs Crawford. Mrs Crawford had already admitted adultery with Captain Forster, who had admitted it, too. So Mr Crawford could have his divorce. What did it matter if Mrs Crawford had committed adultery with two people, or only one?

For that matter, Dilke had admitted adultery with Mrs Eustace Smith; so why not with Mrs Crawford? What did it matter, whether he had committed adultery with two people, or only one?

The judge hammered the last nail into Dilke's political coffin. He drew the jury's attention to Dilke's reluctance to take the stand in the first trial and asked: 'If you were to hear such a statement made involving your honour... would you accept the advice of your counsel to say nothing? Would you allow the court to be deceived and a tissue of falsehoods to be put forward as the truth?'

Upstanding Victorian gentlemen to a man, the jury took just 15 minutes to answer 'no'. They found that the *decree nisi* was not pronounced contrary to the justice of the case. Dilke had failed to get it overturned. Although no real evidence had ever been put that he had committed adultery, it was generally assumed that he had and was deemed to be lying.

Dilke did manage to get himself re-elected to Parliament for the Forest of Dean in 1892. He remained in Parliament until his death in1911, but never again held office. Virginia Crawford began a political career of her own. She became a writer and a Labour councillor, and became such a vociferous campaigner against Fascism that she was blacklisted by Mussolini. She died in 1948.

13 ❖ The Dreyfus Affair

For five years, Alfred Dreyfus languished in a primitive hut on the fever-infested Devil's Island, off the coast of French Guyana, watched day and night. Meanwhile, France was torn apart from top to bottom over the fate of what turned out to be an innocent man.

Dreyfus was born into a Jewish family in the disputed territory of Alsace in 1859. His father was a wealthy textile manufacturer. Instead of going into the family business, in 1882 Dreyfus joined the army, determined on a military career. He rose to the rank of captain and was appointed to the War Ministry. In 1889, he married and started a family.

He was not always popular with his fellow officers. He was haughty and well educated, speaking both Italian and German, which invited suspicion. Worse, however, he was Jewish, and the army hosted a hotbed of anti-Semitism.

On 15 October 1894, he was arrested and charged with selling military secrets to the Germans. The French had an agent inside the German Embassy, a cleaner who had retrieved a note, said to be in Dreyfus's handwriting, offering to sell information.

On such flimsy evidence, Dreyfus was tried and convicted of treason. Stripped of his military honours, he was sent to Devil's Island in January 1895. No one seemed to doubt his guilt. As he was led away, protesters shouted: 'Death to the Jew'.

However, in 1896, the now chief of military Intelligence, Lieutenant-Colonel George Picquat, discovered that the note had actually been written by an officer still serving in the army, Major Marie Charles Ferdinand Walsin Esterhazy. A gambler and a womanizer, Esterhazy was constantly in need of money. On 20 July 1894, he had casually strolled into the German Embassy and offered to sell the astounded military attaché, Colonel von Schwarzkoppen, any information about the French army he required. By September, Esterhazy was passing over details of manoeuvres, equipment and intelligence reports.

Picquat's discovery was greeted with dismay by the High Command. Defeat in the Franco-Prussian war had left them more than a little sensitive about their honour. The conviction of Dreyfus had not been unpopular. No one wanted to admit that a dreadful mistake had been made at the court martial, so they began a cover-up.

Alfred Dreyfus and his family

Picquat was posted to North Africa and later, when he still proved troublesome, arrested. Esterhazy and another officer, Major Henry, began manufacturing new evidence against Dreyfus. They forged documents naming Dreyfus as a spy. Others showing him to be innocent were suppressed. Both of them made great play of the code of honour of the French Army. It was plainly disloyal to accuse either of them and they even called their tampering of evidence 'patriotic forgery'.

However, as the evidence against Esterhazy grew, he was charged with treason. But at his trial, the courtroom was packed with a sympathetic mob, which booed anyone who spoke in Dreyfus's defence. Esterhazy was a fine orator, and when he talked rousingly of the code of honour that binds soldiers together, his fellow officers applauded enthusiastically. The judge was sympathetic, too. He took just three minutes to find Esterhazy not guilty.

But a number of independently minded intellectuals had been following the case. They had their doubts. The most influential, the novelist Emile Zola, then crystallized the issue with an open letter published in the newspaper, *Aurore*, on 13 January 1898. Under the headline 'J'accuse', it named the men who had helped convict an innocent man and those who had helped acquit an innocent one.

The newspaper sold 200,000 copies that day. 'J'accuse' split the nation into two camps: the Dreyfusards and the anti-Dreyfusards. The anti-Dreyfusards were of an authoritarian bent and believed that the nation had been rescued from a dastardly foreign conspiracy and that Dreyfus, innocent or guilty, was a necessary sacrifice. The Dreyfusards – intellectuals, socialists and radicals in the main – believed that the freedom of the individual was sacrosanct. They feared that anti-Dreyfusards in the Army and the Church were undermining the Republic, in the hope of setting up a new authoritarian regime.

Zola was sued for libel and sentenced to one year in jail. As the case went to appeal, there were violent clashes on the streets. Major Henry slit his throat after admitting his part in forging and withholding documents. Realizing the game was up, Esterhazy fled to Belgium, where he took a partnership in a brothel. Later he moved to England, where he lived under the name, Comte de Violemont.

In his tiny hut on Devil's Island, Dreyfus was unaware of the controversy his imprisonment was causing back home in France. But continued public pressure forced a retrial and in 1899 he was returned to France, a haggard and prematurely aged figure.

To public consternation, the new trial upheld the original verdict. But realizing the political fallout the country risked if the scandal dragged on any longer, the President of the Republic gave Dreyfus a full pardon. Dreyfus was grateful, but he felt that honour had not yet been satisfied. He began a long campaign which, seven years later, resulted in a second retrial. This time his conviction was overturned. He was reinstated in the army and awarded the *Légion d'Honneur*. He went on to fight in World War I and died in 1935.

14 ❖ Diamonds are Forever

Many otherwise reasonable nations support unpleasant dictators abroad as part of the game of global politics. In the 1970s France had one of the more unpleasant African dictators heading up their client state, the Central African Republic.

But Jean Bedel Bokassa was not content to be a president, like his old friend President Valéry Giscard d'Estaing of France. He wanted to be an emperor like his hero Napoleon, and France had to stump up most of the £10 million bill for the coronation.

For several days before the ceremony, the inner circle of 600 of the 2,500 invited guests were treated to lavish meals in leading restaurants. They were housed in top hotels, all at the French taxpayers' expense.

On the day of the coronation, Bokassa rode to the 'coronation palace' – the capital Bangui's new stadium – in a coach drawn by 14 of the 16 imported Normandy horses that had survived the shock of the change in climate.

Bokassa wore an ankle-length tunic, a 30 ft crimson velvet, gold-embroidered, ermine-trimmed mantle, which weighed over 70 lb, and shoes made of pearls. He ascended to the red velvet imperial throne, on the back of which was a huge gold eagle.

Like Napoleon, Bokassa crowned himself with the heavy gold crown on his head. He buckled on a ceremonial sword, held high an ebony rod and swore a solemn oath to continue the Central African Empire's democracy.

Then the Empress Catherine, a white woman swathed in gold, knelt at his feet while he crowned her. She was the favourite of his nine wives, who had given him 54 legitimate children.

While serving as a sergeant in the French army in Indochina, he had fathered several illegitimate children. As Head of State, he had sent word that the children he had had with Vietnamese girls could come and live with him in the Central African Republic. But when a bunch of Vietnamese refugees turned up, he discovered that they were probably not his kids at all and they disappeared.

The coronation was consecrated with a High Mass in Bangui's Notre Dame Cathedral, during which the archbishop read greetings from the

Pope. Then there was a banquet for 4,000 guests. The food was French, of course. A French navy band played while Bokassa I, in the uniform of a Marshal of France, took to the floor with Empress Catherine, who wore a couture gown from Paris. But that was the end of the fairy-tale.

In May 1979, it was reported that Bokassa had ordered the killing of between 100 and 200 school-children, because their parents were too poor to afford the compulsory school uniform. The clothes were available only from a shop owned by one of Bokassa's wives. When the children demonstrated in protest, they were rounded up and herded into prison. Some suffocated in the airless cells. The rest were clubbed to death and they were buried in mass graves. An eyewitness said he saw Bokassa personally kill 39 of the children.

So why was the French government bankrolling this monster? The official reason was that if they didn't, Bokassa would turn to the Soviet Union for support. French companies would then lose control over the country's uranium deposits, as well as the country's ivory and diamonds. This was a particularly important consideration since Giscard d'Estaing had installed his relatives, including his brother Jacques, in key positions in the country and he himself owned businesses and property there. So while most countries in the world boycotted Bokassa's farcical coronation, Giscard d'Estaing was happy to be seen embracing the dictator at the airport.

Bokassa – whose name translates as 'butcher's boy' – denied the accusation, but Amnesty International confirmed the story. He then said that the whole thing had been got up by Marxist students and declared 1979 'Year of the Child'.

France denounced the massacre, but continued to support the Bokassa regime financially. But when a five-man international inquiry team confirmed that Bokassa had personally participated in the atrocity, France was forced to announce it was cutting its foreign aid. Meanwhile, Bokassa contested the findings of the inquiry and had 40 witnesses who had testified against him killed.

On 21 September 1979, Bokassa was deposed by his nephew, David Dacko. French troops were standing by and flew in to support the coup. A search of the Kologa Palace led to the discovery of human corpses stuffed with rice and prepared for eating.

Bokassa fled to his delightful 18th-century château near Paris with £500 million looted from the Central African Republic's coffers. More lurid tales came out of Bangui. The remains of 40 people were found around the palace crocodile pond and it was said that Bokassa's coronation guests had been served human flesh. Bokassa had kept a jam jar full of diamonds in his study and gave handfuls to foreign visitors. One of them was President Giscard d'Estaing, who publicly owned up to taking £250,000 worth on French television during the presidential election campaign in 1981. But, he said, they were just 'normal gifts between heads of state'. No one in France seemed much bothered about it. Most people thought that, in Giscard d'Estaing's position, they would have done much the same. However, Giscard d'Estaing's opponents travelled the country, sticking huge paper diamonds over his eyes on his election posters and he was voted out of office.

The French authorities then revoked Bokassa's asylum and he moved to the Ivory Coast. Living in exile seemed to make him even more crazy than when he was in office. He changed his name to 'M. Christian Sole', dressed in a white cassock and, carrying a cross given to him by Pope John Paul II, he went home to face trial.

Naturally he lost the case and was condemned to death, but the sentence was mysteriously commuted to 10 years' imprisonment. Released after seven years in 1993, he lived on in straightened circumstances in Bangui.

Meanwhile, the French authorities were pursuing him for £300,000 in back taxes. To raise the money, Bokassa sold his château to the National Fighters' Circle, a group of ultra right-wing veterans of the French colonial war. The National Fighters' Circle, which is associated with Jean-Marie Le Pen's anti-immigration party, had been renting the château since Bokassa left France in 1986.

15 ❖ Haute Couture Call Girls

Omar Bongo, President of the West African state of Gabon since 1967, was implicated in a good old-fashioned sex scandal by a court case in Paris in April 1995. The court was told that Bongo was regularly supplied with prostitutes by the Italian couturier who made his made-to-measure suits.

The trial of Francesco Smalto, the Paris-based menswear designer, gave an insight into the ferocious competition in the fashion world to secure celebrity clients. It also painted a deeply unflattering portrait of Bongo.

The court was told that Smalto hired the prostitutes and sent them to

Gabon. But they were terrified of having sex with Bongo because he refused to wear a condom. Bongo was not in court to defend himself, but his
Parisian lawyer and doctor denied the charges on his behalf.

The Paris police had been investigating a de luxe call girl ring when
Smalto got caught in their net. Part of the ring was a model agency run by
a young woman named Laure Moerman. She supplied Smalto with models
for his collection.

Several of the models said that they were sent to Gabon's capital,
Libreville, with Smalto's collections of suits. Their job was to help the
Gabonese President out of his clothes.

The presiding judge read out the testimony of a girl named Monica,
who had been on one of the trips to Libreville.

'It went very badly that evening,' she said. 'Bongo didn't want to wear
a condom, and as he had a friend who had died of AIDS, I refused to make
love to him.'

Another girl, Chantal, testified that she had been told that the going
rate for sex with Bongo was £1,200 with a condom and £6,000 without.

Although these prices may seem a little over the top, money meant
little to Bongo. He was one of the richest men in Africa. When the society
jeweller's, Chaumet, ran into financial difficulties, it was discovered that
Bongo owed them £500,000.

**Albert Bernard Bongo –
speaking to the press**

Initially, Smalto had denied all knowledge of the girls' allegations. But he then told the court that Bongo was his best customer. He spent £300,000 a year on suits and other clothes and he had been frightened of losing him to a rival.

'We knew that President Bongo was sensitive to a feminine presence,' Smalto told the court. 'That is why we sent a girl on every trip. I suspected that he kept her to sleep with, but I wasn't sure.'

That was not true. The transcript of the recording of a telephone conversation between two prostitutes named Ariane and Sarah was read out:

'Marika telephoned me, she had to go to Libreville. I told her that's dramatic. His [Bongo's] friend died of the thing,' said Ariane.

'AIDS? That's disgusting,' said Sarah.

'Yes, the worst is, a great couturier proposed it,' Ariane replied.

Smalto, who had been known as 'the king of tailors and tailor to kings', was ruined. Bongo went elsewhere to buy his suits.

16 ❖ Rainbow Warrior

The French have fewer scandals than most other countries for two reasons. Firstly, it is expected that any man with a position in society would have at least one mistress, so to discover that a politician has fathered an illegitimate child is no scandal. Secondly, there are strict privacy laws, which prevent the details of a person's private life being aired in the press. This is why French scandals tend to centre around military matters.

The French are particularly proud of their nuclear bomb. When everyone else in the world had given up testing them, the French still took great pride in blowing up small islands in the Pacific. This did not sit well with the environmentalist organization, Greenpeace. In 1985, it sent its ship *Rainbow Warrior* to harass the French military, who were planning a nuclear test on Mururoa atoll in French Polynesia.

On 10 July 1985, *Rainbow Warrior* was preparing to set sail from Auckland harbour when there was a terrific explosion on board. One crew member died in the blast and the ship sank. It soon became clear that the explosion had been caused by a bomb.

Two days later, New Zealand police arrested Alain and Sophie Turenge who had been seen 'acting suspiciously'. They claimed to be Swiss tourists, but telephone numbers found on them connected them to the French Secret Service. They turned out to be two French agents named Alain Mafart and Dominique Prieur.

President Mitterand was informed, but he did nothing, hoping that the affair would blow over. It didn't, so on 8 August, when fresh revelations were imminent, he ordered his Prime Minister, Laurent Fabius, to instigate a rigorous inquiry under Bernard Tricot into what Mitterand called this 'absurd and criminal affair'. Naturally, the inquiry would leave no stone unturned and Tricot was ordered to track down those responsible, 'no matter how high their status'.

After just two and a half weeks, Tricot reported back. Five agents including Mafart and Prieur, he said, had been sent to New Zealand to gather information about Greenpeace's intention, and he had no reason to believe that they had overstepped their brief.

'Everything I have heard and seen makes me certain that, at governmental level, no decision was taken to damage the *Rainbow Warrior*,' he said.

Few were convinced that he had really got to the bottom of the matter. Meanwhile, journalists began their own investigations. On 17 September, *Le Monde* published a story saying that a third team of agents, whom Tricot had not been told about, had planted the bomb on the *Rainbow Warrior* and escaped undetected. The Minister of Defence, Charles Hernu, who had ordered the surveillance of the Greenpeace vessel, had apparently either approved the bombing or, at the very least, failed to prevent it. The Chief of the General Staff and the head of the Secret Service were both implicated; and President Mitterand's own military advisor had approved the funding of the operation.

Hernu repeatedly denied that the attack had been ordered by his department. Then he changed his tune. It had been ordered by his department, he admitted, but the truth had been concealed from him personally. On 20 September, he was sacked. The head of the French Secret Service was also removed for refusing to answer questions.

On 23 September, Laurent Fabius conceded that the agents who had blown up the *Rainbow Warrior* had indeed been following orders. He offered compensation to the family of the Greenpeace photographer who had died, and to the government of New Zealand. However, the French government refused to return the agents who had actually done the bombing to stand trial. So the New Zealand authorities tried Mafart and Prieur for being party to the plot. They were found guilty of manslaughter and sentenced to 10 years. The French were outraged. They threatened to bar New Zealand butter from the European Union.

New Zealand backed down. A deal was brokered under which Mafart and Prieur would serve three years on an isolated atoll in French Polynesia. In return, France would pay compensation and make a public apology.

France did not live up to its side of the agreement. In 1987, the Chirac government repatriated Prieur without New Zealand's consent. On the eve of the 1988 election, Mafart was returned home, too, contrary to the agreement.

New Zealand protested and the matter went to international arbitration. In 1990, the panel brought in a split decision. France, it said, was wrong to have returned Prieur early, but conceded that it was too late to send her back into exile. In lieu of compensation, France was ordered to establish a fund to promote peace and understanding between the two countries.

Journalists continued to look into who ordered the sabotage. In 1987, Hernu admitted responsibility for conducting an 'action of the State' against *Rainbow Warrior*, but he maintained to his death, in 1989, that he was a scapegoat that had been sacrificed by his colleagues. Indeed, there was no evidence found that he ordered the bombing in as many words. However, on a memorandum by a senior admiral on the effects of Greenpeace's activities on the nuclear test programme he underlined the word 'forestall'.

Although the money for the operation came from the Elysée Palace, no 'smoking gun' was found to link the sinking of the *Rainbow Warrior* to President Mitterand. However, many people believe that authorization for such an operation could have come only from the very highest level.

17 ❖ P-2

The Italians' political scandals are more often connected with the Mafia and with the Catholic Church. And that is exactly what they got in 1981 when they discovered that a mysterious lodge of Freemasons called P-2 – *Propaganda Due* – was acting as a state within a state. Not only were its leaders prominent members of the establishment, some had links to organized crime. And one of them – Robert Calvi – was known as 'God's banker' because he organized the financial affairs of the Catholic Church.

During the 1970s, Italy was plagued by left-wing terrorism. P-2 posed a threat from the right which Italy's Prime Minister, Giovanni Spadolini, called a 'creeping coup'. No one can be sure just how much of a threat it was. That the lodge was a government-in-waiting may well have been one of the grander delusions of its head, Licio Gelli. It mainly used its political influence to secure favours and cut through red tape. Businessmen used P-2 as a way of fixing up contracts and dealing with Italy's labyrinthine bureaucracy.

In fact, few of the members knew what was going on. Gelli and his deputy, Umberto Ortalini, were highly secretive. They held their initiation ceremonies in anonymous hotel rooms and it was only when the scandal broke and the membership lists were published, that members discovered who the other members were. Although they came from all political parties, ranging from the socialist PSI to the neo-Fascist MSI-DN, members tended to be rightward leaning. Gelli himself held dual Italian-Argentinian nationality and had been a friend of Argentine dictator, Juan Perón.

Freemasonry has long been entwined with Italian politics. During the 19th century its secret network and anti-clericalism made it the perfect vehicle for Italian nationalism, which culminated in the unification of the country.

The Masonic lodge P-2 had been in existence for a long time. It was part of the Grand Orient rite of the freemasonry. However, when Gelli took over in the 1970s, it was expelled, and when the scandal was revealed orthodox Freemasons denied any connection.

The existence of P-2 only became known to the public in 1981, when investigating magistrates in Milan were trying to untangle the affairs of the disgraced Sicilian financier, Michele Sindona. Sindona had used the contacts he had made through P-2 to build a financial empire. He was an expert in evading Italy's banking laws – having set up foreign companies, through which money could be laundered. One of his P-2 contacts was Roberto Calvi.

Calvi was born into a Catholic family in Milan in 1920. At the age of 26, he joined the Ambrosiano bank, rising to become its head in 1975. It was around that time he joined P-2. The Sindona empire was already in ruins by then. Sindona had skipped the country in 1974 to avoid arrest on charges of fraud and false accounting and Calvi picked up the pieces. Banco Ambrosiano quickly became the biggest private bank in Italy. Much of its growth was on paper only though. Calvi transferred money at lightning speed between companies, artificially inflating their share price. In the process, billions of lire left Italy illegally for accounts in Switzerland, Peru and Argentina. Calvi was secretive, a law unto himself. No one else in the bank knew what was going on and no one in charge thought to ask – just as long as Calvi continued making money.

One of the major clients Sindona introduced to Calvi was the Instituto per le Opere di Reglione – the Institute for Religious Works, the Vatican bank. Calvi's involvement with IOR earned him the nickname, 'God's banker'. The IOR's head, Archbishop Paul Marcinkus, allowed Calvi access to massive amounts of cash and turned a blind eye to his activities. This was because Calvi's money laundering techniques allowed the Catholic Church to support, for example, the banned Polish trade union Solidarity. But Calvi was just as happy using the Vatican's money to invest in Communist-controlled companies and in other enterprises that the Church would certainly not have approved of.

The Bank of Italy was investigating Ambrosiano. But the national bank was itself involved in a scandal in 1979, and the investigation was proceeding at a snail's pace. A number of people who got in Calvi's way were gunned down in Mafia-style shootings. Pope John Paul I's mysterious death after just 30 days on the papal seat was even attributed to Calvi. The new pontiff had threatened to clean up the Vatican's financial affairs.

Although Sindona had escaped arrest in Italy in 1974, he was not so lucky in New York in 1979. Arrested for fraud and for staging his own kidnapping, he was sentenced to 25 years. The authorities began looking into his Mafia ties. An informant mentioned Sindona's connection to Gelli. Gelli's office was raid by the customs police. In a briefcase, they found files detailing P-2's activities and the names of its 962 members. These included media barons, businessmen, judges, two serving cabinet ministers, a former head of the civil service, the chief of the general staff, the head of military intelligence, the past and present head of the customs police and banker Roberto Calvi.

It was clear that P-2 had not just used its influence and inside knowledge, but had also used blackmail and extortion as a means to its ends. It was also implicated in the Bank of Italy scandal of 1979 and the 1980 bombing of the railway station at Bologna by a neo-Fascist group.

The Christian Democrat government immediately set up a commission of inquiry into the activities of P-2. But with two of its own ministers members of the lodge, this had little credibility. The Christian Democrat's coalition partners withdrew their support and the government fell – not an unusual event in Italy. The new prime minister was Giovanni Spadolini, leader of the Republican Party. This was the first time since 1945 that Italy had had a prime minister who was not a Christian Democrat.

P-2 was branded a secret society, and thus outlawed under the Italian constitution. The head of the customs police and his chief of staff were arrested for their part in an oil tax evasion scam, fined 50 billion lire each and sentenced to seven years in jail. The military chiefs were reshuffled. Directors of radio and TV news were sacked; the editor of the influential newspaper *Corriere della Sera* resigned. The owners of the *Corriere della Sera* Rizzoli group were under investigation. The company's senior executives were P-2 members. Angelo Rizzoli and the managing director, Bruno Tassan Din, were arrested and charged with fraud and concealment of debt. Their interests in the firm were later seized by the authorities. Rizzoli had been used as a front by Calvi, whose company, La Centrale, had a 40 per cent stake.

Calvi was arrested and charged with the illegal export of currency. He was found guilty, fined 16 billion lire – some £8 million – and sentenced to four years in jail. Out on bail pending appeal, he went back to work at Ambrosiano. The bank had lent some $774 million to foreign subsidiaries that could not be recovered. A further $1.3 billion had disappeared, after being lent to Panamanian-registered front companies.

The Bank of Italy wrote to Calvi, demanding that he inform his fellow directors of the bank's true position. When he did, he lost the support of the board for the first time. On 10 June 1980, Calvi disappeared from his flat in Rome. At first, it was feared that he had been kidnapped. His disappearance shook what was left of the bank's credibility and the UK's Midland Bank and others forced Ambrosiano's overseas network into liquidation.

Using a forged passport, Calvi had fled to London with Flavio Carboni, a Sicilian building contractor with Mafia connections, and Silvano Vittor, a small-time smuggler who acted as Calvi's bodyguard.

On 11 June, Calvi booked into a cheap hotel in Chelsea. He stayed in his room, making frantic phone calls to his family and business associates. On the night of 17 June, he went out, seemingly on his own. The next morning he was found dead, hanging by a rope from some scaffolding beneath Blackfriars Bridge. In his pockets there were bricks and £7,000, mainly in lire and US dollars.

Initially, his death was thought to be suicide. But it seemed improbable that a 62-year-old man would go to the trouble of clambering out across scaffolding and weighing himself down with bricks before hanging himself when he could have killed himself in his hotel room. However, there were no marks of violence on his body. How he died remains a mystery, and an open verdict was recorded by the coroner's court. Elaborate theories about ritual Masonic killings have been advanced. Murder was an obvious possibility. But Calvi had so many enemies that the Metropolitan police hardly knew where to start and, with Italy still reeling over the P-2 scandal, the Italian authorities were less than helpful.

On the day Calvi died, his devoted secretary, Graziella Corrocher, was killed when she fell from the fourth floor of the Banco Ambrosiano building. Appalled by his fraud, she left a note saying that she hoped Calvi 'be cursed a thousand times for the harm he has done to everyone at the bank, and to the image of the group we were once so proud of'. Clearly, she knew nothing of what her boss was up to.

The authorities were still trying to unravel what had happened when Gelli was arrested in Geneva, trying to withdraw $55 million from a Swiss bank account. The money had come from one of Banco Ambrosiano's foreign subsidiaries. Suspicious bank staff called the police. Gelli was in disguise. He was immediately jailed for travelling on a false passport. But before he could be extradited back to Italy, where he faced charges of political conspiracy, criminal association, extortion and fraud, he escaped from his maximum security Swiss prison with the help of a warder, who drove him across the French border to a waiting private jet.

The Ambrosiano bank collapsed, putting its 4,200 employees out of work. Ten of the bank's directors and officials were convicted of illicit share dealing and contravention of foreign exchange controls.

But Archbishop Marcinkus went unpunished, even though he was on the board of several of Banco Ambrosiano's overseas companies and the Panamanian front companies where $1.3 billion had gone missing. Some of Ambrosiano's subsidiaries were found to be owned directly or indirectly by the IOR, but where the money went to the authorities never discovered.

Italy's Treasury Minister, Beniamino Andreatta, accused the Vatican of being responsible for the collapse of Banco Ambrosiano, and IOR officials were forced to stay within the confines of the Vatican City, afraid that they would be arrested if they set foot on Italian soil.

In an effort to rebuild the relationship between the Catholic Church and the Italian government, the Pope set up a joint commission of inquiry. But the Church remained as secretive as ever. In May 1984, the Vatican agreed to pay 109 creditor banks some $250 million of the $1.3 billion outstanding, in recognition of its 'moral involvement' in the scandal. However, the IOR refused to accept responsibility and the Vatican only handed over the money when the banks agreed to drop their claims for any other outstanding debts.

18 ❖ The Prime Minister and the Air Hostess

In Greece, Andreas Papandreou scandalized the nation when the 70-year-old Prime Minister divorced his wife of 37 years to marry a 35-year-old air hostess. Worse, he was embroiled in a financial scandal and several members of his government were in jail at the time. Acquitted after a long corruption trial, Papandreou bounced back into power, only to create yet more scandal.

Andreas Papandreou had left Greece for America in 1939. He took American citizenship and rose to become professor of economics at Berkeley. Divorcing his Greek wife, he took an American one, who gave him four children.

He returned to Greece in 1959 to become an advisor to the National Bank of Greece. Then he went into politics, entering Parliament in 1964 in the election that made his father, George Papandreou, Prime Minister.

As head of the Pan-Hellenic Socialist Party, Andreas Papandreou became Prime Minister himself in 1981. But he was unable to put his socialist policies into practice because of a steep downturn in the Greek economy.

Papandreou met the air hostess, Dimitra Liani, in 1986. Soon, she was

Greek Prime Minister Andreas Papandreou, who caused uproar when he divorced his wife to marry a 35 year old air hostess

accompanying him to summit meetings and other official functions in place of his wife. In 1988, Papandreou had to go to London for a heart-valve transplant operation, which involved a two-month convalescence. Dimitra went with him. This caused a scandal in the Greek newspapers.

At the same time, a financial scandal surrounding George Kostotas was erupting. Kostotas was a Greek-American who had moved to Greece in 1983. He bought two right-wing newspapers, *Kathimerini* and *Vrathini*, with the aim of turning them into mouthpieces for Papandreou's PASOK Party. He set up the publishing company Grammi, took over a football team, bought a radio station and a great deal of property, and became President of the Bank of Crete, Greece's second largest bank.

Kostotas was introduced to Papandreou in 1986 by Papandreou's son, George, who was Minister of Education in the PASOK administration. They only met three times, but Kostotas gave money to George Louvaris, a close friend of Papandreou's who handled property deals for him.

Rumours concerning irregularities in the running of the Bank of Crete had already begun to surface, but Papandreou's government changed the law to hamper any investigation. This, it was said, was why Kostotas had given Louvaris – and by implication, Papandreou – money.

Nevertheless, it came to light in the bank's accounts that two invest-ments with major investment banks were forgeries. Kostotas was charged with forgery and embezzlement to the tune of $200 million. He was also accused of obstructing justice by refusing to release documents detailing payments to leading members of the government, including Papandreou's son.

Kostotas was barred from leaving the country and was kept under surveillance by the security forces. Even so, he managed to escape to Brazil, which does not have an extradition treaty with Greece. The Minister for Public Order resigned. Fearing for his life, Kostotas flew on to the United States, where he was arrested. In an interview with *Life* magazine, he claimed that the Bank of Crete had poured large sums of money into the coffers of PASOK. This indirectly implicated Papandreou and Athanasios Koutsogiorgas, the Minister for Justice, who tendered his resignation. However, Papandreou immediately promoted Koutsogiorgas to Minister in Charge of the Prime Minister's Office and sacked the Minister for Education and Religious Affairs, Stephanos Tzoumakas, for criticizing the government. Five other ministers promptly resigned, citing the govern-ment's lack of response to the corruption charges.

In the midst of all this, Papandreou announced his marriage plans. Just 30 days after his divorce from his second wife, he married Dimitra in an

Papandreou talking to the press

Orthodox ceremony in a suburb of Athens. None of Papandreou's children attended.

Although the marriage stemmed press criticism of his sex life, Papandreou came under increasing fire over the Kostotas scandal and he was swept from power in 1989. The new government called for the prosecution of Papandreou and three of his ministers.

Papandreou was accused of taking money from Kostotas, via Louvaris. One of Papandreou's bodyguards had seen the money being slipped into a ministerial car. Papandreou was also charged with funnelling government money into the Bank of Crete, even though he knew it was insolvent and under investigation. Papandreou faced other charges of using government money in his private affairs. His government was also accused of selling firearms to South Africa illegally. In addition, he was implicated in covering up the Yugoslavian corn scandal. In 1986, 20,000 tonnes of Yugoslavian corn was shipped on to other European Community countries, thereby avoiding £600,000 in duty. Greece was fined $2.5 million by the EC and Papandreou's Deputy Finance Minister, Nikos Athanassopoulos, was sentenced to three and a half years in jail for fraud. Lastly, a commission of inquiry was set up into illegal phone tapping, said to have been done on the orders of Papandreou.

Koutsogiorgas was accused of accepting bribes and helping a criminal escape when it was discovered that £2 million had been paid into a Swiss bank account in his name by Kostotas. He claimed that he had no idea how the money had found its way into his account. The Minister of Transport and the Minister of Economics were also charged with corruption.

In 1991, Papandreou went to trial. After six months of convoluted hearings where numerous other corruption charges were made, he was acquitted and immediately called for an election. He managed to line his campaign coffers with money from Time International, owners of *Life* magazine, when he won a suit for defamation.

In October 1993, PASOK won the election and Papandreou gave his wife the job of running his private office. His son George became Minister of Education again. In 1995, Papandreou became ill again. Dimitra had to be dissuaded from flying a sacred icon to his bedside in Athens. As his condition worsened, she manoeuvred for power. George also declared that he was ready to take over when his father died.

To curb the ambitions of Dimitra, the press published nude photos of her. This damaged Papandreou so badly that he fell from power. Papandreou's children blamed Dimitra for their father's downfall. They were even more miffed when they discovered, when he died, that he had cut them out of his will and left everything to Dimitra. A battle royal then ensued over his estate.

19 ❖ I Was a Drug Smuggler for the CIA

Panamanian strongman General Manuel Noriega worked for the CIA. But when the CIA discovered that he was a double agent, also providing intelligence to Cuba and to the Soviet Union, it used his connections with drug barons in Florida to bring him down. But to make the arrest it had to stage a full-scale invasion of Panama.

The country of Panama had been founded in 1903 by a break-away province of Colombia. The US government backed the succession so that a sympathetic government there would allow it to build the Panama Canal.

Born in a poor *barrio* of Panama City in 1938, Noriega joined the army and rose swiftly through the ranks of the National Guard. In 1969, he foiled a coup against the then dictator, Brigadier-General Omar Torrijos, and was appointed head of military intelligence. In 1981, Torrijos was killed in an air crash. Noriega was appointed commander of the Panamanian Defence Forces and *de facto* head of state. He then used his powerful military intelligence network to subvert the opposition, and to blackmail and intimidate the electorate. When that failed, he simply stuffed the ballot boxes.

In 1987, allegations came to light that Noriega was involved in drug smuggling. The US Senate passed a resolution, asking him to step down while the allegations were investigated by the CIA. Noriega's second-in-command, Roberto Dia Herrera, broke ranks and accused him of murdering Torrijos, conspiring to murder the opposition leader, Hugo Spadafora, and rigging the 1984 elections. Herrera quickly found himself out of a job.

Federal grand juries sitting in Miami and Tampa issued indictments against Noriega. They accused him of turning Panama into one 'vast criminal empire', a staging post for the Colombian cartel that was smuggling drugs into the USA. Noriega, they estimated, had made $4.6 million from this racket.

The US applied economic sanctions against Panama. The nominal head of state, President Eric Delvalle, a Noriega appointee, announced that Noriega had been sacked, but the Panamanian Legislative Assembly promptly sacked Delvalle, too. The resulting election was declared null and void when it became clear that the results were running against Noriega.

Then the army turned against him. Rebel troops held Noriega captive in the headquarters of the Panamanian Defence Forces for four hours, until troops loyal to Noriega surrounded the building. Leaders of the abortive coup were executed – some say by Noriega personally – and the army was purged.

Although US troops from the Canal Zone had offered the rebels some assistance, Congress now criticized the administration for not doing more. On 15 December 1989, Noriega had himself officially declared President by the Panamanian National Assembly and declared that Panama was at war with the USA. This was not a good move.

The following day an off-duty US Marine was killed by a Panamanian soldier. Another US soldier was beaten up and his wife threatened.

On 20 December, the USA invaded. Some 9,500 troops were airlifted in from the USA to join the 3,500 already stationed there. US tanks rolled out of the Canal Zone. The Americans destroyed the headquarters of the Panamanian Defence Forces and seized key installations. For the first time in its history, the Panama Canal was closed.

The following day, the Pentagon announced that resistance had been crushed. The US had lost 23 men. Nearly 300 Panamanian troops had been

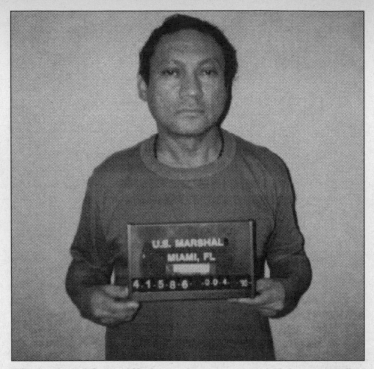

US mugshot of General Noriega, who was accused of drug smuggling

killed and 1,500 taken prisoner. The number of civilian dead stood at 230.

Although sporadic action continued for several days, the USA congratulated itself on its victory. However, Noriega – whose arrest had been the object of the invasion – was nowhere to be seen.

Four days later, it was discovered that he had taken refuge in the papal nunciature in Panama City and was claiming sanctuary. The Americans insisted that the papal authorities hand him over. The Vatican said they would not. US troops tried to force him to surrender by playing loud rock music outside the nunciature day and night. It worked. Two weeks after the invasion, Noriega walked out and was arrested by the US authorities.

He was flown to Miami where he was arraigned on drug-smuggling charges. A legal battle ensued. Noriega's defence claimed that the manner of his arrest was illegal and the coverage of the invasion made it impossible to get a fair hearing.

Some $20 million in Noriega's bank accounts world-wide were frozen. This sparked more actions in foreign courts. Some of the money was later unfrozen so he could pay his spiralling legal bills.

Noriega himself threatened to release documents that would be embarrassing to the CIA. It came up at the hearings that the CIA had indeed used Noriega to spy on his own people. Noriega also claimed that he had delivered Exocet missiles to the Argentines during the Falklands War on the orders of the CIA.

Nevertheless, in April 1992, he was found guilty on drug smuggling charges. His position was hardly enhanced by his wife, who was arrested during the trial for stealing buttons off designer clothes. Noriega was jailed for 40 years.

20 ❖ The Longs of Louisiana

The Long family dominated politics in the state of Louisiana for 50 years. The Longs were 'poor white trash', but Huey Long, their sixth child, was an avid reader and managed to get himself a place in university.

To see himself through college, he worked as a travelling salesman, selling kerosene lamps and laxatives. By the time he was 25 he knew the state and its people like the back of his hands.

Desperate to get into politics he managed to get a seat on the State Utility Regulatory Board. The cabal of vested interests that ran Louisiana was horrified by Long. He was a country hick with no table manners and no social graces. If he saw something he fancied on someone else's plate, he would simply lean over and grab it. He was also regarded as a rabble-rouser, but his hectoring style of campaigning won over the common people. They recognized him as one of them.

Long ran for governor in 1924, but was narrowly defeated. He ran again in 1928 and won. His wife found his lack of finesse embarrassing enough at home, but in the governor's mansion it was intolerable. She moved out, taking the children with her. Long lived in a series of hotels for the rest of his life.

Dressing in colourful suits, he was a flamboyant popularist. 'Every man a king' was his slogan. And he called himself 'the Kingfisher'. He stopped the state's unpopular poll tax, improved the roads and bridges, supplied school-children with free textbooks and introduced a free night-school for adults.

However, all this was accomplished by methods that can only be considered fascist. He brooked no opposition. He censored newspapers and banned meetings of more than two people. Cities were placed under martial law at a whim. In New Orleans, no one except the police and politicians were allowed to carry guns. A climate of fear gripped Louisiana. Long had to be accompanied by a posse of bodyguards wherever he went.

As a monument to his reign, he built a 24-storey Capitol building and a mansion that was an exact replica of the White House. That way, he said, he would know where every light switch was when he was elected president.

To that end, he installed one of his flunkies as Governor of Louisiana in 1931 and got himself elected to the US Senate. His platform was a plan called 'Share the Wealth'. He proposed that the federal government levy a tax that would prevent anyone earning over $1 million a year. The money raised would be used to guarantee every American family a 'homestead' worth $5,000 and an annual income of $2,000. He also proposed college grants, old-age pensions, a 30-hour working week and a month's paid leave a year.

Across the country victims of the Great Depression resented the affluence still flaunted by the wealthy few. They rallied to Long's banner. 'Share the Wealth' societies were set up in every state and, by 1935, Long had four and a half million supporters.

The Democrats were running scared and it was thought that Long, as a third party candidate, would harm Franklin Roosevelt's chances of re-election. Long had other enemies. Those on the right saw him as a socialist; those on the left saw him as a fascist. Long was gunned down by Dr Carl Weiss, leader of an anti-Long faction, outside the Louisiana House of Representatives in 1935, before his plan could be put to the test.

The following year, Huey Long's brother, Earl, was elected Lieutenant Governor and, when the Governor quit over a political scandal, Earl stepped into his shoes. He was elected Governor in 1948 and again in 1956. Earl was cut from the same cloth as Huey.

'You have to watch Earl,' Huey had once said. 'If you live long enough, he'll double-cross you.'

Earl introduced free school lunches, raised teachers' pay, upped the pension and built new hospitals. But he was restrained from his brother's totalitarian excesses by Huey's son, Russell Long, who was elected to the State Senate in 1948.

Like his brother, Earl was a man of the people. He travelled around the state, buying up soft drinks, snacks and live hens. He was also addicted to power. He spent a lot of time trying to figure out how to get around the state law that prohibited anyone standing for more than two terms as governor.

He planned to quit just a few days before the election and stand as an ordinary citizen instead of the incumbent. But he never got a chance to see

Huey Long, part of the Long family who dominated politics for 50 years in the deep south of America

whether this would work. He was in hot water long before then.

Louisiana was in the Deep South and famous for its Jim Crow laws. Earl wanted to change all that. He tried to force new voter registration rules through the state legislature, allowing blacks to vote – on the theory that they would be so grateful that they would vote for him. But after a bitter and foul-mouthed debate, the bill was thrown out.

Earl also had problems at home. His wife, the matronly Miz Blanche, began having public fights with him. Rather than return to her at night, the Governor sought solace in a striptease club in New Orleans called the

Sho-Bar. It was there that the 65-year-old politician set eyes on Blaze Star, the club's headline stripper who had been voted 'Queen of the Burlesque' the year before. He fell instantly in love with her. He told her that Miz Blanche had denied him sex for two years. Blaze was prepared to do something about that and, in gratitude, Earl set her up in the Flamingo Hotel, just outside town.

When they were caught together there, the scandal hit the headlines. Miz Blanche was fuming, but Earl was not about to come to heel. In front of the astonished audience at the Sho-Bar, Governor Long asked the betassled stripper to marry him.

Miz Blanche and Russell Long then drew up papers to have Earl committed to a mental hospital. He was dragged from the governor's mansion, flown to Texas and locked up in a clinic. A judge ruled that he could return to Louisiana, provided he check into another clinic there.

When Earl arrived back in New Orleans, he walked into the front door of a clinic, then straight out the back. He headed for Baton Rouge, but was intercepted on the orders of Miz Blanche and returned to hospital. Finally, he got a judge to release him, and when he got out he fired the director of the Louisiana Department of Hospitals.

From then on his behaviour became increasingly bizarre. Once, when eating out with Blaze, he put a paper bag over his head and kept his false teeth beside him in a jar.

Since he could not run for governor again, he ran as lieutenant-governor but lost. For his farewell party at the governor's mansion, he invited all the strippers from the Sho-Bar. Miz Blanche fled and Blaze did a strip. Then they stuffed all the goodies they could carry in the car and went back to Blaze's flat.

Earl then ran for Congress and got elected. He died the following day

21 ❖ Iran-Contra

The Iran-Contra scandal was a much more serious scandal than Zippergate and a bigger scandal than Watergate. It was clear that numerous illegal acts had been ordered by the President. However, the 70-year-old Ronald Reagan – who was diagnosed as suffering from senile dementia when he left office – said that he could not remember a thing. And, terrifyingly, everyone believed him.

Iran-Contra began with a scandalous revelation in the Lebanese magazine, *Al Shiraa*, on 3 November 1986. It said that President Reagan's National Security Adviser, Robert McFarlane, had secretly travelled to Tehran and supplied the Iranian government with military equipment. This was scarcely credible. Since the Islamic revolution in 1979, Iran had been an international pariah. President Reagan himself had called the Islamic Republic a 'terrorist state' and supplying arms to Iran was illegal.

However, on 4 November 1986, the speaker of the Iranian parliament, Hojatolislam Hashemi Ali Akbar Rafsanjani, confirmed that it was true, but claimed that the American delegation had been arrested, detained in their hotel for five days, then expelled. The Iranian government could hardly admit to dealing with America, whom they cast as the 'Great Satan', either.

It was soon clear that there was more here than met the eye. In the Lebanon, it was said that the object of the arms deal was the release of David P. Jacobsen, a US hostage held by a pro-Iranian faction in Beirut. The US routinely condemned bargaining for hostages. Then it was revealed that the secret dealings with Tehran had not ended with Bob McFarlane's resignation the previous December. The new National Security Adviser, Vice-Admiral John M. Poindexter, had continued the trade through an official of the National Security Council named Oliver North.

Ten days after the story first broke, President Reagan was forced to admit publicly that the US government had secretly sold 'defensive weapons and spare parts' to Iran. But this was not a deal for hostages, he said. It was a covert operation designed to encourage moderate elements in Iran; and it was working. President Reagan boasted proudly: 'Since US government contact began with Iran, there's been no evidence of Iranian government complicity in acts of terrorism against the US.'

Three days later, Secretary of State George Shultz flatly contradicted this. By that time, the White House was in a state of confusion. Reagan issued a statement claiming that no third country was involved in this arms deal. This was almost immediately contradicted by a White House statement saying that Israel had been involved.

The following day, 20 November, Attorney General Ed Meese was called in to investigate. Just five days later, Meese announced that Poindexter had resigned and North had been dismissed when it had been discovered that profits from the deal – some $10–30 million – had been diverted to aid the right-wing rebels in Nicaragua known as the Contras.

It was no secret that the Reagan White House backed the Contras, who were trying to overthrow the left-wing Sandinista government in

President Reagan, who apparently suffered from senile demensia throughout the Iran-Contra affair

Managua. But Congress had specifically banned any aid to the Contras, so North was breaking the law. Worse, Meese discovered that Poindexter knew of North's activities and so did McFarlane, but only after he had left office. The obvious question was that, if the President's National Security Adviser knew North was breaking the law, did the President know as well?

Unfortunately, when Meese uncovered the Contra dealings on 23 November, he did not seal North's office. That was not done until the press started baying for blood on 25 November. In the intervening two days, North and his secretary, Fawn Hall, spent day and night shredding documents.

Reagan sought to rescue the situation by appointing Senator John Tower of Texas to investigate the role of the National Security Council in the affair. As head of the National Security Council – assuming he was awake at their meetings – Reagan should have known what was going on. This did not satisfy Congress, which pressured Reagan into appointing an independent council to investigate the scandal. Then Congress set up its own joint House–Senate committee to look into it.

The problem was that despite the Watergate fever on Capitol Hill, there was not very much to look into. Everything was known in the first few weeks. Apart from Poindexter and North, the only other casualty was White House Chief of Staff, Donald Regan. He resigned after the Tower Commission report said that 'he must bear primary responsibility for the chaos that descended upon the White House'. Ironically, it was Regan who had sought to alert the President to the problem. He later claimed that his plan to handle the crisis was overruled by the President's wife, Nancy, on the advice of her astrologer.

However, the investigation into the Iran-Contra scandal revealed deep divisions within the administration. Secretary of State George Shultz and Secretary of Defense Caspar Weinberger had both warned against selling arms to Iran at an early stage and had believed that the deal had been cancelled on their advice. The CIA grew cold on the operation because of the shady middlemen employed to broker the deal. One of them, expatriate Iranian Manucher Ghorbanifar, even failed a CIA lie detector test. So the only people left to put the plan into operation were the NSC staff and the ever-compliant Colonel Oliver North.

President Reagan had been elected to power over Jimmy Carter's mishandling of the 1980 Iranian hostage crisis. North – a gung-ho military man – knew that his Commander-in-Chief was coming under similar pressure over the number of hostages being taken in Lebanon, just as he knew that Reagan backed the Contras, despite the liberals' opposition in Congress.

It came out during the hearings that North had had a nervous breakdown during the Vietnam War and was something of a fantasist. The whole Iran-Contra operation was characterized as a renegade plan by North, his sidekick Major-General Richard V. Secord and Secord's Iranian-born business partner, Albert Hakim. Secord had had a chequered career, resigning from the Defense Department when the FBI discovered his business connections to rogue CIA operative, Edwin Wilson, who had been jailed for 52 years for selling arms to Libya.

Donald Regan told the Tower Commission that President Reagan had only approved the weapons shipment retrospectively. Reagan himself said that he could not remember, but when Bob McFarlane said that he had approved the shipment as early as 1985, Reagan stood corrected. He told the American people: 'A few months ago I told the American people I did not trade arms for hostages. My heart and my best intentions still tell me that is true, but the facts and the evidence tell me it is not. What began as a strategic opening to Iran deteriorated in its implementation into trading for hostages.'

Poindexter pointed out that this was the opposite of the truth. His memo on the affair, which was signed by the President on 5 December 1985, talked only of trading for hostages. The first reference to the trade being a 'strategic opening' occurred only in a memo of 17 January 1986. Unfortunately, the documents concerned had been shredded. But whichever the case was, at the very time that North and McFarlane were flying arms into Tehran, the USA was trying to sure up an international arms embargo against Iran. Since 1984, Iran had been on the State Department's list of countries that supported terrorism, a country it became illegal to export arms to under the Diplomatic Security and Anti-Terrorism Act that Reagan signed into law in August 1986.

But all this was becoming too complicated for the public to follow, particularly because of the involvement of Israeli intelligence and competing factions in Tehran. So the interest turned to the Contra end of Iran-Contra in a search for the 'smoking gun'. But this end was messier still. Aid to the Contras had been banned in 1984 by the Boland Amendment, when it was discovered that the CIA had been mining Nicaraguan harbours. If it could be shown that Reagan had used the money from the arms shipment to Iran to send aid to the Contras, deliberately thwarting the will of Congress, it would be a very serious matter indeed.

However, Poindexter and North said that they did not think that the Boland Amendment applied to them, only to the CIA. And Poindexter said that he never told the President about sending support to the Contras.

'Although I was convinced that we could properly do it and the President would approve if asked,' Poindexter said, 'I made a very deliberate decision not to ask the President so that I could insulate him from the decision and provide some future deniability for the President if it ever leaked out...

'On this whole issue,' Poindexter announced, 'the buck stops with me.'

North said that he had never communicated directly with the President about the matter. He had sent some memos to Reagan via Poindexter, but they had not been acknowledged and North had put his copies through the shredder. Reagan told *Time* magazine that North was 'a national hero'.

Also in the firing line was William Casey, head of the CIA. He was eager to break free of the shackles applied to the agency by Congress after the House had investigated its activities in the aftermath of Watergate. It was then that the CIA's successful plot to overthrow the government of

Robert Macfarlane -
President Reagan's
National Security
Advisor

Salvador Allende in Chile and its ludicrous attempts to assassinate Fidel Castro came out. But Casey could hardly argue that the Boland Amendment did not apply to the CIA.

Casey claimed that he only knew of the diversion of funds to the Contras after Meese had told him. However, before he could testify, Casey was struck down with a brain seizure on 5 December 1986 and died in May 1987. Bob Woodward, one of the *Washington Post* reporters who had unearthed the Watergate scandal, said that Casey had told him on his deathbed that the CIA had been involved from the start. Casey's wife spiked his guns, saying that Woodward had never been anywhere near her husband's bedside.

However, when Oliver North was hauled in front of the Congressional Committee in July 1987, he told the same story as Woodward. He said that Casey had envisaged the arms-for-Iran deal financing, not just the Contras, but any other activity for which they did not want to ask Congress for funding. The Boland Amendment, naturally, had caused him some problems, but they had both agreed that if anything should go wrong North would be the fall guy.

America watched the televised hearing riveted as Ollie North wrapped himself in the flag in front of the Congressional Committee. He was a soldier just doing his job. After all, the Contras he funded were 'freedom fighters'.

When George Shultz referred to him as a 'loose cannon' at the NSC, North looked directly into the eyes of the congressmen and said: 'That wasn't what I heard while I worked there, people used to walk up to me and tell me what a great job I was doing.'

However, it turned out that North and his cronies were not as selflessly patriotic as they made out. The deal had made some $48 million in all. Albert Hakim had $8 million, which he was unwilling to surrender. Secord resisted all requests by the US government to look into his Swiss bank accounts. The committee noted that he drove a Porsche and owned a private jet. North himself had had a $16,000 security fence, paid for by Secord, installed around his house. When the scandal broke, he readily accepted backdated invoices for the work.

With the NSC, which had effectively been making foreign policy, now in disgrace, Secretary of State Shultz seized the opportunity to reassert the power of the State Department, which had known of the Iranian arms deal only when officials read about it in the Lebanese press. Now assured the ear of the President, he fulsomely acknowledged the Constitutional authority of Congress and the Boland Amendment on behalf of the administration. Caspar Weinberger did the same thing for the Defense Department, saying that he had only learnt of the arms deal through the intelligence service of another government.

The Congressional Committee's report blamed North, McFarlane and Poindexter. Although the President was ultimately responsible for allowing a 'cabal of zealots' to take over, it stopped short of accusing him of complicity or any impeachable offence. A minority report issued by the Republican members of the committee concluded that there was 'no systematic disrespect for the "rule of law", no grand conspiracy and no administration-wide dishonesty or cover-up'. The Republicans were still smarting from Watergate and did not want to see another of their number go that way.

However, someone had to pay the price. McFarlane, a broken man who attempted suicide in 1987, pleaded guilty to misleading Congress when he had said that North was not sending aid to the Contras. He got a small fine and two years' probation. This was part of a plea bargain with the Special Prosecutor. He turned state's evidence against North, Poindexter, Secord and Hakim, who faced a portmanteau of charges, which included conspiracy, fraud and embezzlement – but no charges relating to gun running.

Although the Special Prosecutor wanted the four to be tried together, the judge ruled that they must be tried separately. North would go first. President Reagan continued to make nice noises about North's high motives, but the White House refused any help. In response, North refused to be the fall guy. He demanded that the administration hand over documents relating to various intelligence operations and gave notice that he intended to call President Reagan and Vice-President George Bush as witnesses at his trial. This forced the Special Prosecutor to drop some of the more wide-ranging conspiracy charges.

The trial was a tedious affair, unearthing no new evidence. North's defence was that he had been obeying orders, or thought he was obeying orders, when he sent money to the Contras. After 13 days of deliberation, the jury agreed. They found North not guilty on the nine most serious charges, including conspiring to conceal the funding of the Contras from Congress. However, they found him guilty of shredding government documents, falsifying records and accepting an illegal gratuity in the form of the security fence. A penitent North was given a suspended three-year jail term and 1,200 hours of community service, and fined $15,000. This got George Bush, who was now President, off the hook. Had North been jailed, Bush would have come under a great deal of right-wing pressure to pardon him.

With his exaggerated sense of patriotism, North had become a right-wing icon and was being mooted as a congressional candidate by the Republicans. But due to the nature of his offences, the judge banned North from running for public office.

Secord and Hakim pleaded guilty to minor charges on a plea bargain and were given two years' probation and a fine. Hakim also promised to hand over $7.3 million worth of profits from the deal, which he had stashed in a Swiss bank account. Poindexter was sentenced to six months' imprisonment, largely on the testimony of North, who said that he had supervised the arms shipment in November 1985, although he had told Congress that he had only found out about it in January 1986.

North's convictions were eventually overturned. The Archbishop of Canterbury's special envoy Terry Waite, who had been sent to Beirut as a hostage negotiator, was taken hostage himself. Eventually, the hostages were released and the Sandinistas were defeated in an election.

22 ❖ A Nazi at the UN

In June 1986, Kurt Waldheim was elected President of Austria. As a former two-term secretary-general of the United Nations, he was internationally respected. However, the following April he was banned from entering the United States, under a US statute barring former Nazis. Other nations followed suit and soon, the President of Austria was reduced to performing a purely domestic role.

In the run-up to the 1986 presidential election, the magazine, *Profil*, had drawn attention to crucial omissions in Waldheim's autobiography – his membership of a number of National Socialist organizations and his role in the Nazi occupation of the Balkans. Waldheim supporters claimed that this was part of a 'stop Waldheim' smear campaign organized by Jews and Communists.

The latent anti-Semitism in the Austrian election soon brought condemnation from the World Jewish Congress in New York. But the Austrian electorate resented what it saw as outside interference in its own elections. The economy was in a parlous condition due to the mismanagement of the country's numerous, top-heavy nationalized industries, and Waldheim was seen as the man who could sort it out.

Waldheim won the second ballot with 53.9 per cent of the vote and became the first non-socialist to become Austrian president since World War II. He was not particularly unpopular, even with his socialist opponents, once the election was over. The new socialist Chancellor, Franz Vranitzky, even managed to form a coalition with Waldheim's ÖVP, despite the dissatisfaction of some of his more radical followers.

While Waldheim was fêted by Arab countries, he came under fire from Jewish organizations and Nazi hunters. Records were released that showed that he had been involved in interrogations in the Balkans and had referred some detainees for 'special treatment'. He had also known of Nazi reprisals against Yugoslav civilians, although had been powerless to stop them.

An international historians' commission was set up to investigate Waldheim's war record. It concluded that he was not a war criminal and was not implicated in the Holocaust nor the numerous Nazi atrocities that took place in the Balkans. He was simply a careerist with a more than usually selective memory. But Waldheim continued to draw criticism, largely because his presidential term spanned the 50th anniversary of the 1938 *Anschluss*, when Nazi Germany had annexed Austria. After that, however, the Austrian people grew tired of the scandal and few challenged Waldheim's right to remain in office.

However, the United States and others remained wary of contact. This drew criticism from the Czech President when the West boycotted a summit in Salzburg, which he and the German President attended.

Waldheim had developed good relations with the Arab nations during his time at the UN and, at the beginning of the Gulf War in 1990, he managed to rescue 80 Austrians held hostage by Saddam Hussein. This was much criticized by other nations, who saw it as a break in Western ranks.

The month after the return of the hostages, Waldheim was found guilty of perjury over his testimony on his Nazi past in a court case held in 1987 and was fined. When that conviction was upheld by an appeal court in 1988, Waldheim announced that he would not be seeking a second term in office.

23 ❖ Evita

Thanks to Andrew Lloyd Webber, the whole world knows that Argentina's most famous First Lady was once a prostitute. But if that was not scandalous enough, her husband, Juan Domingo Perón, was eventually kicked out of office for being a paedophile.

Perón was born in 1895 in Lobos, a small town about 60 miles southwest of Buenos Aires. His parents were Creole and unmarried. At 15, he was sent to military school, where he had his first sexual experiences with prostitutes.

'In the era when we were boys,' he said, 'we weren't accustomed to going to social parties, and it would not have occurred to us to go to a home and make love to a family girl.'

At the age of 33, he married a respectable school teacher. They had no children and after 10 years of marriage his wife died.

In 1939, he was posted to Rome as military attaché and he was very impressed by Mussolini and his methods. Travelling extensively throughout Germany, Hungary, Austria, Spain and Portugal, he concluded that Fascism worked. But he would never have been able to put what he had learnt into practice without the help of his second wife, the celebrated Evita.

Born Marma Eva Duarte in the small town of Los Toldos in 1919, she was the daughter of the wealthy local landowner, Juan Duarte, and his mistress of 15 years' standing, Juanita Ibarguren. When Evita was seven, her father died and her mother was left to fend for herself. She made ends meet by running an *amoblados* or 'love hotel'.

The prospects for young girls in a dusty pampas town like Los Toldos were bleak. At the age of 14, Evita agreed to sleep with the small-time tango singer, José Armani, if he would take her the 150 miles to Buenos Aires. Later, she claimed her first lover was the far more famous singer, Agustin Magaldi.

When she first arrived in Buenos Aires, Evita had little choice of career. She became a prostitute and modelled for pornographic photographs. But she was burning with ambition. Five feet five, with brown eyes and bleached-blonde hair, she was determined to become an actress. At the age of 15, she became the mistress of Emilio Kartulovic, publisher of the movie magazine, *Sintonia*. Kartulovic had all the contacts she needed. Evita soon turned her attention to the impresario, Rafael Firtuso, owner of the Liceo theatre. He cast her in one of his productions, which was sent out on a provincial tour. The play was called *The Mortal Kiss*, a rousing melodrama about the evils of promiscuity – sponsored by the Argentine Prophylactic League in response to Argentina's soaring illegitimacy rate.

On her return to Buenos Aires, Evita landed a number of small parts in lacklustre Argentine movies. To make ends meet, she would spend her evenings in clubs with wealthy businessmen. Her nights would often end in one of the city's numerous love hotels and a ride home in a cab with an extra 50 pesos in her purse.

Evita's big career breakthrough came when she got on the radio. She quickly became queen of the soaps and appeared on the covers of the radio listings magazines.

In June 1943, a number of ambitious officers, including Juan Perón, staged a military coup. With her eye on the main chance, she began bedding the Minister of Communications, Colonel Anibal Imbert. Showing off in front of her fellow actresses in the rehearsal room of Radio Belgrano, she phoned Government House and spoke to President Ramirez, who invited her to dinner. The owner of Radio Belgrano promptly upped her salary from 150 pesos a month to 5,000. She was going up in the world.

Colonel Imbert moved her out of the rough Boca district into a smart apartment off the fashionable Avenida Alvear. When an earthquake destroyed the town of San Juan in January 1944, Evita persuaded him to stage a benefit concert for the victims to be broadcast nation-wide. Of course, Argentine's favourite soap star would be guest of honour.

Also present was Juan Perón, the rising strongman of the new regime. He arrived with Argentina's loveliest movie star, Libertad Lamarque, on his arm. But when Libertad stood up to do a bit at the microphone, Evita slipped into the empty chair beside him. The 48-year-old Perón already had a reputation for liking young girls. Evita was already 24, but she knew how to please a man and it took little effort to seduce him.

A few days later, Evita marched into Perón's apartment and evicted his teenage mistress. Perón had let it slip that he and a few like-minded officers were plotting to oust the civilian president. They planned to put Fascism into action without making the mistakes they thought Mussolini had made.

Evita was convinced that Perón could be the leader of the coup this time, if he had her help. And she moved into his apartment block to keep an eye on him. She realized that the traditional source of popular power in Argentina was the gauchos, the cowboys who had once inhabited the pampas and had now migrated to the shanty towns around the cities in search of work. As Minister of Labour, Perón was in a perfect position to mobilize their support. He introduced a minimum wage, sick leave, paid holidays and a bonus payment every year before Christmas. On the back of his growing popularity, Perón formed the *descamisados*, a paramilitary organization modelled on Mussolini's blackshirts.

His growing popularity among the poor brought a swift reaction. Moneyed interests forestalled his coup with a coup of their own. Perón, by then Vice-President and Minister of War, was arrested. Evita quickly rallied the labour unions. Hundreds of thousands took to the streets in protest. On 17 October 1945, Perón was released. Together, Perón and Evita were taken to the presidential palace where he addressed a crowd of 300,000. It was more of a coronation than a coup. A few days later, they were married.

Now President, Perón used his powers to conceal the sordid details of Evita's past. The pornographic photographs she had posed for were collected and destroyed. The regime invested a good deal in her popularity. Although she dressed in jewels and furs, she was portrayed as a woman of the people. In posters, she appeared as the Virgin Mary, the personification of Perónist beauty.

But many were not fooled. Argentinian poet and leading opponent of the regime, Jorge Luis Borges, said: 'Perón's wife was a common prostitute. She had a brothel near Junín. And it must have embittered him, no? I mean, if a girl is a whore in a large city that doesn't mean too much, but in a small town on the pampas, everybody knows everybody else.'

One day, when protesters taunted her while she was riding in an official car with an elderly Italian admiral, she turned to the admiral and said: 'Do you hear that? They are calling me a whore.'

He said: 'Yes, I quite understand. I haven't been to sea for 15 years and they still call me an admiral.'

However, Evita did try to legalize prostitution and regulate the red light district. At the same time, she used her women's welfare organizations to siphon off millions of pesos into her Swiss bank accounts.

While she boasted that her husband rewarded her work with just 'a kiss on the forehead', it was said that she maintained her position in the regime by using her womanly wiles on a network of men. The Perón regime used torture to suppress political opponents and the collection of rebel leaders' testicles that Evita kept on her desk was used to intimidate those who came to petition her.

In 1947, Evita made a trip to Italy where she made love to Aristotle Onassis in his villa on the Italian Riviera. Afterwards, she made him an omelette and he gave her a cheque for $10,000 for charity. He said later that it was the most expensive omelette he had ever eaten.

Moving on to Rome, she was greeted by crowds shouting 'Perón, Perón' and giving the straight-armed Fascist salute outlawed since the War. The riot police were sent in.

Evita died of cancer of the uterus at the age of just 33. Her death plunged Argentina into mourning. Moves were even made to have her canonized. Sadly, her husband could not live up to her virtuous image.

He was now 56, but his taste for teenage girls had not diminished. He began to take an inordinate interest in the Union of Secondary School Students, especially its young female members. There were branches in every school and young girl recruits were sent to luxurious 'recreational centres' where they entertained high-ranking government officials. Teams of doctors were on hand to cope with venereal diseases and unwanted pregnancies.

At Perón's private recreational centre, he would while away the hours watching teenage girls swimming or playing basketball. At least one of them, 13-year-old Nellie Rivas, became his mistress.

Nellie was the daughter of a worker in a sweet factory and slept on a

Eva Peron "Evita" Argentina's most famous First Lady, and one-time prostitute

sofa at the end of her parents' bed. One day, at the Union of Secondary School Students, she was told that she would be having lunch with the President. More lunches followed. Soon she moved into the love nest he had built in the basement of one of his villas. It had mirrored walls and white bearskin rugs on the floor.

As well as making love to her, he would teach young Nellie the rudiments of culture. He offered to send her to Europe to learn about the world, but she said she did not want to leave him.

'The very thought of leaving the residence brought me to the brink of madness,' she said later.

Rumours about Perón's underage mistress soon spread. With the economy in ruins, stories that Perón was staging orgies with young girls in the presidential mansion spread. Many thought he had besmirched the memory of the saintly Evita. Supporters deserted him in droves. Deposed, Perón had to seek refuge on a Paraguayan gunboat that had put in at Buenos Aires for repairs. Before it took him into exile, he scribbled one last note to Nellie.

'My dear baby girl,' it read, 'I miss you every day, as I do my little dogs... Many kisses and many desires. Until I see you soon, Papi.'

Perón was tried *in absentia* in a military court for paedophilia. Their torrid correspondence was read out and subsequently published. His reputation in ruins, Perón was stripped of his rank for 'conduct unworthy of an officer and a gentleman'.

Summing up, the judge said: 'It is superfluous to stress the horror of the court at the proof of such a crime committed by one who always claimed that the only privileged people in the country were the children.'

Nellie was sent to a reformatory for eight months, then went into exile with her parents in Montevideo. The new regime had Evita's remains dug up and sent to Italy, where they were hidden to prevent them becoming an object of veneration.

Perón himself was in exile in Spain when he met and married his third wife, Isabel Martínez, an Argentinian dancer. In 1971, there was yet another coup in Argentine. This one promised a return to democracy and, as a gesture of reconciliation, Evita's remains were returned to Perón in Spain.

In 1973, Perón returned to Argentina to run in the presidential elections with his wife as his running mate. They romped home, but Perón was already dying. His widow succeeded him into office in 1974, but she could not hope to live up to the image of Evita. In a last-ditch attempt to rally support, she had Evita's remains flown home from Spain and interred next to her husband's in a crypt in the presidential palace.

In many eyes, this seemed only to confirm her illegitimacy. In 1976, the Air Force seized power. Isabel was held under house arrest for five years. In 1981, she was banished back to Spain, where she died in 1985.

24 ❖ Imelda Marcos and the Scandal of the Shoes

Imelda Marcos, long-serving First Lady of the Philippines, will always be known for the 3,000 pairs of shoes she left behind in Manila when she and her unscrupulous husband, Ferdinand, were driven from power in 1986. However, these are a symbol only of the scandalous self-indulgence of a regime that had systematically robbed the National Bank of billions and had the temerity to gun down the opposition leader, who was returning from exile, in front of a plane-load of journalists.

Ferdinand Marcos was born in Luzon in 1917. In his highly fanciful autobiography, *Rendezvous with Destiny*, he claimed that he had distinguished himself as a highly decorated resistance leader during the War, against the Japanese. In fact, he had collaborated with the Japanese, but that did not matter: as President of the Philippines, he could give himself any decoration he liked. Not only that, as a fervent anti-Communist and one of America's few allies during the Vietnam War, he forced the Americans to award him the US Medal of Honour, as well as a vast amount of foreign aid, even though they knew the truth.

As a politician, Marcos had already done the seemingly impossible. He had got himself elected to Congress after being convicted of murder. Jailed for killing a political opponent, Marcos had used his incarceration to study the law. He had passed the bar exams and argued his own case in front of the Supreme Court. There he got lucky. The chief justice himself had been convicted of murder at the age of 18 and had successfully argued his case in front of the Supreme Court. Marcos walked free.

Marcos first met Imelda when he gave an address at her high school in Tacloban, on the island of Leyte. Although she was one of the island's powerful Romualdez clan, her side of the family was poor. For a time, they had lived in a car port and, as a child, she had gone barefoot – which might explain why she needed so many shoes later on.

At 16 she was a considered beauty. She fell in love with Victoriano Chan, the heir of a wealthy Chinese family. They considered her unsuitable. Then she was pursued by a rich saw-mill owner, Dominador Pacho. To escape his attentions, she fled to Manila with just five pesos in her purse.

She got a job in a bank, where one of the customers was Ferdinand Marcos. He paid her no attention. However, the editor of the Sunday supplement *This Week* noticed her and put her picture on the cover of the magazine's Valentine Day's issue. Suddenly, she was a star, and welcome at the Manila home of her kinsman, Congressman Daniel Romualdez. There, she was courted by an up-and-coming young politician named Benigno Aquino. But when he learnt of her humble origins, he dropped her.

In an attempt to make her way in the world, she entered the Miss Manila competition. Her family, who were strict Catholics, were shocked. They assumed that she would have to sleep with the judges. Presumably she didn't, as she lost to 20-year-old Norma Jimenez from Pangasinan province.

Realizing her mistake, Imelda appealed to Mayor Arsenio Lacson, who was well known for his wide-ranging sexual interests. It was said that he took 'Chinese tea' every afternoon with two Chinese girls thoughtfully provided by a constituent – a case of two for tea, perhaps?

When Lacson tried to overturn the judges' decision, it was assumed that Imelda was his latest conquest. However, the judges stuck by their original choice for Miss Manila, so Lacson simply named Imelda the 'Muse of Manila'. Both girls went forward for the Miss Philippines' contest, but neither won.

Imelda consoled herself by becoming the mistress of Ariston Nakpil, one of Manila's wealthiest men. Unfortunately, he was married.

It was then that she met Ferdinand Marcos once more at an ice-cream party. He began pursuing her. The following week, when she took off to Baguio with two girlfriends, he followed with a marriage licence that he had already signed just in case.

A religious girl, Imelda would go to Mass each morning. Ferdinand would sit beside her and tell her how golden their future would be together. She did not believe him, until he took her to see his bank deposit box, which contained the best part of $1 million in cash. They had a small private wedding conducted by a Justice of the Peace. From meeting to marriage had taken just 11 days. Her wedding ring had 11 diamonds set into its white gold, one for each day of their courtship.

Imelda thought her father would be angry about the marriage, but he took to Ferdinand immediately and forgave his daughter – provided they had a proper church wedding. Marcos did better than that. He arranged a wedding in the cathedral in Manila in the presence of the President of the Philippines, Ramon Magsaysay. Imelda wore a couture gown, comprising acres of white satin and tulle, embroidered with seed pearls and sequins.

Among the 3,000 guests at the reception in Malacanang Park, across the river from the presidential palace, were numerous senators and congressmen. The wedding cake was a model of the Congress building.

'It was a very political wedding,' said Imelda's sister, Conchita.

The Marcoses had a very public honeymoon in Baguio. This was vital since there was already one Mrs Marcos. Her name was Carmen Ortega. Four years before his marriage to Imelda, Ferdinand had offered to sponsor Carmen for the Miss Press Photography contest. When she became his full-time mistress, he moved her into the house he shared with his mother, Doña Josefa. Marcos even announced their forthcoming nuptials in the press. Neither a civil nor a church wedding ever took place, but around Manila she was known as Mrs Marcos. Even Imelda knew her as such. Marcos had once brought her into the bank where Imelda worked to withdraw $50,000 for a shopping trip to the USA and had introduced her.

Doña Josefa considered Carmen her son's real wife. Imelda was merely a political mistress in her eyes. At the time, Marcos was planning to run for the Senate. He needed the backing of the Romualdez family, both politically and financially.

This fact was brought home painfully to Imelda. While they were away on their honeymoon, Marcos had Carmen and their three children moved out of the family home into a larger house in the suburbs. Imelda would now move in with Marcos and Doña Josefa. If the associations with Carmen there were not bad enough, the house was on Ortega Street. Imelda insisted that they sell up and move immediately. Marcos and his mother refused.

Worse, Marcos continued to see Carmen. Imelda paid her a visit and insisted that Carmen stop seeing her husband as she was destroying her happiness. Carmen said that it was Imelda who was ruining her happiness. At the time, Carmen was pregnant with Marcos's fourth child.

Imelda was now between a rock and a very hard place. In a Catholic country like the Philippines, she had no chance of an annulment, so there was no chance of making another lucrative match. She had no money of her own, and she could not stop her husband seeing his mistress.

Imelda had a nervous breakdown. Marcos sent her to New York for treatment. She spent three months in Manhattan's Presbyterian Hospital, but no amount of therapy changed the situation. She must either leave her husband and return to a life of penury, or bite the bullet.

There was only one thing a good Catholic woman could do. She flew back to the Philippines by way of Portugal, where she visited the shrine of Our Lady of Fatima and prayed for fertility. She gave birth to her first daughter, Imee, during Marcos's congressional campaign the following year. Two years later, their second child, Bong Bong, was born. Their third child, Irene, was born during Marcos's 1959 senatorial campaign.

Imelda suffered migraines and other recurring psychiatric symptoms, but she clung on. By the time Marcos was running for the presidency in 1965, Imelda was warming up the audience at his political rallies with stirring, patriotic Filipino songs. During that campaign Imelda emerged as a political figure in her own right, but she was still unused to the rough and tumble of political life. When the opposition circulated a nude photograph of her, claiming that it came from Marcos's private collection, she collapsed in a state of shock. Marcos supporters insisted that Imelda's head had been superimposed on another woman's nude body.

For Imelda, the best revenge was to be installed as First Lady in the Malacanang Palace. Nevertheless, Imelda remained unsure of herself and demanded inordinate deference from all those around her. When the Beatles turned up in Manila in 1966, she invited them to come and perform in the Malacanang Palace. They respectfully turned down the invitation, but invited her to come and see their public concert like other Filipinos. Imelda took this as an insult. They found themselves unceremoniously expelled from the country. As they left, they were punched and kicked by Imelda's hired thugs on the way to their plane.

The nude photo scandal had revealed a weakness in Imelda that political enemies sought to play on. The Governor of Negros, Alfredo Montelibano Jr, installed a two-way mirror in the lavatory of his hacienda. When Imelda came to his house for a party, he invited a number of guests into a back room to watch the First Lady pee. He took a photograph, which was circulated. Benigno Aquino kept a copy in his wallet until shortly before he died.

Marcos modelled himself on John F. Kennedy and Imelda was only too happy to play Jackie. Like Kennedy, Marcos liked to show off his pretty young wife. He was also an inveterate womanizer. This was still painful for Imelda and it was politically dangerous for Marcos. In 1969, he began showing an interest in Gretchen Cojuangco, wife of Eduardo Cojuangco, who controlled the Philippines' multi-million-dollar sugar-producing corporation. Imelda was determined to put a stop to the affair. She wrote Gretchen a note. Although what it said has never been revealed, when Gretchen read it she could not stop weeping.

Cojuangco took another approach to keep Marcos away from his wife. He suggested that Marcos's dire book, *Rendezvous with Destiny*, was feature film material. He had contacts in Hollywood and set to work immediately.

Imelda Marcos, Long-serving First Lady of the Phillipines, whose passion for shoes was legendary

In *Rendezvous with Destiny*, the fearless guerrilla fighter claimed that his Filipino-American lover, Evelyn, had sacrificed her life to save his, by stopping a Japanese bullet meant for him.

A producer at Universal was employed to recruit girls to audition for the part of Evelyn. One of them was an actress called Dovie Beams. When she arrived in the Philippines, Marcos seduced her. He installed her in a house in the Green Hills suburb and claimed that he had been sexually estranged from Imelda for years. She was frigid and suffered, he said, from 'virginitis'.

Things went swimmingly until Dovie discovered Marcos was still seeing Carmen Ortega, who was now pregnant yet again. Dovie began recording their love-making sessions and when Marcos took her to the presidential palace while Imelda was away, Dovie searched his desk and took documents.

Imelda grew suspicious and began to have them followed. Marcos insisted that Dovie move out of the house in Green Hills and into a hotel. She later discovered that Marcos had given the house to Carmen Ortega, as he had planned all along.

Dovie was determined to get even. Marcos had bought a Polaroid camera and began taking pictures of their love play. He also asked her for a lock of her pubic hair. She consented to give him one, provided he gave her a lock of his. She sent this with a collection of the photographs, the tapes and the documents to the USA for safekeeping.

By then, Marcos was getting tired of her. He told Dovie that she had been miscast for the role of Evelyn and he wanted to audition some new actresses. She packed her bags and flew back to California.

She later returned to the Philippines on the pretext of making a travelogue. She was given $10,000 to buy silence. Although she took it, she insisted that her silence was worth more like $100,000. When that was refused, she asked for $150,000. That night, she was grabbed by the secret police and taken to a house where Marcos was awaiting. There was a row. He tried to make up with her. She spurned him and was beaten up and tortured by the secret police.

When they allowed her to go to the bathroom, she gave them the slip and called a friend in Los Angeles, who contacted influential people Dovie knew in the USA. One of them was former movie actor, Ronald Reagan, then Governor of California. He called the State Department while Dovie checked into a private clinic under a false name.

Meanwhile, Imelda had learnt about everything and had her cohorts combing the island for Dovie. The American ambassador turned up at Dovie's bedside with an offer from Imelda – $100,000 tax free if she kept quiet. But things were not going to be quite as easy as that. Dovie told the ambassador about the incriminating evidence she had on Marcos and said that she believed her life was in danger.

The US ambassador realized that the only way to keep Dovie safe was to make the scandal public. He arranged a press conference. Dovie spilt the beans, referring to Marcos throughout as 'Fred' so that journalists could report the story without falling foul of the recent restrictions preventing the publication of anything critical of the President. She even played one of the tapes that featured bedsprings creaking, murmurs, moans and a man's voice crooning an Ilocano love song, which the whole of the Philippines knew was one of Marcos's favourites. Pirated versions of the tape were soon changing hands at $500 a time.

When the students at Manila University got hold of a copy, they looped the tape and played it over and over on the University radio station. Everyone's favourite section was the part where Marcos begged Dovie to perform oral sex on him. Even the troops sent to shut down the radio station could not keep a straight face. Senator Benigno Aquino, tongue buried firmly in cheek, called for a congressional investigation.

Imelda was now fighting mad. The US authorities had to spirit Dovie out of the Philippines. She was taken to Hong Kong, where the British Secret Service held her in protective custody for five days.

Back in the USA, Dovie published an account of the affair called *Marcos' Lovie Dovie*, which included some of the nude Polaroids. Mysteriously, the books vanished from the bookshops. Even the Library of Congress's copy went missing.

When Imelda cooled off, she realized that she now held the whip hand. If she dumped Marcos now, he would be finished. She told him that she would not ask for a divorce, provided he gave her everything she wanted – everything. He had no choice. He wrote an open cheque. It was then that the shopping started in earnest.

But it was not enough for Imelda to be personally wealthy. She wanted respect. She was First Lady of a small poverty-stricken state. For her to be anything in the world, the Philippines would have to raise its profile. She planned to stage a Manila Film Festival, which she hoped would rival the glamour of Cannes. As part of the project, she planned a 100,000-seater stadium, the construction of which fell badly behind schedule.

To speed up its building, she demanded that the structure be erected before the concrete floor had dried. Predictably, the upper floors collapsed, killing 168 building workers. Imelda simply ordered their remains to be concreted over so that building work could begin again, before their relatives had time to collect their corpses.

Marcos continued his womanizing ways, starting an affair with the wife of a US Navy officer, jeopardizing Filipino-American relations. There followed a liaison with the Filipino singer, Carmen Soriano. Imelda caught up with her in San Francisco in 1970. Arriving at her apartment with her financial adviser, Ernesto Villatuya, Imelda insisted that Carmen sign a declaration promising never to go to bed with Marcos again. When Carmen refused, Imelda took a swing at her. She ducked and Imelda floored Villatuya. Soon after, he was made President of the Philippine National Bank, a position he held until 1972.

With Marcos and the national exchequer in her pocket, Imelda roamed the world as the Philippines' roving ambassador. In Libya, she claimed that Colonel Qaddafi made a pass at her, but to friends she confided he was gay. There were gay rumours about Imelda, too. She travelled everywhere with Cristina Ford, wife of Henry Ford II, and it was said they were lovers. Others say that she went to bed with the permanently tanned actor George Hamilton. And why not? Everyone else did.

According to the Philippines' constitution, the President can hold office for only two four-year terms. In 1973, Marcos considered putting up Imelda as his successor, thereby holding on to the reigns of power for eight more years. But with Imelda constantly away on state-sponsored shopping sprees, he felt she might leave a power vacuum. Instead, he declared martial law.

Popular frustration soon turned to violence. At an open-air awards ceremony, one of the recipients lunged at Imelda with a cane-cutting blade. She instinctively protected her breasts and was slashed on both forearms. The would-be assassin was slaughtered on the spot by her bodyguards.

The assassination attempt had a profound effect on her. She called in voodoo advisers to protect her from hostile spells. Old clothes were hoarded and no personal items were thrown away, lest they fall into the hands of those plotting against her. She began wearing a scarf around her neck to ward off the danger of decapitation. And she surrounded herself with handmaidens, whom she called her 'blue ladies' because they were dressed identically in a traditional Filipino *termos* with a blue sash. They were hand-picked for their loyalty and owed their elevation from the grinding poverty that was now engulfing the country solely to Imelda.

Imelda travelled around the world in her private jet, which had a bathroom with gold fittings. She carried with her an entourage of freeloading socialites, supping on champagne and caviare. On one shopping trip that took in New York, Copenhagen and Rome, she spent more than £3 million. Admittedly, that did include a £2-million Michelangelo. And she bought some bath towels costing £8,000. After her plane took off from Rome, Italian air traffic control received a message from the pilot asking permission to return. Fearing some life-threatening technical problem, the air traffic controller asked what the problem was.

'We have no cheese,' said the pilot.

Wherever she stayed, there was a standing order that the hotel would furnish her suite with £500 worth of flowers. Whenever she returned to the Philippines, Manila airport was closed down, the red carpet was rolled out and the local school-children were turned out to cheer and wave.

At home, she was hardly more frugal. She had a plane-load of sand flown in from Australia when she decided that the natural Philippine sand around her summer house wasn't quite the right shade of white. The entire 5,000 sq ft basement of the Malacanang Palace turned into her private wardrobe. Along with her breathtaking shoe collection she had 1,500 handbags, 35 racks of fur coats, 500 brassieres – one bullet proofed – and 1,200 hand-sewn designer dresses, each of which had been worn only once.

When the Philippine ambassador in London failed to get her an invitation to the wedding of Prince Charles and Lady Di, she sacked him. In 1983, she tried to outdo the splendour of St Paul's with the wedding of her daughter, Imee. New façades were put on the houses around Manila Cathedral to make them look like seventh-century Spanish colonial homes. For the reception, she hired a luxury liner to house the 500 guests. The entire beanfeast ran out at £7 million. And this was in a country that was practically bankrupt.

But it was not these excesses that brought the Marcoses down, it was sexual jealousy. Since Marcos had introduced martial law, the Leader of the Opposition, Benigno Aquino, had fled into exile in the United States. Ronald Reagan was now in the White House and the Americans were beginning to get a little worried about the dictatorial methods of Ferdinand Marcos. To placate the Americans, Marcos called elections. The US government insisted that Aquino be allowed to return to the Philippines so that he could stand, and they brokered a deal with Marcos. However, they had counted without Imelda. Still smarting from her rejection 30 years earlier, she ordered that Aquino's feet should never again touch Philippine soil. When he flew into Manila airport with a plane-load of journalists, Imelda's henchmen shot him as he came down the steps of the plane.

Ferdinand was horrified. He knew his number was up. In desperation, he blamed the assassination on rogue elements in the army and fixed the presidential election. Strikes and public demonstrations followed. The media slipped its yoke and the Philippines teetered on the brink of anarchy.

Somehow the Marcoses clung on. In 1986, Ferdinand called another election, again to placate Washington. This time he faced Benigno Aquino's widow, Corazón. He claimed victory but it was plain that he had won only by ballot rigging. There was an international outcry. Hundreds of thousands of people took to the streets of Manila. They stood in the path of tanks and Marcos's troops in a demonstration of 'people power', while the Marcoses were airlifted to safety in Hawaii.

Once order had been restored, the new government under Cory Aquino began to untangle the web of corruption the Marcoses had left behind, and discovered that an estimated $10 billion was missing from the treasury.

Apart from the money the Marcoses had squandered on high living, the rest seemed to be in Switzerland. But after interminable court battles the Swiss were prepared to return only about $2 million.

The Aquino government had more luck in the USA. There, the courts were prepared to freeze the Marcoses' assets. The US authorities maintained that the Marcoses had broken US laws by transferring Philippine government money into private accounts on US soil. Ferdinand and Imelda failed to answer subpoenas to appear before a Grand Jury in New York, and in October 1988 they were indicted under the Racketeer-Influenced and Corrupt Organizations Act.

Ferdinand Marcos never stood trial. He had long suffered from lupus and his health had deteriorated since he had been ousted. He was excused the trip to New York for his arraignment. Imelda appeared alone. She was charged with stealing a mere $200 million from the Philippines and illegally investing it in the United States. She was also charged with fraudulently obtaining loans from the USA and obstructing justice. Pleading not guilty, she was released on $8.5 million bail.

In September 1989, Ferdinand Marcos died. Cory Aquino refused permission for his body to be returned to the Philippines for burial.

In March 1990, Imelda stood trial in New York. Her co-defendant was Saudi arms dealer, Adnan Khashoggi, an old pal of the Marcoses and reputedly the richest man in the world. He was charged with fraud and obstructing justice by helping Imelda hide some of her ill-gotten gains.

The prosecution accused Imelda of systematically looting her country. The charges related particularly to four skyscrapers that the Marcoses had bought in Manhattan between 1981 and 1983 as a nest egg should something go wrong in Manila. When the US authorities froze the Marcoses' assets in 1987, it was alleged that Khashoggi drew up bills of sale and backdated the purchase to 1985.

The prosecution called 95 witnesses. One of them was Oscar Carino, the manager of the Philippine National Bank's branch in New York. He claimed that when Imelda was in town, she used the National Bank like her own 'personal piggy bank'. He regularly delivered up to $100,000 in cash to her hotel room as loose change for her shopping sprees. When state investigators examined the books, they found unreimbursed withdrawals totalling over $22 million.

The defence called no witnesses. Instead, Imelda's attorney, the flamboyant Gerry Spense, who wore a Stetson and cowboy boots in court, delivered a *tour de force*. He focused the jury's attention on the 3,000 pairs of shoes. This was not as extravagant as it may seem, he pointed out. Shoe manufacturers regularly deliver dozens of free samples as courtesy. Most of them did not fit.

It was true, he said, that Imelda 'may have been a world-class shopper, but she was also a world-class decent human being who was guilty only of loving her husband'.

The jury acquitted both defendants of all charges.

With a personal fortune estimated at $7.5 billion – every penny obtained honestly, she says – Imelda went on to become queen of the chat shows. Her defence was her beauty.

'They call me corrupt, frivolous,' she said. 'I would not look like this if I were corrupt. Some ugliness would settle on my system.'

Interviewers are too polite to point out that her beauty is fading.

Slowly, the courts in Switzerland and the USA ordered the return of some of the money the Marcoses had embezzled. More went to the victims of torture and human rights abuses and to the families of the estimated 10,000 killed during Marcos's presidency. Imelda's jewellery and shoes were auctioned off, but she still had plenty of money left to buy more.

Imelda kept Ferdinand's body on ice in Honolulu until 1993, when she was allowed to return it to the Philippines for burial. She then stood in the presidential elections, but stood down after being accused of cheating. However, she was elected to the House of Representatives in 1995.

25 ❖ The Empress of South America

Eva Perón was not the first prostitute to be a First Lady in Latin America. Her distinguished predecessor was an Irish courtesan, who became Empress of South America as the consort of Francisco López, one of the most scandalous dictators even that benighted continent has ever seen.

Born in 1827, Francisco López was the son of the Perpetual Dictator of Paraguay, Carlos Antonio López. Francisco was a thoroughly repulsive figure, whom the US ambassador to Asunción described as follows: 'Short and stout, always inclined to corpulence. He dressed grotesquely, but his costumes were always expensive and elaborately finished. His eyes, when he was pleased, had a mild expression; but when he was enraged the pupils seemed to dilate till they did not appear to be that of a human being, but rather a wild beast goaded to madness. He had, however, a gross animal look that was repulsive when his face was in repose. His forehead was narrow and his head small, with the rear organs largely developed. His teeth were very much decayed, and so many of the front ones were gone as to render his articulation somewhat difficult and indistinct. He apparently took no pains to keep them clean, and those which remained were unwholesome in appearance, and nearly as dark as the cigar that he had almost constantly between them. His face was rather flat, and his nose and his hair indicated more of the negro than the Indian. His cheeks had a fullness that extended to the jowl, giving him a sort of bulldog expression.'

He was not a pretty sight then, and the girls were hardly queuing up for him. But that did not bother Francisco. He would seize any woman he fancied and jail her father if she resisted.

Francisco fell for the beautiful young Pancha Garmendia, who was known as the 'jewel of Asunción'. He could not jail her father since the latter had already been executed by Carlos López's predecessor, El Supremo, the First Perpetual Dictator of Paraguay. So Francisco jailed her brothers instead. But still she resisted, threatening suicide if he ever laid a finger on her. He kept her in chains until she died 20 years later.

Next his attention turned to Carmencita Cordal, but she was engaged to be married to her cousin Carlos Decoud. He was the son of one of the leading families of Paraguay. Francisco and Carlos fought and Francisco was given a humiliating thrashing. The night before their wedding, Carlos's mutilated body was hurled through the window of Carmencita's home. She spent the rest of her life dressed in black, praying at desert shrines and picking flowers by moonlight.

Such behaviour did not go down well with the population of Asunción. Anyone with a daughter and enough money to emigrate was soon applying for a passport. To rescue the situation, Carlos López sent Francisco to Europe to buy a navy – not that they needed one, since Paraguay is landlocked.

In Paris, Francisco started spending the money he had been given to buy ships on, as the American ambassador put it, 'his natural licentious propensities, and... the vices of that gay city'.

Francisco saw himself as the Napoleon of South America and was eager to meet the great man's nephew Napoleon III. He was presented at court, but when he kissed the fastidious Empress Eugénie's hand she found him so revolting that she turned away and vomited over an ormolu desk. The Emperor apologized for his wife, explaining that she was pregnant.

Naturally, much of the money Francisco was squandering was spent on courtesans. One of the most famous at the time was Eliza Lynch. Born in County Cork in 1835, her family moved to France in 1845 to escape the potato famine. At the age of 15, she married an officer in the French army who was old enough to be her father. He took her to Algiers, where she was raped by her husband's commanding officer. A career officer, her husband did nothing to defend her honour.

She was rescued by a dashing young Russian cavalry officer. He killed her assailant and took Eliza to Paris. They set up home together in the chic Boulevard Saint Germain, but the Crimean War had just started and he went off to fight.

Eliza could not have been more different from Francisco. An Argentinian journalist wrote of her: 'She was tall with a flexible and delicate figure with beautiful and seductive curves. Her skin was alabaster. Her eyes were of a blue that seemed borrowed from the very hues of heaven and had an expression of ineffable sweetness in whose depths the light of Cupid was enthroned. Her beautiful lips were indescribably expressive of the voluptuous, moistened by an ethereal dew that God must have provided to lull the fires within her, a mouth that was like a cup of delight at the banqueting table of ardent passion. Her hands were small with long fingers, the nails perfectly formed and delicately polished. She was, evidently, one of those women who make the care of their appearance a religion.'

Added to that, Eliza had a quick wit and a flair for languages. At the age of 19, she became a courtesan. Soon every man of substance was beating a path to her door.

One of Francisco's lieutenants had visited Chez Lynch. When he raved about her, Francisco decided to go and see her for himself. Eliza knew a mark when she saw one. She whisked Francisco into the bedroom. This was a new experience for Francisco. He had never before had a lover who did not put up a struggle. He told her of the riches of his country and of his plans.

Eliza had no idea where Paraguay was, but she had an eye to the main chance. When she expressed an interest, Francisco offered to make her the Empress of South America.

Eliza immediately gave notice to her landlord and they set off on a shopping trip around Europe. On their way, they dropped by the battlefields of the Crimea, perhaps to see how her Russian lover was getting on. In Rome, Eliza held a 'wickedly obscene' dinner party for the Pope. They also dropped by on the notorious Queen Isabella of Spain.

Laden with trunks full of jewellery and expensive clothing, Eliza set sail for Paraguay with Francisco. Unsure of the reception that awaited them in Asunción, Francisco and Eliza stopped off in Buenos Aires. In Paraguay, Carlos had already heard that his son was returning with *una ramera Irlandesa* – an Irish prostitute. Francisco's mother and two sisters were outraged, but Carlos was getting old and needed his son and heir back in the country.

Francisco and Eliza began the 1,000-mile trip up the Amazon. When they arrived in Asunción, she was pregnant. Francisco's mother and sisters

**Don Fransisco
S Lopez**

would have nothing to do with her, but the beauteous Eliza, dressed in the latest low-cut gowns from Paris, caused a sensation.

Eliza did not have the field to herself. Francisco maintained his former lover and their two children in his town house. He also took it as his right, like any other Latin male, to take as many other lovers as he could handle. Since she could not stop him, Eliza took charge. She chose his new lovers carefully for him. Although she would not marry him herself, feeling it would weaken her position, she would make damn sure that he would marry no one else.

Francisco continued with his brutal seduction technique. When the daughter of Pedro Burgos, a magistrate from the small provincial city of Luque, refused him, Francisco threatened to confiscate her father's property. This did not work because Burgos was a friend of Francisco's father, who was still in power. So Eliza stepped in. Once she had ascertained that there was no danger of Burgos's daughter marrying Francisco, she persuaded Burgos to surrender her, on the promise that he would be amply rewarded when Francisco took over.

Unfortunately, he never got to enjoy the patronage. Francisco had Burgos summarily executed when he thought he was plotting against him.

By manipulating his love life, Eliza wielded power over Francisco. Since he had promised to make her Empress of South America, she thought

she had better have a capital worthy of the title. Asunción was to be trans-
formed into an imperial city.

Francisco began an extensive building programme. The centrepiece
was a replica of Napoleon's tomb at *Les Invalides* in Paris. This was to be his
own mausoleum.

Eliza then gave birth to a healthy son. Francisco was so delighted that
he organized a 100-gun salute. This caused 11 buildings in downtown
Asunción to collapse, five of which were newly built under Francisco's
urban development plan. One of the guns, an English field piece, had not
been cleaned properly. It backfired, killing half the battery and putting the
other half in hospital.

To secure her son's position in his father's affections, Eliza wanted him
baptised in Asunción's *Catedral de la Encarnacion*. Francisco's mother and
sisters objected to this and Carlos banned it. In addition, Carlos's brother,
who was the Bishop of Paraguay, threatened to excommunicate any priest
who performed the ceremony. But Eliza was not to be put off. She found a
corrupt priest named Father Palacios and promised to make him Bishop of
Paraguay when Francisco came to power.

Francisco himself was worried about getting on the wrong side of
Carlos, so Eliza threatened to take his son back to Europe and have him
baptised a Protestant – worse, an Anglican. When Francisco said that he
would simply stop her leaving the country, Eliza replied that if she told his
father of her plans he would certainly give her safe passage to the border
and money, too, if she promised not to return. The baptism went ahead
although no one, apart from the priest and the child's parents, turned up.

There was a constant battle between the López family and Eliza, but
she usually got the upper hand. When Francisco's new opera house was
opened, the Lópezes were ushered into the 'Royal Box', which they then
discovered was a small box to the left of the stage. Eliza and Francisco
occupied the large box in the centre of the auditorium.

Eliza also held regular salons. The ladies of Asunción snubbed them,
but they could not stop their husbands from going – lured there by Eliza's
magnificent figure and low-cut gowns.

Francisco was still determined that the ladies of Asunción, particularly
his mother and sisters, accept *La Ramera Irlandesa*. He had started a disastrous agricultural project upstream in the Rio de la Plata region of
Paraguay, and organized an official visit there for the diplomatic corps and
Paraguayans of rank. The men would travel there by horse; the women by
boat. Madame Lynch was to be the official hostess on board.

Resentfully, the womenfolk embarked, pointedly ignoring Eliza. Soon after they cast off, a huge buffet was laid out. As hostess, Eliza tried to officiate, but the other women would not let her near the table. So she got the captain to moor the boat in the middle of the stream and ordered him to throw all the food and wine overboard. The women of Asunción were then stranded there in the boiling heat without food or drink for the next 10 hours, until Eliza gave orders for the boat to return to the quay.

When Carlos López died, Francisco called a National Convention and had himself appointed President for the next 10 years. He then ordered that 'Madame Eliza Lynch should enjoy the same privileges as those usually accorded the wife of a head of state'. Soon, half the population of Asunción were in jail or in exile for the simple crime of opposing Francisco. Good to her word, Eliza made Father Palacios Bishop of Paraguay – not only had he baptised their son he had also passed on vital information gleaned in the confessional about those plotting against Francisco.

The British ambassador began calling Eliza 'the Paraguayan Pompadour'. She lived openly with Francisco, although he maintained a number of other houses where he entertained prostitutes. At last, the ladies of Asunción began to call on her and she held magnificent balls where she outshone them all.

Francisco began to let ambition get the better of him. If he was to become Emperor of South America, he should marry into royalty. The beautiful young Princess Isabella of Brazil seemed like a suitable bride, but Eliza was not going to let him get away with this. She demanded equal status and forced Francisco to legitimize their children. When she heard this, Princess Isabella decided to marry one of the French royal family instead.

To celebrate the first anniversary of Francisco López coming to power, Eliza organized a great circus with bullfighting, dancing and entertainments in a specially constructed hippodrome on the waterfront. Wine and *caña*, the local firewater, flowed freely and, as one observer put it, the population of Asunción 'actively engaged in raising the birth rate'.

The ambition to be Emperor of South America still haunted Francisco. Brazil and Argentina were squabbling over Uruguay at the time. Seizing his moment, Francisco intervened, only to have all three countries declare war on him simultaneously. As part of his imperial plan, he ordered a disastrous offensive.

Despite Paraguay's decisive defeat, Eliza organized a Victory Ball, where the wealthy ladies of Asunción were expected to hand over their baubles to aid the war effort. She caused more scandal by personally throwing open the doors to the city's prostitutes, saying 'all classes mingle as one on so festive an occasion'.

When Francisco went to the front to organize the retreat, he left Eliza as Regent. Her first act was to impound what remained of the ladies' jewellery, and the gentlemen of Asunción were forced to part with their gold to prove their loyalty or face imprisonment as traitors.

The war went so disastrously that every able-bodied man was called up. Women had to plough the fields and the only men left in Asunción were the police. Not only was the Paraguayan army hopelessly outnumbered, Francisco turned every rout into a greater disaster by summarily shooting his own men for cowardice. A truce was offered, but a precondition was that Francisco had to go into exile in Europe. He refused, and imprisoned, tortured and killed any Paraguayan who spoke in favour of it.

If the odds were not stacked against him enough already, Francisco turned on Paraguay's foreign residents. Britain, America, France and Italy all sent gunboats.

The only thing Francisco had on his side was Eliza. She used her not inconsiderable charms to woo foreign envoys. She also reassured Francisco that the military reverses were not his fault. They were the fault of people conspiring against him and she fed his paranoia so that she could seize the wealth of those she accused.

In the face of the advancing armies of the Triple Alliance, Francisco was forced to evacuate Asunción. He had already tortured and killed his two brothers who, he said, had plotted against him. His mother and sisters were imprisoned in a bullock cart. The 'jewel of Asunción', Pancha Garmendia, still in chains, was dragged along behind. Occasionally, his sisters were let out so that they could grovel at his feet, make new confessions and submit themselves to a flogging. Francisco also ordered the flogging of his mother, even though she was over 70.

Eliza carried her booty with her. But she had to abandon one of her prized possessions, her grand piano, at what is now Piano, Paraguay.

Francisco withdrew into the jungle, where he sought to make treaties with the Indians, but the Brazilian army pursued him relentlessly. Shortly before the last attack, he sentenced his mother and sisters to death, although he did not have time to see the sentence carried out.

While his men made a human shield, Francisco tried to escape on horseback. The horse got stuck in the mud of a river bed. The Brazilians had been ordered to capture Francisco alive if possible, but he pulled a gun so they hacked him to death. Eliza and her sons were forced to dig Francisco's grave with their bare hands.

In Asunción there was a huge celebration. Eliza, her sons and the López women were taken there on a Brazilian gunboat. The Provisional

Government demanded that Eliza be handed over for trial. Not only had she conspired to kill tens of thousands of Paraguayans in an unwinnable war, she had also made off with most of the country's wealth. But the Brazilians took pity on her, took her to Buenos Aires and put her on a ship to Europe.

In London, there were 4,000 ounces of gold on deposit in the Bank of England in Eliza's name. It had been smuggled out by the American and Italian ambassadors, both of whom fancied her. The Brazilians also let her take most of her booty with her.

She put her children in school in England, then began to recover the loot she had left behind through the English courts. When the Paraguayan government seized more of her assets, she went back to take up the matter in the courts there. But her presence in the country caused such unrest that the government asked her to leave.

Eliza returned to Paris, where she died in 1886. She was buried in the famous cemetery of Père Lachaise. In 1961, her remains were disinterred and taken back to Paraguay, where she now lies under a monument proclaiming her to be the Empress of South America.

26 ❖ The Flower Child First Lady

Pierre Trudeau was the first French-speaking Prime Minister of Canada. He served from 1969 to 1979, and again from 1980 to 1984. Although a Liberal and progressive, he defeated the French-speaking separatists who wanted Quebec to secede.

No scandal there then. That's true, but when Trudeau came to power he was a handsome and eligible bachelor. On holiday in Tahiti, he met Margaret Sinclair, the daughter of a wealthy politician. She was 29 years his junior and, in the spirit of the time, a flower child. They married in 1971.

Everything was fine to start with, but it gradually became clear that Margaret Trudeau was not going to settle into the life of a politician's wife. She remained, at heart, a flower child, and wanted a career of her own.

She became a photojournalist and, in 1977, while Pierre was baby sitting in Ottawa, she travelled the 240 miles to Toronto to photograph the Rolling Stones who were on tour. As much photographed as

Margaret Sinclair with Pierre Trudeau. Their marriage caused scandal because she was 29 years his junior and a "flower child" of the sixties

photographing, Margaret Trudeau sported a tight-fitting blue boiler suit. She danced to the Stones' music and sat at Mick Jagger's feet as he sang.

It was also noted by the press that she had turned up to the concert in Jagger's limousine. She spent the night in their hotel in a room next to Keith Richards, who had recently been charged with drug offences in Canada. She was also seen hanging around the hotel corridors in a white bathrobe, and seemed happy to pose for photographs with the band.

The Rolling Stones' drummer, Charlie Watts, summed up the feelings of most Canadians when he was heard to comment: 'I wouldn't want my wife associating with us.'

The next night she attended another Stones' concert, arriving with Jagger in his limousine once more. Afterwards, she went to a party with Jagger and Richards that lasted until 7 a.m.

But it did not end there. Margaret Trudeau followed the Stones to New York like some groupie. By that time, she seemed to have developed a closer relationship with guitarist, Ron Wood. On the foreign exchange markets, the Canadian dollar dropped one and a half cents.

Even the Stones were embarrassed by the affair. They were still trying to live down their disastrous gig at Altamont, where a young black man named Meredith Hunter was stabbed to death within feet of the stage by the Hell's Angels the Stones had hired as security.

'The last thing in the world the Stones want is any scandal, any crazies,' said their press spokesman, Paul Wassermann. 'Their whole energy is needed for new albums. Jagger and the others are in New York for specific things. Mrs Trudeau and the group have completely different interests in New York.'

Jagger himself simply shrugged off the growing scandal.

'We just had a passing acquaintance for two nights,' he told the media. 'She just wanted to be introduced. Princess Margaret wanted to be introduced in London. Lee Radziwill followed us. These ladies are charming to have around. There is no question of anything more.'

But it did not look like such a small thing the other side of the 50th parallel.

'Someone should control the lady,' said one Toronto newspaper, pointing the finger at the Premier. 'It is unacceptable for the wife of the Prime Minister to be cavorting with a group like the Rolling Stones. Most of them have, at one time or another, been involved with drugs.'

Embarrassed by the situation, Margaret Trudeau was defiant. Instead of meekly returning home, she went to stay with Princess Yashmin Khan, the daughter of Aly Khan and the movie star Rita Hayworth.

'I don't want to be a rose in my husband's lapel,' she said. 'I've had enough. After six years, I abdicate.'

What made the scandal all the more embarrassing was that Trudeau was awaiting an official visit from the British Prime Minister, James Callaghan, and the Foreign Secretary, David Owen, both of whom were bringing their wives. Margaret was persuaded to return home. She arrived the day before the official visit, wearing dark glasses. But the following day, she refused to entertain Mrs Callaghan and Mrs Owen, while their husbands held high-level talks.

This provoked a blazing row and things were thrown. Two days later, Margaret appeared with a black eye.

'Pierre said I deserved a good spanking,' she explained. 'He belted me. But that night we made love and it was wonderful. I don't think it had ever been so good before.'

Or again. They separated. After a half-hour meeting at an airport, it was decided that Pierre should have custody of their three children. Margaret moved to New York where she set up as a freelance photographer, using her maiden name, Margaret Sinclair.

The Prime Minister's office issued a brief statement: 'Pierre accepts Margaret's decision with regret and both pray that their separation will lead to a better relationship between themselves.'

Margaret's name was soon linked with those of King Hussein, Senator Edward Kennedy and Ryan O'Neal. She had a brief career as a movie actress, then published her autobiography, *Beyond Reason*, just in time to embarrass her husband at a general election.

It repeated all her greatest *faux pas*, like the time she sang a dreadful song of her own composition to the President of Venezuela's wife at the state banquet in Caracas. During an earlier general election, she had turned up at her husband's hotel in the middle of the night, grubby and barefoot, and had demanded to be taken to the Prime Minister's suite.

She had shocked the guests at a formal dinner in Washington by wearing a micro-miniskirt. Unfortunately, she had had a ladder in her tights. At a New York luncheon, she had inflicted herself so gauchely on Princess Margaret that the normally sociable royal had frozen her out.

She proudly announced that she had shown her tits to Prince Charles. She had tried to get him to come over to Paris when she was on a photo assignment there, but when he had called her hotel he had asked for Margaret Trudeau. The feisty Mrs Trudeau had checked in as Ms Sinclair.

But it was her flirtation with drugs that scandalized her husband's Liberal Party more than anything.

'Of course, I smoked marijuana in Morocco,' the flower child announced proudly. And, although she said that she steered clear of hard drugs, she admitted: 'I still smoke marijuana from time to time.'

Canada may be a laid-back place, but it's not that laid-back.

27 ❖ Victorian Values

The governments of Margaret Thatcher were dogged by scandal. Although she prided herself on her adherence to 'Victorian values', she surrounded herself by those who did not. Or if they did, it was to those values that meant one out of every four women in Victorian London was a prostitute.

The first casualty was Sir Nicholas Fairbairn, whom Mrs Thatcher appointed as Solicitor General for Scotland. In October 1981, the 47-year-old MP's 34-year-old ex-girlfriend tried to commit suicide in spectacular fashion. The press said that the spurned lover had been found hanging from a lamp-post outside Fairbairn's London home. She denied this, saying: 'I wouldn't even have the energy to climb up a lamp-post.'

However, she admitted the affair. It had begun when she was a secretary in the House of Commons and he was still married to his first wife, Elizabeth McKay. He had wooed her with red roses, passionate love letters and proposals of marriage. Unfortunately, on the last item, he did not come through.

When the scandal broke over Christmas, Mrs Thatcher had no comment to make on whether Sir Nicholas's values were Victorian or not. It was, she said, 'a private matter' between 'two single people'.

The press pursued Fairbairn to Fordell Castle, his Scottish home. They found the drawbridge up and camped outside. Eventually, the laird appeared in a blue and white dressing gown. They had got the story the wrong way round, he told them. It was the lady who was the ardent suitor, not he. It was she who had suggested marriage.

Fairbairn had only just survived this scandal, when he walked right into another one. In January 1982, he decided not to pursue the prosecution of three Glasgow youths in a controversial rape case. Unfortunately, he announced his decision in the *Glasgow Daily Record* the day before he told the House of Commons. MPs will not stand for this discourtesy. The next day, Fairbairn was summoned to 10 Downing Street. Mrs Thatcher already had his letter of resignation drawn up. She handed him a pen and said: 'Sign here.'

He showed no bitterness, later describing Thatcher as 'probably the warmest and kindest human being that those who have met her have ever encountered'. Fairbairn was probably happier on the back benches where he could spend more time 'making love, ends meet and people laugh' – the hobbies he had once listed in *Who's Who*.

One of his greatest laughs came from his parliamentary put-down of Edwina Curry, who was embroiled in the salmonella-in-eggs controversy at the time. He rose to remind the Honourable Lady that she had once been an egg herself and Members on both sides of the House regretted that it had been fertilized.

In October 1982, Fairbairn was back in the headlines when he was cited in a divorce case. Unrepentant, he furiously attacked the press's hypocritical moral crusades. He told *The Times*: 'Scandal may be good copy, but it adds nothing to the integrity of our institutions. I do not think they were any worse, indeed I think they were probably much better, when those who ruled us were known and seen to have healthy sexual liaisons with many mistresses and lovers.'

Mrs Thatcher's reaction was not recorded.

IN 1983, Mrs Thatcher lost another of her favourites to sexual scandal. Cecil Parkinson was the golden boy of Tory politics in the early 1980s and Mrs Thatcher had been grooming him as her successor.

'In some ways, he seems too good to be true,' said *The Times* in October 1981. 'Tall, handsome, charming and likeable... the perfect constituency MP, intelligent without being intellectual, self-made, brilliantly supported by a politically committed wife – is there no flaw?'

There was – a fatal one.

Born in 1931, the son of a railwayman, Parkinson went to Royal Lancaster Grammar School and won a scholarship to Emmanuel College, Cambridge. In 1955, he met Ann Jarvis, daughter of a wealthy building contractor. When they married in 1956, her father set up Parkinson with his own building firm in Stockport. From these humble beginnings, he became a millionaire with homes in Hertfordshire, Pimlico, Cornwall and the Bahamas.

He entered Parliament in 1970 and was quickly seen as the model Thatcherite man. In her first administration in 1979, Mrs Thatcher made him Minister of State for Trade. In 1981, he became Chairman of the Conservative Party and, in 1982, Chancellor of the Duchy of Lancaster. This brought him into the cabinet, and during the Falklands War, he was one of the inner cabinet that engineered the Argentine defeat.

Everything was right on track until 9 June 1983, when as Party Chairman, he delivered her a landslide victory. A few hours before they were seen together waving to gleeful supporters from the upstairs window of Conservative Central Office, Thatcher had offered him any job in her cabinet that he wanted. She knew he had always hankered after the Foreign Office, but instead of asking to be appointed Foreign Secretary, he admitted to a 'serious personal problem'.

In 1971, Parkinson had begun an affair with Sarah Keays, a House of Commons secretary. The affair had continued until July 1979, when she went to Brussels to work for Roy Jenkins, who was then a commissioner for the European Community. When she returned to London in October, the affair had resumed. They were nearly discovered. One night his car was stolen from outside her house in a Southwark muse. It was recovered, but since his ministerial red boxes had been in the car, he had had to own up to the Home Secretary, Willie Whitelaw. Whitelaw was supportive.

'There but for the grace of God go many of us,' he said.

A month before the 1983 election, Keays announced that she was pregnant. Parkinson told Thatcher that he could hardly expect to be in her cabinet under these circumstances.

'Mrs Thatcher was immensely sympathetic, not at all censorious,' Parkinson wrote later. Rather than Foreign Secretary, she offered him the more junior post of Secretary of State for Trade and Industry until the dust had settled. As to the baby, Mrs Thatcher 'was sure that as sensible people we could sort it out'.

While Parkinson and his wife went off for a well-earned rest in their holiday home in the Bahamas, journalists from the *Daily Mirror* began pursuing the heavily pregnant Sarah Keays, demanding to know whether Parkinson was the father.

While on holiday, Parkinson decided to stay with Ann, his wife of 27 years and mother of his three grown-up daughters. This put paid to his political career. As we know, politicians who divorce their wives and marry their paramours can keep their jobs – even if they are Foreign Secretary, as Robin Cook proved in Tony Blair's administration. Those who stay after having erred are often forced out.

When he returned to England, Parkinson broke the news to Keays. There was a row and they agreed that all future communication should be via their solicitors.

It was then that Sarah Keays' father took a hand. He wrote to Mrs Thatcher, warning her of an imminent public scandal. In preparation, Parkinson stepped down as Party Chairman on 14 September. The then unknown John Selwyn Gummer took over.

On 5 October 1983, the satirical magazine, *Private Eye*, ran a gossip piece saying: 'Why was Cecil Parkinson asked to step down as Tory Party Chairman? I can assure readers that it had nothing to do with his marital difficulties which have recently raised eyebrows in Tory circles. Now comes the news that Parkinson's fun-loving secretary Ms Sarah Keays is expecting a baby in three months' time.'

Although libel writs were issued and the magazine paid out damages, the damage had been done.

Parkinson issued his own statement that day at 11.45 p.m. It read: 'To bring to an end rumour concerning Miss Sarah Keays, and her family, I wish, with her consent, to make the following statement. I have had a relationship with Miss Keays over a number of years. She is expecting a child, due to be born in January, of whom I am the father. I am of course making financial provision for both mother and child. During our relationship I told Miss Keays of my wish to marry her. Despite my having given Miss Keays that assurance, my wife, who has been a source of great strength, and I have decided to stay together and to keep our family together. I regret deeply the distress I have caused to Miss Keays, to her family and to my family.'

Mrs Thatcher made no comment, again saying it was a 'private matter'. The press reaction was generally favourable. Parkinson had done the right thing, he had stayed with his wife and he had provided for his ex-lover and their child.

'Men who tell the truth and face their responsibilities are, in my view, far more worthy of public office than men who take the easy way out,' wrote Mary Kenny in *The Times*. 'I trust Cecil Parkinson more for having done the brave thing.'

The editorial in *The Times* agreed with Mrs Thatcher that it was a 'private matter'. *The Daily Telegraph* even suggested that the problem would be best solved with an abortion.

The public was sympathetic, too. Parkinson's office received 16,000 letters of support and 46 against.

In confessional mode, Parkinson went on the BBC's flagship current affairs programme, *Panorama*. For the moment, he would stay on in office. But 'if ever I ceased to be an asset and become a liability, and the Prime Minister felt so, then of course I would leave immediately,' he said.

But hell hath no fury like a woman scorned. And Sarah Keays was not just scorned, her ambitions had been thwarted. She, too, had set her heart on a political career. She had stood unsuccessfully as a councillor in Southwark and had been runner-up in the selection for the Conservative candidate in the nearby constituency of Bermondsey.

When a by-election had been called in Bermondsey, the candidate whom the constituency party had selected could not run. They had asked Conservative Central Office whether they should then take the runner-up – Keays – or start the selection process all over again.

The decision had fallen to Parkinson, who could hardly declare an interest. If he had opted for the former, he would have been open to charges of nepotism; if he had chosen the latter, he risked alienating his lover. As it was, he had decided that Bermondsey should reselect. They did, and chose a young man called Robert Hughes.

In fact, Parkinson had done Keays a favour and saved her from a very unsavoury campaign. Bermondsey was a rock-solid Labour seat and the

Labour Party had selected as a replacement for the sitting Member, Bob Mellish, who had died, a young Antipodean firebrand named Peter Tatchell. During the hustings, Tatchell was outed as a homosexual, which did not sit well with the working-class voters of Bermondsey. The Liberal candidate, Simon Hughes, had romped home and the Conservatives had never stood a chance.

After Parkinson's statement, Keays bided her time. She waited until he went to the Conservative Party conference at Blackpool the following week. He delivered a low-key speech, but he garnered enough applause to believe that the party would, if not condone what he had done, at least forgive him.

It was then that Keays blew him out of the water. She issued the following statement:

'I agreed for the sake of my family that we would not discuss with the press the statement made by Mr Parkinson last week. I hoped that it would not become necessary for me to say anything. However, I now feel that I have a duty to do so.

'On Friday, October 7, *The Times* said that "Mr Parkinson had made a sad and silly blunder". Like the government, the editor believes that this should have remained a "private matter".

'For *The Daily Telegraph* (Monday, October 10) "the moral logic is that a quiet abortion is greatly to be preferred to a scandal". I was not aware that political expediency was sufficient grounds for an abortion under the 1967 Act, quite apart from the fact that I could not have contemplated it.

'On Monday night, in spite of the understanding expressed in his statement, Mr Parkinson saw fit to answer questions about the matter in a much publicized *Panorama* programme. It appeared from that programme that the Prime Minister had been kept fully informed and that the statement issued by Mr Parkinson contained the full facts.

'The full facts have *not* been made public. Press judgements and public opinion have been influenced by inadequate information, speculation, and the Government's desire to restore Mr Parkinson's position – as someone else put it, to "rehabilitate" him.

'1. It had been implied that I tried to trap Mr Parkinson into marriage;

'2. that I sought to destroy his reputation; and

'3. that the matter should have remained private.

'The last presumes that I should hide from public view and declare on the baby's birth certificate "father unknown", so casting further doubt on my reputation and denying the child his fundamental right to know the identity of his father.

'According to the view expressed in *The Telegraph*, I should have sacrificed my baby's life for Mr Parkinson's career and the Government's reputation.

'I wish therefore to make known the following chronology of events:

'1. My baby was conceived in a long standing, loving relationship which I had allowed to continue because I believed in our eventual marriage. It has been suggested that Mr Parkinson only asked me to marry him after I became pregnant, when in fact he first did so in 1979.

'2. In May, when I knew I had to accept the fact that he was not going to marry me, I could not deny my baby his right to know the true identity of his father.

'3. I did, however, implore Mr Parkinson, during May and early June, to inform the Prime Minister because his name and mine were sufficiently linked in political circles for speculation to be inevitable and it was essential that the Prime Minister was made aware of the situation before forming her new Government. He would not agree to this.

'4. On polling day, Mr Parkinson sought a reconciliation and asked me to marry him. I gladly accepted. He said that he was about to see the Prime Minister to inform her of our relationship and to tell her that he would be getting a divorce in order to marry me. That evening he told me he had so informed her.

'He also told other members of my family his intention. He asked me to give him time to arrange matters and to leave my job at the House of Commons, which I did at the end of June. I and my family assured him of our full co-operation and that we would give him such time as he needed.

'5. On August 5, Mr Parkinson went on holiday abroad with his wife and family, having reassured me of his intention to marry me.

'6. On August 23, I was visited at my London home by reporters from the *Daily Mirror* who demanded to know if it was true that I was pregnant by Mr Parkinson. At that very same moment others from the same newspaper called on my father and sister.

'Later that night, as I was driving a girlfriend to her home, I was pursued by two cars which I believed to be driven by reporters from the *Daily Mirror*, who tried to force me to stop and one of their cars collided with mine. I had to take refuge in Rochester Row Police Station.

'7. On August 24, I informed Mr Parkinson, who was still abroad, of the incident with the *Daily Mirror*. I assured him that neither I nor any member of my family had told them anything, but I was concerned that the press would shortly confront him.

'He advised me to leave London, which I did, and he said he would speak to me again on his return to England the following week. He gave me no indication that matters between us had in any way changed.

'8. On September 1, Mr Parkinson asked me to meet him secretly in an office in London, where he informed me that he was not going to marry me after all. Later that day I telephoned him to say that I thought it essential that he should inform the Prime Minister.

'9. I subsequently instructed solicitors with a view to Mr Parkinson and myself issuing a joint statement. In the ensuing weeks it became clear that other newspapers were pursuing the story and that it was being talked about in political circles.

'10. On Wednesday, October 5, when I was informed of what had been published in *Private Eye*, I telephoned Mr Parkinson and told him that if he did not issue the statement which solicitors had been discussing for some weeks, that I would be obliged to defend myself.

'Press comment, government pronouncements, and continued speculation about this matter have put me in an impossible position. I feel that I have both a public duty and a duty to my family to put the record straight.'

THAT, of course, was only Sarah Keays' side of the story, but it was damning. The timing was perfect, too. Publication of the statement would coincide with Mrs Thatcher's victory speech at the party conference, when Parkinson was sure to be on the rostrum by her side. *The Times* sent a copy of the statement to the Imperial Hotel, Blackpool, where the Parkinsons and the Thatchers were staying. After reading it, Parkinson walked the few yards to Thatcher's suite. They talked for about 15 minutes, then, at 2 a.m., he resigned. He was replaced by Norman Tebbit, his one-time deputy at Hemel Hempstead Conservative Association.

The following day, Parkinson was noticeably not at Thatcher's side when she gave her victory speech. He and his wife had already left for Hertfordshire. Thatcher made some last-minute amendments to her speech. Although she praised 'the man who so brilliantly organized our campaign', she did not name him.

On New Year's Eve 1983, Sarah Keays gave birth to an 8 lb 3 oz girl she named Flora. Parkinson did not visit the mother or the child, but issued a statement wishing his daughter 'peace, privacy and a happy life'. Although Parkinson was criticized for denying his daughter any contact, Sarah Keays revealed on the radio that the child was handicapped and said that the publicity attendant on any visit from her father would be cruel and confusing for her.

But that did not mean that she was not going to have her pound of flesh. By 1985, things had cooled sufficiently for Mrs Thatcher to consider having Parkinson back in her government. But on the eve of the 1985 Conservative Party conference, Keays serialized her autobiography in the *Daily Mirror*, banishing him to the political wilderness once more.

In the 1987 election, Parkinson was returned with an increased majority and Thatcher felt that she had an electoral mandate to return him to the ranks of her ministers. She gave him the junior cabinet post of Energy Secretary. Two years later, he was made Transport Secretary. But he had lost his sparkle. The scandal had knocked the wind out of his sails. No one mentioned him as a potential leader again. He quit the cabinet when Margaret Thatcher stepped down in 1990. He did not stand again in the 1992 election and was elevated to the Lords.

In his autobiography, *Right at the Centre*, he devotes just seven pages to 'The Keays Affair'. One only wishes that Sarah Keays had done the same.

THEN followed a couple of gay scandals for the Conservative government. Michael Heseltine's Parliamentary Private Secretary, Keith Hampson MP, was arrested by a plain-clothes police officer in a gay club in Soho and charged with indecent assault.

Although Hampson resigned his position as Heseltine's PPS, he insisted that he had done nothing wrong. He had accidentally brushed the policeman's thigh, he said. And he had only been in the club because he had been drunk. He said he had downed five pints of beer before completing a speech for Heseltine then, with time to spare before meeting his wife, he had chanced upon the Gay Theatre in Berwick Street, which promised a non-stop male strip show. Naturally he went in.

This story was somewhat undermined by the club's manager, Russell McCleod, who said mischievously that Hampson was a regular client, along with a number of other MPs.

Hampson's wife claimed that her husband was a red-blooded heterosexual and, despite calls for his resignation, he decided to tough it out. At the trial, the policeman said that Hampson had grabbed his buttocks with one hand and his groin with the other.

In his defence, Hampson wheeled out former Speaker of the House of Commons, Lord Tonypandy, as a character witness. The judge, if no one else, was impressed. He told the jury that to say that Hampson was a homosexual was 'absurd and unthinkable'. His story about finding himself in a gay club was plausible since 'the history of mankind is littered with the debris of men who have acted more stupidly than anyone else would have thought possible at the time'.

Nevertheless, the jury came back after five hours and said that they could not agree on a verdict. The Attorney General, Michael Havers, then stepped in. Due to the widespread publicity the case had received, it would not be possible to stage a retrial. So a verdict of not guilty would be recorded. Hampson stayed on as an MP and co-ordinated Michael Heseltine's bid for the leadership in 1990.

CONSERVATIVE MP Harvey Proctor's sexuality first became apparent in 1981 when he locked his long-standing boyfriend, Terry Woods, out of his Fulham flat. Woods shot his mouth off to journalists. *Private Eye* ran the story and soon the newspapers began a hue and cry.

Proctor claimed that the allegations against him was 'a campaign of political character assassination'. He had certainly made himself a target. He voiced right-wing views about immigration, and was generally viewed as 'one of the Thatcher praetorian guard'.

The trail went cold until 1986, when *The People* ran a story about a young male prostitute who claimed that Proctor had employed him for spanking sessions. The paper alleged that Proctor paid rent boys £35 a time to spank them while he watched by-election results on the television.

Although Proctor had previously sued *The People* and won – when the paper had falsely claimed that Mrs Thatcher was refusing to call Proctor 'my Honourable Friend' – this time he did not sue. The paper then ran a six-week campaign against Proctor, during which it was claimed that he had used an underage boy for sex who had tape recorded their spanking sessions. The rent boy concerned was 18, but it is clear from the tape that he told Proctor he was over 21. The newspaper handed over its evidence to the police.

Even with an election looming on the horizon, Proctor managed to secure the backing of his constituency party.

Then the *Daily Mirror* broke the story that on a trip to Morocco, a naked Arab youth had been found under Proctor's bed in his hotel room. Proctor protested that the youth concerned was 25 and he was not naked – at least not at the time he was found. That story had hardly died down when Terry

Woods found himself locked out of Proctor's flat again, this time clad only in his underpants.

The police, led by Chief Superintendent Marvin, then began a series of raids on his flat. These were unfailingly attended by a gaggle of journalists. On 11 May, the day the Prime Minister announced the date of the1987 general election, Proctor was charged with four counts of gross indecency.

With the election campaign now underway, Proctor had no alternative but to resign. His solicitor, Sir David Napley, pointed out that although Proctor had believed that all the rent boys he employed were over 21, some had not been. In homosexual cases, the reasonable belief that someone was not underage was not enough. Proctor pleaded guilty and was fined £1,450 with £250 costs.

Even then the scandal did not die down. When Chief Superintendent Marvin retired from the Serious Crime Squad, he sold his story to *The Sun*, which happily printed more sordid details of Proctor's private life.

However, his colleagues rallied around. Michael Heseltine, Tristan Garel Jones, Tim Yeo and Neil Hamilton – both of whom came to grief in the Major government – helped him set up a high-class menswear shop in Richmond called 'Proctor's Shirts and Ties' When it featured in a *Spectator* cartoon with a sign saying 'Shirtlifters will not prosecuted', Proctor bought the original and proudly displayed it in the store.

NOT all scandals during the Thatcher years centred around sex. One concerned the conduct of the Falklands War and the fate of the Argentine cruiser, *General Belgrano*, which had been sunk by the British nuclear submarine, *Conqueror*, on 2 May 1982 with the loss of some 370 lives.

In December 1982, veteran backbench MP, Tam Dalyell, published a book called *One Man's Falklands*. In it, he alleged that the government's decision to sink the *Belgrano* also sank any peaceful resolution of the conflict. The day before the sinking, Dalyell maintained, the leader of the Argentine junta, General Galtieri, had agreed to withdraw from the Falklands under a peace plan brokered by Peru. The Thatcher government knew this and went ahead anyway. What's more, the *Belgrano* was outside the 30-mile exclusion zone the British had declared around the islands, and it was heading back towards its home port. Even so, the Ministry of Defence claimed that the cruiser 'posed a major threat to our ships'.

When the President of Peru confirmed that the Argentine junta had indeed been on the point of accepting the peace plan when they had received news of the sinking, 150 Labour MPs asked for a full inquiry. For the government, Cranley Onslow, Minister of State at the Foreign and Commonwealth Office, insisted that Peruvian proposals had only reached London, via Washington, three hours after the *Belgrano* went down.

Interest was revived when Dalyell revealed that he had some leaked documents showing that a secret internal inquiry, ordered by the Secretary of State for Defence, Michael Heseltine, had confirmed his accusations.

An assistant secretary at the Ministry of Defence, Clive Ponting, was charged with offences under the Official Secrets Act. In court, he freely admitted handing classified material to Dalyell, but he argued that Dalyell was 'a duly elected MP and a man of considerable integrity who had been systematically mislead', and it was 'in the wider interests of Parliament to be told how it had been misled and how the government was now proposing to mislead it'. Ponting was acquitted.

In 1985, a Commons Select Committee issued a majority report, which said that the sinking of the *Belgrano* was justified. Four Labour MPs issued a minority report, which said that the government had tried to cover up 'a hasty and unjustifiable decision to risk many lives and possible disaster in order to ensure the life of an administration which itself was palpably negligent'.

It is now generally conceded that Dalyell was right. But the war was long over and victory had returned Margaret Thatcher as one of the most popular prime ministers ever.

After the Falklands War, the Thatcher government adopted a decidedly gung-ho approach. In 1984, the Deputy Chief Constable of Greater Manchester, John Stalker, was asked to investigate whether the Royal Ulster Constabulary had adopted a 'shoot-to-kill' policy to combat terrorism in Northern Ireland.

In September 1985, he submitted an interim report, saying that such a policy was in operation and that seven senior RUC officers should be prosecuted for conspiracy to murder and for attempting to pervert the course of justice. Stalker suddenly found himself on an enforced leave of absence, while he was investigated for unspecified allegations unrelated to Ulster. His place on the 'shoot-to-kill' inquiry was taken by Colin Sampson, Chief Constable of West Yorkshire, the same man who was also charged with the investigation of Stalker.

The allegations against Stalker amounted to his long-standing friendship with Manchester businessman, Kevin Taylor, who was allegedly an associate of known criminals. Sampson recommended that Stalker appear before a disciplinary tribunal. The Greater Manchester Police Authority rejected Sampson's report and reinstated Stalker, but he had had enough and resigned from the force.

Meanwhile, following the Stalker–Sampson report on the 'shoot-to-kill' policy in Northern Ireland, the Attorney General Sir Patrick Mayhew told the House of Commons that no RUC officers would be prosecuted, despite the fact that the Director of Public Prosecutions for Northern Ireland had concluded that there was evidence that there was a conspiracy to pervert the course of justice. The Attorney General said that national security considerations and the public interest must have priority. No RUC officers faced disciplinary procedures.

Kevin Taylor was eventually cleared of fraud charges and John Stalker was exonerated.

ONE place where there certainly was a 'shoot-to-kill' policy in action was Gibraltar. Three IRA terrorists – Daniel McCann, Mairead Farrell and Sean Savage – were shot by members of the British secret service, after the Spanish police had warned that they intended to car-bomb the changing of the guard ceremony outside the governor's house on Gibraltar.

The IRA confirmed that the three were part of an 'active service unit'. However, the car they had parked outside the governor's residence did not contain a bomb and the three people killed were found not to be carrying guns.

A 140 lb bomb, bomb-making equipment, timing devices, ammunition and false passports were found in two other cars the three had rented on the other side of the border. Nevertheless, the Irish government said that it was 'gravely perturbed' at the gunning down of three unarmed Irish citizens. Amnesty International described the killings as 'extrajudicial executions'.

An inquest held in Gibraltar concluded that the three had been unlawfully killed. Six secret servicemen, identified only by the letters A to F, appeared at the inquest behind a screen. They maintained that their intention had been to arrest the three but, fearful that they might detonate a car bomb by remote control, had shot them.

More disturbing were witnesses who said that they had seen McCann and Farrell put their hands up before they were shot, or that they were shot while they were lying on the ground.

Thames Television's award-winning *World in Action* programme had first opened up the story. In Mrs Thatcher's reorganization of independent television, Thames lost its franchise to the anodyne Carlton. Some suspected that it was part of a vendetta.

THE Thatcher government's fearful attitude to the truth came to world attention once more with the scandal surrounding the publication of the book, *Spycatcher*.

The book was the memoirs of Peter Wright, a long-serving member of the British intelligence outfit, MI5, who had retired in Tasmania. In it, he alleged that Sir Roger Hollis, head of MI5 from 1956 to 1965 was a Soviet double agent, that MI5 officers and others had plotted to remove Prime Minister Harold Wilson from office, and that the organization was generally treacherous, bungling and incompetent.

Spycatcher could not be published in Britain due to the Official Secrets Act. Its publication in America could not be prevented, but when Wright tried to publish it in Australia the British government obtained an injunction.

The British Cabinet Secretary, Sir Robert Armstrong, was sent to Australia to make the case for the government. He argued that Wright owed a duty of confidentiality to the Crown; that the book would put at risk the lives of other intelligence officers and their families; that it would damage liaisons with other friendly intelligence services since confidentiality could not be guaranteed; and that it would aid the enemies of Britain.

In March 1987, the court found in favour of Wright and publication. It ruled that although Wright was bound by a duty of confidentiality, most of what was in the book was not confidential since it had been published elsewhere. Disclosure of the other information, it judged, was not damaging to the UK or MI5. The court also found that since the Australian security forces liaised with the British, publication in Australia was in the public interest. That way, people could judge how competent MI5 was. The British government appealed, and lost. *Spycatcher* went on sale in Australia in October 1987.

The British government continued to fight the battle against *Spycatcher* in the British courts, however. From 1986 to 1988, the government had obtained injunctions against *The Guardian*, *The Independent*, *The Sunday Times* and the London *Evening Standard* in an effort, often not very successful, to prevent them publishing extracts from the book.

In February 1988, the Court of Appeal ruled that the government could not maintain a permanent ban on publication of material from the book, now that it was being published world-wide. The court pointed out that the government had not gone to such great lengths to prevent the dissemination of more important material in other books and TV programmes. But with typical Thatcherite grit, the government took the *Spycatcher* case all the way to the House of Lords – and lost. However, their Lordships noted lamely that the members of the security services did have a lifelong obligation of confidentiality, as enshrined in the Official Secrets Act.

BUT it was not just the Tories who involved themselves in sex scandals in the 1980s. The 33-year-old firebrand George Galloway, who ousted the SDP's Roy Jenkins from his Edinburgh Hillhead constituency in June 1987, also managed to land himself in hot water.

But the scandal over 'Gorgeous George' began with certain financial irregularities. Before being elected, Galloway was head of the charity, War on Want. Although his flamboyant management brought in a massive 25 per cent increase in revenue, there were questions over his expenses. However, in March 1987, the auditors cleared him of any impropriety, dishonesty or bad faith.

After he was elected, some of War on Want's executive members went to the Charity Commissioners, who again cleared him of any wrongdoing but recommended tightening up the procedures. Galloway agreed to repay £1,720, including £525 to attend a 'World Marxists Review' seminar in Athens and £850 in minicab fares to take him to work and back.

BBC Scotland then attacked his running of the charity. He hit them with a libel writ for six-figure damages and called a press conference. This was an ill-judged move. Journalists began to question him on his sexual conquests during his all-expenses paid trip to Greece for a seminar that grappled with the Horn of Africa. Galloway was unrepentant.

'I spent lots of time with women,' he said. 'I actually had sexual intercourse with some of them.'

Such candour earned him the headlines: 'Gorgeous George: I bonked for Britain' and 'My Sex Orgy – By MP'.

This did not please his wife, who was at home in Scotland with their five-year-old daughter, nor his girlfriend who lived with him in his one-bedroomed flat in London's East End. Two days later, this arrangement hit the headlines, too. His domestic affairs, Galloway protested, had never been a secret.

But there were more clouds on the horizon. A Channel 4 documentary accused Galloway and three other Labour MPs of illegally transferring funds from three of Dundee's Labour social clubs into the coffers of the Labour Party. However, a police investigation found that one of the club's managers was responsible for the missing money.

Nevertheless, his local party executive passed a vote of no confidence in him. However, Galloway managed to get himself reselected and re-elected. He also won massive libel damages from the *Daily Mirror*.

RON Brown MP was another loony left-winger from Edinburgh. The Parliamentary Labour Party knew it was in for a rough ride from the first moment he arrived in Westminster. In his maiden speech, which are by tradition non-controversial, Brown declared a class war on Mrs Thatcher.

In 1981, when the Russians invaded Afghanistan, Brown flew over to congratulate the invading forces, stopping for a photo opportunity by a tank. Frequently suspended from the House of Commons, Brown took his fight against Mrs Thatcher to the streets. When she visited Glasgow in 1982, he lunged at her and shouted: 'You're not welcome here.' He was fined £50 for a breach of the peace.

If his Afghanistan trip had not made him unpopular enough with the Labour leadership, in 1984 he went to visit Colonel Qaddafi, only months after WPC Yvonne Fletcher had been murdered outside the Libyan Embassy in London.

In 1988, Brown tried to emulate Michael Heseltine and swing the ceremonial mace. But he fumbled and dropped it. Asked whether he had been drunk, he said: 'I'd only had a pint of Younger's Tartan. The bloody thing was heavier than I expected.'

He offered to get the Amalgamated Engineering Union, who sponsored him, to mend it. The union dropped its sponsorship. The following day he refused to read an apology that he had agreed with the Speaker, 10 times. Three times the Speaker ordered him to leave the chamber and he refused. Eventually, a burly Labour whip bundled him out. He was suspended from the Commons for 20 days and Labour withdrew the whip. A private prosecution of criminal damage was later brought against him, but the Director of Public Prosecutions put a stop to it.

The night the PLP upheld the decision to withdraw the whip, Brown was caught naked in a shower with a woman at the House of Commons. The woman, Brown's researcher, Norma Longden, denied shouting: 'I want your baby.'

Brown said that Longden had wandered into the men's shower room by mistake and denied having an affair with her.

'I may be bonkers but I wasn't bonking,' he told the press. 'Because I drop the mace, I also drop my trousers?... I can assure you that at my age, 47, I have sex weekly – very weekly according to my wife... My credentials certainly leave something to be desired. That's why I keep my trousers up.'

A few weeks later, he denied rumours that Longden was pregnant by him.

'It would be physically impossible,' he said. 'A doctor can examine me if he wishes.'

In January 1990, Brown appeared at Lewes Crown Court, charged with theft and causing £800 worth of criminal damage to Longden's flat in St Leonards. He admitted having a three-year affair with Longden that had ended the previous March. Longden claimed that Brown was seeking a reconciliation when he turned up at her flat on the way back from the TUC conference at Eastbourne, blind drunk. Brown went berserk and she fled with her new boyfriend. When the police arrived, Brown had gone, leaving the one plaintive word 'love' scrawled across a mirror in lipstick.

Brown said that he had only dropped by the flat to pick up some documents and tapes. The damage, he said, was caused by Longden's new boyfriend who threw things at him.

The trial lasted six days. Brown was acquitted of theft, but fined £1,000, with £2,500 costs for criminal damage. He was also ordered to pay £628 compensation. Brown supped champagne with his wife on the courtroom steps to celebrate what he claimed was a 'moral victory'.

In Edinburgh, his local party secretary said: 'People here think he's a bit daft but at least he's a bit daft on behalf of us and they are prepared to forgive him.'

They weren't. The rest of his constituency party turned against him and deselected him. He fought them in the courts all the way up to the Court of Sessions, Scotland's highest civil court, but still lost. In the 1992 general election, he stood as an independent and trailed home second to last, trounced by the official Labour candidate.

Later, it was disclosed that Brown had had a long association with the KGB controller in London and Soviet double agent, Oleg Gordievsky. Brown admitted passing on information about Labour colleagues, but only things that the Soviet spy could have 'read in *The Beano*'. Sadly for Brown, any sensitive information would have been passed to MI5, too, and may well have reached the ears of Mrs Thatcher.

ONE of the other left-wingers with Ron Brown on the Afghanistan trip was Allan Roberts, Labour MP for Bootle. When he got back, *Private Eye* ran a story about another less publicized trip the MP had taken to Berlin, the previous Easter.

The rogue MP had visited a gay bar called the Buddy Club. According to Roberts's companions, he had been supping at the bar when a man in an SS uniform had approached him and asked him what his name was. Roberts said: 'Allan.'

'Nein,' shouted the SS man. 'It is Rover.'

Then he had attached a dog lead to the studded collar the MP for Bootle was already wearing around his neck. Roberts was then dragged around the floor and while the other S&M fans looked on the SS man had flogged him. When he had finished, Roberts, who was bleeding profusely, reportedly said: 'That was beautiful, baby.'

Next stop was the hospital, where he had left without paying the bill.

Roberts told his constituency club: 'I was a bit drunk... it is true that I was in the club, but the suggestion that I was dressed in a dog collar and whipped is complete and utter rubbish.'

He said that he had fallen over and cut himself. So he had gone to hospital, where the wound required one stitch. However, the doctor who administered the treatment told *Private Eye*: 'I declined to administer any sutures as the swelling was so great that additional damage could have been caused.'

The magazine also detailed the MP's injuries. They included 'deep lacerations to the back, buttocks and genitalia, apparently caused by a belt buckle'.

Roberts said that he had neglected to settle the bill because he had thought that there was 'an arrangement between the NHS and Germany'. Fortunately, Tory right-winger, Charles Irving, MP for Cheltenham and Chairman of the House of Commons Catering Committee, happened to be in Berlin 'by coincidence' and paid the bill for him.

This was not the first time Roberts had been involved in such antics. The outrageous parties at his Manchester home were legendary. Once, when Roberts was giving a speech to Manchester City Council, it was noticed that the MP, who usually waved his arms about when he spoke, kept his right hand firmly in his pocket. When a fan rushed up to shake his hand, he was shocked to discover a pair of handcuffs dangling from Roberts' wrist. The MP said 'f***ing key' and left.

Roberts resented the intrusion into his private life and successfully sued both *Private Eye* and the *News of the World* when they reported, falsely, that he was being investigated by the police for sexual offences.

On the other hand, he liked to flaunt it. He turned up for an election night party at the American embassy with a number of friends in leather gear. They were thrown out after one of their number stood on the bar and denounced Ronald Reagan as a homophobe.

IF THE Conservatives can do it, and Labour can do it, so can the Liberals. That's what Paddy Ashdown proved in 1987. Although happily married to the mother of his two children, the MP for Yeovil took a leaf out of Lloyd

George's book – and many another MP who gets elected – and had an affair with his secretary, Tricia Howard.

Had it been known about at the time, it would certainly have damaged his chances of becoming party leader. But he managed to keep it quiet.

Three years after the brief affair, Mrs Howard began divorce proceedings. Terrified that his name might come up in court, Ashdown called his solicitor, Andrew Phillips. Phillips made a note of their conversation in case action was needed later, locked the note in his safe and forgot about it.

In January 1992, his office was burgled. The note fell into the hands of Simon Berkowitz, an ardent Thatcherite who believed in private enterprise and standing on your own two feet. He offered the note to the *News of the World*, initially for £5,000. When they showed interest, he upped the price to £20,000. They refused to pay. Instead they tracked down Tricia Howard.

When reporters turned up at Mrs Howard's Wiltshire home, she called Ashdown, who in turn called Phillips. It was only then that Phillips discovered that his *aide mémoire* was missing.

He obtained an injunction to stop the media publishing the note, since it had been obtained by a criminal act. But Ashdown knew the story was bound to come out. Seizing the initiative, Ashdown held a press conference and confessed all. *The Sun* quickly dubbed him 'Paddy Pantsdown', but otherwise he emerged unscathed. In fact, his approval rating climbed quite sharply afterwards.

A former captain in the Royal Marines, Ashdown had carefully cultivated his 'action man' image. A toy manufacturer rushed out an Ashdown model in army fatigues. They offered a free sample to Mrs Howard. She declined, preferring, one supposes, the real thing.

28 ❖ Back to Basics

John Major should have known better. When he told the Tory Party conference in October 1993 that he wanted to go 'back to basics' he unwittingly delivered the kiss of death to his government, which was eventually driven from office after an unprecedented series of scandals.

He made it perfectly clear what he meant by 'back to basics'. He said that he wanted his Conservative government to stand for 'a country united around those old, common-sense British values that should never have been pushed aside'. This was greeted with rapturous applause by the blue-rinsed delegates.

But under John Major, the Conservative Party had already weathered three scandals. The first occurred in March 1992, when Alan Amos MP, the teetotal anti-smoking campaigner who favoured birching for criminals, got caught in the bushes at a homosexual cruising spot on Hampstead Heath. He denied being gay, but admitted to indulging in 'a childish and stupid act'. Nevertheless, he was pilloried by the press, whom he accused of muckraking. After all, he had not even been charged with anything, let alone tried and found guilty.

It made no difference. The *Daily Star* said: 'Amos is a teetotaller, opposes abortion, and brands smoking a "dirty, dangerous and anti-social habit". Hopefully he is now questioning his judgement in wandering around at dusk, at a place which has been turned into a no-go area for decent families by perverts practising what many people – even smokers – would call another dirty, dangerous and anti-social habit. His downfall must be sad for him. But he should not try to tar us with his own muck.'

His Hexham constituency party turned on him and Amos was forced to resign.

THE next scandal was a real shocker. It concerned David Mellor, a close friend of the Prime Minister's and a fellow Chelsea fan. John Major had appointed Mellor his Secretary of State at the new Department of Heritage, which was quickly dubbed the Ministry of Fun. It soon became known that the 43-year-old minister, who was married with two children, did not leave his portfolio in the office.

Part of his brief was to handle Sir David Calcutt's report on press intrusion into individual privacy. A Privacy Bill had already been mooted and Mellor had warned Fleet Street that it was drinking in the 'last chance saloon'. But it soon appeared that Mellor was imbibing there himself.

The Minister of Fun was having his own private spot of fun with 31-year-old actress, Antonia de Sancha. This was extraordinary hubris since Mellor had been introduced to de Sancha three years earlier by *Private Eye* journalist, Paul Halloran.

De Sancha was the only child of a Spanish father and a Swedish-born mother, who had both died shortly after they split up when she was in her mid-20s. She made her living as a topless model and bit part actress. Her starring role was in a soft-porn film called *The Pieman*, where she played a one-legged prostitute who pays the pizza-delivery man in kind.

It took some time for the affair to develop, but by June 1992 they were lovers. Antonia wrote to her Swedish grandmother saying: 'I am having a marvellous time at the moment. I have met a wonderful politician. I am very happy.'

But she was already concerned about the possibility of exposure. Nosy neighbours, she feared, might spread gossip. Confiding her fears to a friend, she borrowed his flat in Finborough Road, West London, as a temporary love nest. The flat was bugged. Soon, tapes of Mellor complaining that his nights of passion with the young actress were exhausting were being touted to the *News of the World*.

Early in July 1992, Mellor had a call from Sir Tim Bell, PR consultant and former government spin doctor. He informed Mellor of the story and the evidence that the *New of the World* had. Mellor denied that he was having an affair and expressed surprise that a newspaper could handle tapes that had been recorded in such an underhand fashion. This was just the sort of thing that his Privacy Bill would stamp out.

The moment that Bell was off the phone Mellor phoned de Sancha and told her to keep her mouth shut.

Although they were not entirely convinced by Mellor's denials, the *News of the World* put publication on hold. *The People* had no such reservations. On Saturday, 18 July 1992, Mellor was tipped off that *The People* were going to run the story the next day. He phoned the Prime Minister and tendered his resignation.

John Major refused to accept it. He said he would stand by his friend and he saw no conflict between his current plight and his handling of the Calcutt Report. But the press did. The very man who was threatening to shackle them had been caught with his pants down. What's more, because of Antonia de Sancha's career, they had plenty of juicy pictures to illustrate the story with.

Soon, Antonia was besieged by the press. Mellor had to distance himself. He issued the obligatory statement saying: 'My wife Judith and I have been experiencing difficulties in our marriage. We want to sort the situation out for the sake of each other and especially for our two young children.' And there was the photocall with Mellor and his wife and children smiling outside the in-laws, before going in for a cosy family lunch. From a man demanding privacy, this reeked of hypocrisy.

By an unfortunate coincidence, the *Desert Island Discs* radio programme that Mellor had recorded earlier went out that weekend. Mellor's father-in-law, Professor Edward Hall, decided to attack his daughter's errant husband in the media.

'If he'll cheat on our girl, he'll cheat on the country,' he said.

In an effort to defend herself, Antonia de Sancha employed the publicist Max Clifford to handle the press for her. Soon the press was full of stories that Mellor liked to make love in Chelsea strip and that he indulged in toe-sucking as foreplay.

Clifford sold the serialization of de Sancha's story to *The Sun*. They even mocked up the tawdry scene for their readers, complete with the mattress on the floor where the couple had first made love, the bottle of cheap white wine and the lurid red silk bedclothes.

Although Mellor had become a laughing stock, he may have survived this. But more serious allegations came to light. Mellor and his family had holidayed in the Marbella home of Mona Bauwens, daughter of one of the founders of the Palestine Liberation Organization. While they had been there, Iraq had invaded Kuwait and the PLO had backed Saddam Hussein. Mona Bauwens sued *The People*, which carried the story for casting her as a 'social outcast and leper'.

Although the court case failed, it kept Mellor in the limelight. Valiantly, he fought on. He made endless rounds of TV studios and even took the time to attend the National Press Fund's annual reception.

'I was going through a quiet patch so it was good of you to invite me tonight,' he told them.

But his sense of humour did not save him. He admitted that he had behaved foolishly but insisted that what he had done was not a resigning matter.

'Who decides who is to be a member of the British Cabinet, the Prime Minister or the Editor of the *Daily Mail*?' he asked defiantly.

The answer was, of course, the Editor of the *Daily Mail*. With the newspapers against him, Tory backbench support began to go soft. John Major then had no choice but to accept David Mellor's resignation, despite a letter of support in *The Times* signed by many senior figures in the arts whose work he had championed in his ministerial post.

It was a case of 'From toe-job to no job', as *The Sun* so succinctly put it.

There was no chance of him returning to office either. Two years later, the *News of the World* discovered that he had abandoned the wife who had stood by him and was having another affair – this time with Lady Penelope Cobham, a former adviser at the Department of Heritage. Mellor divorced his first wife and married her. He later went on to build up a successful career in the media.

NORMAN Lamont fell from power because ultimately, as Chancellor of the Exchequer, he had to carry the can after the pound had been forced out of the European Exchange Rate Mechanism, costing the country millions of pounds. But by that time he had already been involved in more than his fair share of scandals. As Mrs Thatcher's Trade Secretary, he had once appeared in the House of Commons with a black eye, the result of walking into a door, he said.

Daily Mail gossip columnist, Nigel Dempster, told another tale. He said that the 43-year-old minister, who was married with two children, had paid a late-night visit to the £350,000 Bayswater home of glamorous divorcee, Olga Polizzi, daughter of Lord Forte. Unfortunately, wealthy art dealer Richard Connolly was already there. The result, Connolly confirmed, was the minister's shiner.

After Lamont became Chancellor, the *News of the World* discovered that he had asked a local estate agent to rent out the basement of his Notting Hill home. Unbeknown to Lamont, the new tenant was a freelance 'sex therapist', soon universally known as 'Miss Whiplash'. She denied being a prostitute, although admitted dressing in a number of specialized costumes to administer domination to her clients and stripping naked to perform massage.

Lamont said he knew nothing of her activities and, if the allegations were true, promised to evict her. *The Sun* thoughtfully provided him with a guided tour of the 'vice den', detailing the facilities that he, as landlord, was providing to the sexually deprived of West London. And Lamont, good to his word, kicked her out.

But five months later, the newspapers spotted that the Treasury had provided £4,700 towards the £23,000 legal bill Lamont had run up over the eviction. The rest had been stumped up by 'Tory benefactors'. The Treasury protested that it had paid only for the cost of handling the press enquiries generated. Lamont was a government minister and he would not have incurred these costs if he had been a private citizen. The Tory benefactors turned out to be, not wealthy individuals, but Conservative Central Office. Lamont had not done anything wrong, but it provided another opportunity to rake over the coals of Miss Whiplash.

After the debacle of Britain's withdrawal from the ERM, the papers were out to get Lamont. *The Sun* reported that he had done a bunk from a Brighton Hotel without paying the bill. In fact, his bill, along with those of several other Tory ministers, had been forwarded to Central Office.

Then *The Sun* revealed that he paid his credit card bills late and had received five warning letters from Access – hardly a record of prudence by a Chancellor of the Exchequer. Lamont protested that this was a private matter. *The Sun* responded with 'Threshergate'. Lamont's Access card had last been used at a branch of the off-licence chain, Thresher's. The assistant manager of the branch, in a seedy part of Paddington, said that Lamont had used the card there to buy a bottle of champagne and 20 cigarettes. The Treasury responded by showing the press the Chancellor's credit card receipt. It showed that he had used to it two buy three bottles of wine in a branch in salubrious Marble Arch.

Although Norman Lamont could claim, with justification, that there was a conspiracy in the press to bring him down, he condemned himself out of his own mouth. In October 1992 he said he could see 'the green shoots of economic spring', while everyone else was still feeling the winter chill of recession.

A week after Black Wednesday, when Britain pulled out of the ERM, he casually remarked to a reporter that he had been 'singing in the bath'. He had not meant this as any sort of economic comment – he said his wife had complained about his singing – but that was how it was taken.

In May 1993, there was a by-election in Newbury and Norman Lamont was wheeled out to talk about the government's economic successes. During a televised press conference he was asked which he regretted more – seeing green shoots or singing in the bath? He replied flippantly: '*Je ne regrette rien.*'

The Tories lost the by-election and Lamont lost his job.

WHEN John Major used the phrase 'back to basics', he meant health, education and law and order, along with his Miss Marple image of England as a country full of warm beer and spinsters' bicycles passing the cricket pitch on the village green to the sound of church bells. But the press mischievously interpreted it to mean a call for the Tory *jihad* on sexual immorality. Soon his ministers were lining up with sordid sex scandals.

Transport Minister Steven Norris was the first to go. Married with two children, the 48-year-old minister was said to have not one, but five mistresses. His wife, admiral's daughter Vicky Cecil-Gibson, lived in her own house in Berkshire and was fully aware that her husband was a weekday Romeo.

The 1993 'back-to-basics' Tory Party conference was scarcely over when Norris announced that his marriage was now over and he intended to marry 45-year-old *Times* political reporter, Sheila Gunn, his mistress of three years' standing. It was then revealed that he had been two-timing her with 40-year-old *Harpers & Queen* executive, Jennifer Sharp. Then there was 46-year-old sales executive, Lynn Taylor, who had met him at a party at his Newbury home seven years earlier and had taken over as his mistress from a lady surgeon who had been Norris's lover for the eight years before that. Then out of the woodwork came the inevitable House of Commons secretary, 29-year-old Emma Courtney. She had been dating Norris for 12 months and was 'devastated' to discover that he had not been giving her his undivided attention. However, when the dust settled, they managed to patch it up.

In happier times, Norris would have stayed on. He had done no wrong and was admired by both the press and his colleagues, not least for his sexual prowess. Major did not sack him, but the 'back-to-basics' ground swell at constituency level resulted in an effort to deselect him. He saw that off, but later announced that he would not stand again in the next election.

ENVIRONMENT Minister Tim Yeo, it was said, was so pro-family that he had two of them. On Boxing Day 1993, the press revealed that he had a six-month-old love child with Julia Stent, a Tory councillor in the London borough of Hackney and, now, a single mother.

Mrs Diane Yeo was a proper Tory wife and stood by her husband. John Major declared that Yeo's love life was a private matter and the errant MP headed off on holiday with his wife and their two grown-up children. But while they were sunning themselves in the Seychelles, the back-to-basics mullahs were baying for his head, led by his local Tory mayor, Mrs Aldine Horrigan.

Yeo returned home like a criminal, hiding on the floor of the family car to avoid the press. Just as David Mellor had done, Major insisted weakly that it was he who decided who was in the government – not the tabloids –. But this time Tory activists took a hand. The officers of his constituency party refused to support him and he resigned as a minister, bitterly blaming Mrs Horrigan. Ten days later though, a meeting of the full constituency party backed him, even after it was revealed that he had sired another illegitimate child when he was a student at Cambridge.

Yeo was later seen lunching with his mistress, Julia Stent, at Langan's Brasserie and his wife said that she received hate mail for her loyalty to her husband.

EVEN while the Yeo affair was unfolding, John Major lost another minister, Lord Caithness, a junior transport minister, after his 40-year-old wife killed herself. The newspapers deduced that Caithness had told his wife that weekend of his close acquaintanceship with glamorous divorcée, Jan Fitzalan-Howard.

ONE Tory wife who did not stand by her man was Italian-born Silvana Ashby. She told *The Sunday Times* that her husband, David Ashby MP, had left her because of 'a friendship with another man'. Ashby denied that he was gay, but admitted that he had shared a hotel bed with another man when he had been on holiday in France. They had shared the bed, he said, merely to save money.

The other newspapers happily sniped away at Ashby. But when *The Sunday Times* announced that he had also shared a bed with a young man in Goa – which was not true – Ashby sued. *The Sunday Times* apologized for the Goa story but refused to withdraw the allegation that the MP was a homosexual, a liar and a hypocrite.

At the ensuing libel trial, Ashby's wife Silvana took the stand as *The Sunday Times'* key witness. She insisted that, when they had separated after 28 years of marriage, her husband had admitted to her that he was a homosexual.

Ashby himself insisted that he had not had sex with his wife for four years because he was impotent. His Harley Street physician, Dr Lewis Sevitt, told the court that he had been treating Ashby for the condition but there had been no improvement. His bedmate in France also testified that they had not had sex.

But *The Sunday Times* had a surprise witness. *Times* journalist Andrew Pierce had seen Ashby in a well-known gay pub in Chelsea. He gave a vivid description of it, pointing out that no one could have been under any illusion that he was not in a hang-out for homosexuals.

The jury found in favour of the newspaper. After the judgement his wife tried to hug him, but he shrugged her off. Already a casualty at Lloyd's, Ashby was ruined. He did not, however, resign his seat in the House of Commons. He then cast the decisive vote against the government in the Labour amendment to the Housing Bill, which would let the surviving partner of a homosexual couple inherit the tenancy in the event of the death of the other. For his constituency party, this was the final straw. They deselected him. He railed against the press and 'homophobes' in the constituency party. It was at this point that he decided to come out, and announced on Radio 5's *Out This Week* programme that he was proud to be a gay MP – even though he was soon to be an MP no longer.

IN JANUARY 1994, the *News of the World* announced that church-going bachelor Garry Waller, MP for Keithley, had been kicked off the books of a posh dating agency for claiming that he was unattached. In fact, the 48-year-old

Waller had a long-term girlfriend and a love child by – yes – a House of Commons secretary.

'BACK to basics' then took a dip into black comedy. On 7 February 1994, young high-flying Tory backbencher, Steven Milligan, was found dead in his Chiswick flat by his Commons secretary, Vera Taggart. Naked except for a pair of black stockings and suspenders, he was trussed up with electrical flex. There was a black bin liner on his head and a satsuma jammed between his teeth.

The police investigated his shady private life and discovered that he was another MP who enjoyed the service of a posh dating agency. Although the circumstances of his death were considered unusual, foul play was not suspected.

Apparently, Milligan was indulging in an esoteric sexual practice that involves restricting oxygen to the system. The precise details remain sketchy, although apparently someone at the BBC had some internal knowledge. An internal memo was circulated which said: 'We can now say that he was wearing women's clothing, we can say he had a plastic bag on his head, and we can mention that he was bound with flex. But on no account mention fruit.'

Don't try this at home. How very back to basics.

SIX days after Milligan's body was discovered, the papers broke the story of an affair between Tory MP Hartley Booth and his 22-year-old House of Commons secretary. Although he claimed that it was an innocent infatuation, as a Christian and a pro-family campaigner, he admitted hypocrisy. He resigned as the Parliamentary Private Secretary to Foreign Office Minister, Douglas Hogg, whose wife Sarah was the Downing Street adviser responsible for the 'back to basics' campaign.

In May, it was reported that Michael Brown, Tory MP for Brigg and Cleethorpes, had been on a Caribbean holiday with his 20-year-old boyfriend. Brown resigned, not because he was gay, but because the homosexual age of consent was still set at 21. It would only be reduced to 18 that autumn.

In March 1995, the second wife of junior civil service minister, Robert Hughes, discovered that he was having an affair with his House of Commons secretary. He did the decent thing and tried to sack her. She threatened to take him to an industrial tribunal. He persuaded her not to and she went to the *News of the World* instead.

A few weeks later, the *News of the World* announced that the Conservative

MP for Bury St Edmunds, Richard Spring, had enjoyed a three-in-the-bed love romp with a Sunday school teacher and a pension fund manager. He resigned as Parliamentary Private Secretary to the Northern Ireland Secretary.

Next, Rod Richards resigned from the Welsh Office when an affair came to light with Julia Felthouse, a public relations officer 20 years his junior. Married with two children, Richards was another keen supporter of the family who found himself all over the pages of the *News of the World*.

NOT that the Tories were the only ones at it. A *News of the World* headline turned hard-line working class Labour MP Dennis Skinner from 'The Beast of Bolsover' – the name parliamentary sketchwriters had saddled him with – to the 'The Beast of Legover'. The object of his affections was his House of Commons researcher, Lois Blasenheim.

Skinner's wife was 61, a working class Northern lass who lived in their semi-detached council house in the Derbyshire village of Clay Cross. His lover was 47, an American heiress living in Carlyle Square, Chelsea, where her neighbours included Felicity Kendal, David Frost and the Duchess of Portland.

The Beast of Bolsover had long boasted his no-nonsense attitude by claiming that he did not even have a passport. It came out that his mistress was teaching him to drive. The working class Northern boy had been corrupted at last.

Skinner had long lived a separate life from his wife. But the situation was made all the more ludicrous by the furtive nature of his new relationship. Instead of walking straight up to his mistress's front door and ringing the bell, he would go to her house in disguise and lurk in the bushes outside. Then, at a pre-arranged time, she would let him in.

APART from this amusing interlude, the Tories kept up their torrent of sex scandals right up until the 1997 election. In the last gasp of the dying government, Piers Merchant, the 46-year-old Tory MP for Beckenham, claimed he was set up when *The Sun* photographed him canoodling in the park with 17-year-old Soho night-club hostess, Anna Cox. Merchant, who had been married for 20 years, claimed that Ms Cox was merely helping him with his campaign.

Meanwhile, the Chairman of the Scottish Conservative Party, Sir Michael Hirst, stepped down following allegations that he had had a homosexual affair with civil servant Paul Martin, who had been involved with Michael Brown, MP for Brigg and Cleethorpes. Conservative candidate

Allan Stewart also stood down – after allegations of a friendship with a woman he had met in a clinic where they were both being treated for alcoholism.

But all this was icing on the cake for New Labour whose candidates, by comparison, looked like choir boys.

29 ❖ Tory Sleaze

With the myopia of hindsight, it might be imagined that Tory sleaze was a condition that affected only the Major government. In fact, it has a long and dishonourable tradition.

Reginald Maudling was Chancellor of the Exchequer when the Conservatives lost power in 1964 and he used the financial expertise he had gained at the Treasury to enrich himself during his time in opposition. After he lost the leadership battle to Edward Heath in 1965, he began taking on directorships. Obviously, a former Chancellor of the Exchequer on the board did a company no harm. Within months, he was earning £20,000 a year, four times his ministerial salary. By the end of the 1960s, he was a name at Lloyd's and a prominent banker, as well as a board member of numerous companies. He owned a home in the country, as well as a Regency house in Belgravia.

But his wealth did not just come from what he earned. As a former Chancellor, he knew the tax system well. He also knew how to get around it. One of his directorships was with Peachey Properties, a company run by a dubious businessman named Eric Miller. Maudling was anxious to avoid income tax and wanted to protect his two homes from the new capital gains tax that the Labour government was proposing to introduce. He offered to work as a consultant for Peachey Properties, but waived his fee. In exchange, Peachey would buy the freehold on his country house. This was already in Maudling's wife's name; he held a lease on the property from her. Peachey would then make repairs and improvements to the house. The deal was worth a year's salary in advance, tax free, to Maudling and was of no commercial advantage to Peachey.

Through Eric Miller, Maudling met the architect John Poulson. His practice was the largest in Europe and he earned over £1 million a year in fees. The tax man saw little of that as a Conservative MP and tax expert had set up an umbrella company as a tax shelter.

Poulson used a number of corrupt practices to secure business and get around bureaucratic constraints. These included building houses for prominent civil servants. He was also in cahoots with corrupt local politician, T. Dan Smith, a prominent figure in the Labour Party in the North of England.

Together they set up a number of public relations firms that employed local councillors. In return, the councillors would put council building projects Poulson's way. Poulson and Smith also had a wide range of contacts politically, socially and in the freemasons. These were all encouraged to give Poulson work, in exchange for free holidays, accommodation, mortgages and other fringe benefits.

The nest of corruption worked because the Labour Party faced no serious opposition in most northern cities. The political network was entrenched and television and the expansion of the national newspapers had enfeebled the local press.

Poulson wanted to expand overseas, and he hired Labour MP Albert Roberts and Conservative right-winger John Cordle to front the organization. But he was still looking for a big name when Eric Miller introduced Poulson to Maudling.

Maudling became chairman of Poulson's overseas operations. Poulson also employed Maudling's son on a healthy salary and gave £8,000 a year to a theatre charity that Maudling's wife ran. It was also agreed that when business started booming, Maudling would be allowed to buy shares.

But boom it did not. Although in a series of trips to the Mediterranean and the Middle East, Maudling was able to open doors for Poulson, only one was converted into a contract. The Maltese government was building a hospital on the island of Gozo. It was partially funded by the British, and Maudling used his influence to win the contract.

Poulson's solicitor put another opportunity Maudling's way and introduced him to Jerry Hoffman, head of the Real Estate Fund of America. REFA was an off-shore investment company, which promised to generate massive tax-free profits out of international property speculation. Hoffman wanted big names to front the company and offered Maudling a seat on the board. Maudling accepted, waiving his fee for 250,000 shares in the venture.

Solely on the strength of Maudling's name, two banks invested in REFA – only to discover, to their cost, that the whole thing was a scam. Hoffman and his associates were taking investors' money and putting down deposits on real estate. They then charged commission and handling fees on the full purchase price. This made Hoffman and his friends rich, while giving the impression that the company was much larger than it really was.

Maudling denied actual involvement in the activities of REFA and later claimed never to have attended a board meeting. But in 1969, when the press started investigating REFA, Maudling pulled out.

In 1970, the Conservatives were returned to power and Maudling became Home Secretary. He resigned his consultancy with Peachey and stepped down as chairman of Poulson's overseas companies. By this time, Poulson was running into difficulties. His corrupt practices effectively front-loaded his contracts, leaving him with increasing cashflow problems. To ease his liquidity problems he simply forgot to pay the taxman. It would all come tumbling down.

In 1972, Poulson filed for bankruptcy. Maudling's name was mentioned during the hearings and he complained stridently. But when the Metropolitan Police Fraud Squad began investigating, Maudling resigned. This, he said, was merely because, as Home Secretary, he was nominally responsible for the police. He made it clear that if he had held any other position in the government, he would not have stepped down.

The police enquiries resulted in a number of corruption trials. These revealed how deeply Maudling was involved. His house was still owned by Peachey Properties. And although he had stepped down from the board of REFA when it began to get flak in the press, he had left the company a great testimonial, saying it was a brilliant concept with a great future. He even held on to his REFA shares for another year, in the hope of capitalizing on what he saw as a 'little pot of gold'.

When the new Labour government came into power in 1974, it promised to tighten up the parliamentary rules on Members' business interests. But MPs look after their own. There was little criticism of those who had had dealings with Poulson, probably because members of both parties were involved. In 1976, the Attorney General announced that the criminal investigation into Poulson's affairs was at an end.

But then a damning article in *The Observer* forced the government to set up a Select Committee to investigate the involvement of Cordle, Roberts and Maudling. Cordle came in for the most criticism. When numerous trips to West Africa had borne no fruit, Cordle had written to Poulson justifying his fee. In this letter, he mentioned that he should be paid because he had taken part in a debate in the House of Commons 'largely for the benefit of Construction Promotion', one of Poulson's firms. This was considered a contempt of the House and Cordle resigned.

All three were criticized for failing to declare an interest at the appropriate time. Roberts complained about being lumped together with Cordle and Maudling, as he had only 'transgressed in shallow waters'. Maudling was also criticized for being less than completely frank in his resignation letter of 1972.

In the debate that followed the publication of the committee's report, Edward Heath described Maudling as an 'honourable man'. Maudling continued to deny any wrongdoing. He was consigned to the backbenches and died in 1979.

KEITH Best, the Conservative MP for Anglesey, was the first casualty of the Thatcher administration, when he subscribed over-enthusiastically to the privatisation of British Telecom.

At the age of 34, he had joined the government as PPS to the Welsh Secretary, Nicholas Edwards, and seemed to be something of a rising star.

The £4 billion sell-off of British Telecom in 1984 was the government's first privatization and they were delighted by its success. The list of those who had made share applications ran to 51,000 pages and the magazine *Labour Research* began the laborious business of checking through them to see if any Conservative MPs had their fingers in the cookie jar.

The rules of the privatization were that any one individual could make only one application. *Labour Research* found Keith Best's name. They also found that of Keith Lander Best and a Lander Best. Not only had he used three different variations on his name, he had used four different addresses – including that of his widowed mother – and six different bank accounts. As a result, he bought six times as many shares as permitted for £6,240, making a clear profit of £3,120.

When the story broke in April 1987, Labour called for Best's resignation and arrest. The Leader of the House of Commons, John Biffen, struck back, describing Labour's demands as 'sanctimonious and distasteful'. Best defended himself, saying that he had not made applications in false names, only variations on his real name. He had made multiple applications, he said, because he was afraid that the sell-off would be over-subscribed and he would miss out.

It was then revealed that he had also made multiple applications in the Jaguar cars sell-off, although this was not illegal. His eager dealings in Mrs Thatcher's other sell-offs – of the TSB, British Gas, Britoil, Cable and Wireless, Enterprise Oil and British Aerospace – all came in for investigation.

In the face of this barracking, Best announced that he would donate the profits from his share dealings to charity. He stepped down as a PPS and said he would not seek re-election at the forthcoming election. The Labour MP Brian Segmore was not satisfied, claiming his resignation was 'political expediency at the expense of parliament'. Labour leader Neil Kinnock turned the guns on the rest of the government, saying he was 'waiting to see if we get a sermon on moral values from Norman Tebbit in the next few days; he has fallen strangely silent'.

Labour Research then discovered that another Conservative MP, Eric Cockham, Member for Ludlow, had bought more than his share of British Gas shares. He claimed that they were for his grandchildren. He, too, said that he would not stand at the forthcoming election. The Crown Prosecution Service said that he would not be prosecuted.

Best was not so lucky. In October 1987, Best pleaded not guilty at Southwark Crown Court and wept in the witness box. It did no good. He was found guilty and sentenced to four months in jail and fined £3,000, with £1,500 costs. After an unpleasant weekend in the hospital wing of Brixton Prison, the prison sentence was dropped, but the fine was increased to £4,500.

Best seems to have learnt his lesson. He moved into charity work and became head of the Immigration Advisory Service.

'CASH for questions' did not begin with the John Major government either. John Browne, Conservative MP for Winchester, blazed the trail in 1970 when he asked a number of seemingly innocent questions about the freezing of certain Middle Eastern assets at Prime Minister's Question Time.

It was only later that *The Observer* and the TV documentary series *World in Action* discovered that, at the time, he was working on a study of the subject for the Saudi Arabian Monetary Agency, which was paying him $88,000 – more than an MP's annual salary.

Browne was also an early exponent of 'cash for access'. He was on the payroll of a firm of Lebanese consultants keen to make contacts in Number 10. They paid him an annual retainer of £2,400, which he failed to declare. Not that he needed the money. He had already hit the headlines with his divorce from his wife of 18 years. She was the daughter of a shipping magnate and he had walked away with a £175,000 settlement.

Although Browne married another heiress, he went back to court to pick up the £65,000 his ex-wife still owed him. She played to the press, clutching a suitcase full of clothes, claiming they were her only possessions. She threw herself on the mercy of the court, saying she had already forked out £200,000 – £110,000 to her ex-husband and £90,000 in legal fees. If she paid any more, it would leave her destitute. Her histrionics did not work and she narrowly escaped going to jail. But the press was sympathetic and dubbed Browne a cad. In response, he tried to introduce a Privacy Bill. It was laughed out of the House.

When the Select Committee looking into *The Observer*'s 'cash-for-questions' allegations found against him, Labour demanded Browne's resignation. He refused to step down. His constituency party deselected him. Mrs Thatcher chastised him from the dispatch box and the Leader of the House, Sir Geoffrey Howe, proposed that he be suspended from the House without pay for 20 days. The motion was unanimously carried.

Browne condemned his treatment by the House as a 'show trial'. The press, he said, were conducting a 'venomous witch-hunt' against him because of 'my divorce, my Privacy Bill and the recent Select Committee report'. He wrote an open letter to his constituents, alleging that he had been pushed out to make way for a minister. And he sought the Attorney General's advice on whether he could bring a case under the UN Convention of Human Rights.

Later, when he won a Commons ballot, he addressed the House at great length on the huge injustice that had been perpetrated on him by all and sundry. When he sat down, the Labour MP John Fraser summed up the feelings of the whole House by describing Browne as 'a public schoolboy, Guards officer, banker, MP – and whinger'.

Browne then seemed to lose the plot totally. He began wearing an oversize top hat, which he took off only when he stood to speak, apparently as some protest over the Ministry of Defence's failure to pay compensation to an ex-Guardsman who had lost his legs. It caused much amusement when a fellow MP sat on the hat and, later, when Browne accidentally sat on it himself.

At the next election, he stood as an independent – and lost.

NORTHERN Ireland Minister, Michael Mates, gave his friend Asil Nadir a £20 watch at a party to celebrate the Cypriot businessman's 52nd birthday. It was a much-needed present. Nadir's Polly Peck empire was under investigation by the Serious Fraud Squad and Nadir's £3,500 Blancpain watch had been confiscated by the SFO during one of its raids.

But Mates made a stupid mistake. He spent £32 having the words 'Don't let the buggers get you down' engraved on the back.

Three days after his birthday, Nadir jumped bail, which had been set at £3.5 million, and fled to his house in Turkish-controlled Northern Cyprus. Turkish-occupied Cyprus is not recognized by the British government and has no extradition treaty with the UK. The press and politicians alike tore into the runaway businessman. Nadir responded by praising Mates's 'unflinching help'. This turned the spotlight on the minister.

When the gift of the watch was revealed, Mates shrugged it off as a 'light-hearted gesture'. But his support for the man who had pulled off one of the biggest frauds in history ran deeper than that. One of Nadir's advisers was a constituent of Mates's and, with the help of Nadir's defence counsel, Mates had written three letters to the Attorney General accusing the SFO of running a witch-hunt against Nadir. Mates insisted that he was within his rights to do so.

John Major, as always, rallied around, saying that Mates's resignation had neither been sought nor offered. The minister clung on. It was then revealed that Nadir had given the Conservative Party £440,000, although his companies owned millions. Party Chairman Sir Norman Fowler said that the gift was stolen money and would be returned.

Nadir was now claiming from Cyprus that there was an establishment conspiracy against him. The press gave little credence to the allegations of the bail-jumping entrepreneur, but the press had a problem. Fraud cases are often so complex that juries, even after months of detailed testimony, are none the wiser. Explaining Nadir's crooked dealings to tabloid readers is next to impossible. Mates was a much easier target.

It was soon discovered that Mates's contact with the Nadir empire had continued, even after Nadir had absconded. He had borrowed a car from Nadir's public relations adviser for his estranged wife and he had been seen dining with him.

Eventually, Mates resigned – not, he said, because he had done anything wrong, but because his continued presence in Major's government was embarrassing the Prime Minister.

In a barnstorming resignation speech, Mates attacked the SFO for trying to put pressure on the judge in Nadir's case. Nine times the speaker warned him that he was intruding into matters that were *sub judice*. This is academic since, at the time of writing, Asil Nadir shows no inclination to return to the UK to stand trial.

IN THE very week Tim Yeo and Lord Caithness resigned for not following 'back to basics', Alan Duncan MP was embroiled in a scandal for showing a little too much good old-fashioned Tory private enterprise.

He had taken advantage of the government's right-to-buy scheme to purchase, not his own council house, but the one next door to his Westminster home. His neighbour, long-standing tenant Harry Ball-Wilson, took advantage of the £50,000 discount he had accrued. Duncan then bought the freehold off him and did up the dilapidated property. His ulti-mate intention was to extend his home through into the next-door building when his sitting tenant passed on.

The deal was perfectly legal. Indeed Mr Ball-Wilson was enjoying a holiday in Hawaii on the proceeds when the story broke. However, as far as the papers were concerned, it was a case of a Tory MP profiting from Tory policies – in other words sleaze.

BY 1994, the Conservatives' 'back to basics' campaign was in tatters. But, al-though catching pro-family Tory MPs bed-hopping was fun, the newspa-pers wanted something more substantial to get their teeth into. It had long been suspected that John Browne was not the first, nor the last, to take cash for questions. *The Sunday Times*'s Insight team decided to investigate.

Posing as a businessman, a *Sunday Times* reporter offered 10 Tory MPs and 10 Labour MPs £1,000 to ask a question at Prime Minister's Question Time, which then took place twice a week in the House of Commons. Two of the Tories, David Tredinnick and Graham Riddick, both Parliamentary Private Secretaries, accepted.

When the newspaper published its scoop, Tredinnick denied the charges. The next day, *The Sunday Times* released a tape of Tredinnick asking for the cheque to be sent to his private address. Riddick, too, had accepted a cheque, but had had second thoughts and sent it back.

Although MPs accused *The Sunday Times* of entrapment, the Chief Whip Richard Ryder suspended them as PPSs. The Committee of Privi-leges suspended them for two weeks and fined Riddick £900 and Tredin-nick £1,800. However, the Press Complaints Commission upheld Riddick's complaint that *The Sunday Times* had used unacceptable methods to lure the MP into wrongdoing.

But more sleaze was about to hit the fan. Northern Ireland Minister, Tim Smith, resigned when it was revealed that he had been paid by Mohamed Al-Fayed to table helpful questions during the Egyptian busi-nessman's battle to take over Harrods. But the Tory Trade Minister, Neil Hamilton, denied similar allegations and issued a writ for defamation against *The Guardian*, which had pointed out that he and his wife had stayed for a week in the Ritz Hotel in Paris, which Al-Fayed owned. They had run up a bill of over £3,000, which had been settled by the management.

Hamilton claimed that he had stayed in the hotel as Al-Fayed's guest, much the same as he would in a private house. On a visit to a biscuit fac-tory in his constituency, he emerged with his wife Christine by his side, holding a biscuit.

'I must remember to declare this in the Register of Interests,' he quipped.

Soon after, he compared his hounding by the press to that of John Major, who had issued a writ against the subversive magazine *Scallywag* when it falsely alleged that he was having a torrid affair with a Downing Street caterer. How Major could have claimed that this allegation damaged him was never tested in court. For one fleeting moment, he almost looked interesting. Plainly, that was the last thing he wanted. Nor did he want to be reminded of the case and he promptly sacked Hamilton from the government.

Hamilton, who at first had been gung-ho about his defamation case against *The Guardian*, inexplicably dropped it. Senior Tories, including the Prime Minister, urged him to stand down. More allegations of sleaze were hurled at him. He admitted accepting £10,000 as a lobbyist. But still his constituency party in Tatton backed him, claiming he was the victim of a media smear campaign. However, in the 1997 general election, the white-suited, whiter-than-white BBC foreign correspondent, Martin Bell, stood against him as the 'anti-corruption candidate'. Hamilton was booted out, but continued, feebly, to try to clear his name.

However, during its investigation into Hamilton and his stay at the Paris Ritz, *The Guardian* had hooked a bigger fish. Jonathan Aitken, Chief Secretary to the Treasury and once tipped as a future Prime Minister, had also been staying there. His £1,000 bill for two nights had been paid, the paper said, not by Al-Fayed, but by a Saudi businessman named Said Mohamed Ayas, who was staying in a £2,000-a-night suite in the hotel.

Aitken claimed that the bill had been settled by his wife, in cash, and he went on the offensive. In the House of Commons, he called for an end to 'sleaze journalism'.

It was true that *The Guardian* had used underhand tactics to obtain a copy of Aitken's bill. The newspaper had mocked up a fax purporting to come from Aitken's office, using House of Commons' headed notepaper requesting a copy of the bill. The Editor of *The Guardian*, Peter Preston, was hauled over the coals. He resigned from the Press Complaints Commission and was kicked upstairs at Guardian Newspapers.

The Independent then renewed the onslaught. It reported that a company on whose board Aitken sat had been exporting arms to Iran, via Singapore, in contravention of an international arms ban. When the Granada TV programme, *World in Action*, repeated the allegations, Aitken called a press conference. He denied everything and turned on his accusers.

'If it falls to me to start a fight to cut off the cancer of bent and twisted journalism in our country with the simple sword of truth, and trusty shield of fair play, so be it,' he said. 'I am ready for the fight.'

He resigned from the government and sued *The Guardian* and Granada TV.

Meanwhile, the *Sunday Mirror* reported that he had had a fling with a prostitute 15 years earlier. His wife, Aitken said, had forgiven him. Later, a love child he had sired with a friend of the family emerged.

By the time he emerged from the Law Courts, Aitken's simple sword of truth and trusty shield of fair play looked decidedly battered. It came out during the libel trial that his wife had not paid his bill at the Ritz. She had not even been in France at the time and Aitken had asked his wife and daughter to perjure themselves to back his story. His case collapsed, leaving him with massive costs. He later admitted perjury and attempting to pervert the course of justice.

In the meantime, John Major's government, which seemed riven from stem to stern with immorality, corruption and sleaze, was swept from power. Tory sleazemeisters could draw only one shred of comfort from their election defeat. Alan Clark was returned to Parliament as Conservative Member for Kensington and Chelsea. The former Defence Minister was a serial adulterer who had told all in his scandalous diaries. He had also admitted his involvement in government wrongdoing over the Matrix–Churchill affair, where the government allowed businessmen to be prosecuted for illegal arms exports even though, via the Secret Service, it had approved it.

30 ❖ All The President's Women (And Men)

Even Alan Clark's scandalous confessions could not match the sordid details teased out of Monica Lewinsky by Special Prosecutor Ken Starr in his best-selling Starr report. But it is worth remembering that President Clinton was not the first president to be involved in a sex scandal.

The first president, George Washington, set a dizzying standard that few presidents have come close to equalling with the 'Washerwoman Kate Affair'. While the father of the nation was busy fighting the British during the War of Independence he had a congressman procuring for him, so that when he returned from the front there was a young woman waiting to administer the comforts of love. Among the congressman's hand-picked comforters was Kate, who was not a washerwoman herself, but the washerwoman's daughter.

The story broke in the *Boston Weekly News-Letter*. It was picked up by the *Gentleman's Magazine* in London and became the basis of a Broadway play – they must have had big billboards. Washington had a reputation as a serial womanizer. His first lover was an Indian squaw. He went on to have a long affair with the wife of his best friend. During the War of Independence, he took an active interest in the daughters of the household wherever he was billeted.

Among the Revolutionary forces, the French General Lafayette set the tone by bedding the wives of fellow officers. General Lee smuggled girls into Valley Forge, and the distraught wife of the disgraced Benedict Arnold would run around Washington's headquarters naked. Only Washington himself could comfort her.

Much of this was known at the time and used in the propaganda war. Rumours were spread that Washington had many mistresses, both black and white. Since he had no legitimate children it was even said that Washington was a woman in drag. However, there were persistent rumours that two of his staff officers were, in fact, his illegitimate offspring. Washington himself fondly imagined that he might one day start a family if his wife Martha died and he had a new young wife.

Washington's interest in women continued throughout his presidency. Love letters written by the first president to the wife of a former mayor of Philadelphia came to light in the 19th century. And, according to the distinguished historian, Arnold Toynbee, Washington died of pneumonia after catching a chill in the unheated slave huts during a passionate encounter with a black woman.

THOMAS Jefferson, who became the third president of the United States, fathered a second family with his slave girl, Sally Hemings. Although some historians have sought to hush this up, at the time the press indulged in the sort of feeding frenzy we see today.

When his father-in-law died, Jefferson had inherited the old man's slaves. One of them, Sally Hemings, was, in fact, Jefferson's half sister-in-law. Like many Southern gentlemen, the old man had made free with his slaves.

After Jefferson's wife died, he was sent to Paris, where he enjoyed an affair with the artist, Maria Cosway, and a number of other married women. When Jefferson's daughter, Mary, came to Paris, 14-year-old Sally travelled with her as her companion. It was there that the affair began.

When Jefferson was recalled to the USA, he urged Sally to stay in France as a free woman. But she returned with him to Virginia, as a slave. She was already pregnant and went on to bear him five children. This was no secret. When Jefferson entered the White House in 1801, his former friend, the rabble-rousing Scots journalist James Callender, rounded on him in the *Richmond Recorder*. First, he revealed Jefferson's youthful indiscretion with a married woman. When that did nothing to dent Jefferson's credibility, Callender attacked Jefferson's ongoing relationship with his 'black Venus'. He wrote that, in Virginia, Jefferson maintained his 'black wench and her mulatto litter'. He kept another 'Congo harem' in the White House, it was said.

Jefferson went about his business and weathered the storm. He went through with the Louisiana Purchase, doubling the size of the United States at a stroke and opening its expansion to the west. Callender died drunk, in penury. After Jefferson's death, Sally and her children were freed.

DURING the 1828 election, it was revealed that Andrew Jackson had married bigamously. His wife's divorce had not been finalized when they were wed. Jackson was a lawyer; he should have checked. The press had a field day. Although Jackson won the election, his wife Rachel died of shame before he entered the White House.

President John Tyler's wife, however, died after he entered the White House. Within months Tyler was wooing the 'Rose of Long Island' Julia Gardiner, a model who advertised soap. Tyler fought off a challenge for her hand from his sons and they married. Tyler was 54; Julia was 24. During his honeymoon, the press pitied the President his 'arduous duties' and urged him to take rest – from the cares of office. The couple had seven children.

Gossip concerning the President's homosexuality was rife during James Buchanan's tenure of office in the late 1850s. His room mate in Washington was William Rufus De Vane King, Vice-President under Franklin Pierce. King was variously known as 'Mrs Vice-President', 'Miss Nancy', Buchanan's 'better half', 'Mrs B' and 'Auntie Fancy'. And smirking references were made to 'Mr Buchanan and wife'.

James Garfield also seems to have had a gay affair, before joining one of the many 19th-century sects in America that encouraged free love. His political career survived an affair with an 18-year-old journalist on the *New York Times* and, during the 1880 election, the allegation that he had slept with a prostitute in New Orleans. He was shot four months after taking office and died, leaving his widow to defend his reputation.

During the 1884 election, Grover Cleveland was forced to admit that he had fathered an illegitimate child. He was also a draft dodger, having paid a young Polish immigrant $150 to fight in the Civil War in his stead.

Cleveland won the election because his Republican opponent, James G. Blaine, was even more corrupt. Then the 49-year-old Cleveland went on to marry his 20-year-old ward while in office. The press pursued them on their honeymoon, watching the couple through telescopes, while editorials speculated on what a man of Cleveland's age and girth could be doing with a pretty young thing.

Scurrilous pamphlets alleging 'bestial practises' lost Cleveland the 1880 election. But he returned to the White House, with his popular young wife, in 1885. They had five children.

The lugubrious President Woodrow Wilson was a serial adulterer. His first wife died while he was in office and Wilson began pursuing a wealthy widow, Mrs Galt. When he asked her for her hand in marriage, Washington gossips quipped that Mrs Galt was so shocked she fell out of bed. The affair hit the rocks when one of Wilson's former *amoretti* published his love letters. Wilson tried to limit the damage with a sickeningly schmaltzy press release.

More trouble ensued when the *Washington Post* made one of the greatest typos in history. When President Wilson presented his fiancée at their first formal engagement, the *Post* reported: 'The President spent much of the evening entering Mrs Galt.' It meant to say 'entertaining Mrs Galt'.

Warren Harding could just about qualify as America's first – and only – black president. He had a Jamaican grandfather. His racial origins, which he never denied, were a major issue in the 1920 election.

This helped distract attention from his compulsive womanizing. His wife caught him *in flagrante delicto* with a young woman in the coat closet in the Oval Office. Had he not died after two years in office, he would almost certainly have been brought down by the drunken orgies he attended with chorus girls in house on H street. His wife tried to salvage his reputation by burning his papers, but Nan Britton, the underage mother of his illegitimate child, wrote a book called *The President's Daughter*. The Society for the Suppression of Vice tried to stop its publication, until campaigning journalist H.L. Mencken of the *Baltimore Sun* rode to the rescue.

But Harding's corrupt administration was known for a much more famous scandal. Known as 'Teapot Dome', it was billed in 1923 as the 'Crime of the Century'. In 1909, President Taft had created three huge petroleum reserves for the Navy, as a hedge against future shortages. One of the richest was at Teapot Dome, Wyoming. As soon as Harding came to office, his Secretary of the Interior, Albert Fall, took control of the reserves from the Secretary of Navy and began selling off drilling rights for suitable kickbacks. The lease at Elk Hills, Nevada, went to the multi-millionaire, Edward Dohney, who sent his son to deliver a $100,000 'cash loan' to Fall. In return, Dohney expected to double his $100 million fortune.

The Teapot Dome contract would go to Harry Sinclair, who was already worth an estimated $300 million. Sinclair was a generous man. He had bailed out Fall's struggling ranch in New Mexico, giving him six prime heifers and a young bull. When Sinclair received his lease in April 1922, he handed over $200,000 in liberty bonds and $100,000 in cash. It was money well spent. When rivals tried to muscle in on Sinclair's concessions, Fall sent in the US Marines.

Naturally, people began to comment on the Secretary of the Interior's new-found wealth. His ministerial salary was a mere $12,000. Harding stood by him.

'If Albert Fall isn't an honest man, I'm not fit to be President of the United States,' he said.

Fall knew Harding well and did not find these words a comfort. He resigned as Secretary of the Interior, saying he had done all he could do in the job. Harding proposed to appoint him to the Supreme Court, but Fall declined, perhaps fearing an investigation into the source of his wealth during the Senate confirmation proceedings.

Half-a-dozen of Harding's other cronies, known as the Ohio Gang, were under investigation, when in June 1923, President Harding set out on a 'voyage of understanding' across America. In San Francisco, he ate some tainted crab meat and died in the Cow Palace Hotel with his wife by his side. It was soon rumoured that his wife had poisoned him to save him from impeachment.

FRANKLIN Roosevelt sailed closer to the wind than any president in history. Always a ladies' man, during World War I when he was Secretary of the Navy, he seduced his wife's social secretary. When Eleanor found out, she said she would stick by him, provided he gave up his mistress. He said he would. This was a lie and he continued seeing her for the rest of his life.

Roosevelt took this accommodation with his wife as *carte blanche* to take other lovers. But when Eleanor took a lover, threatening his chances in the 1932 election, he got one of his own mistresses to seduce his wife's lover, in order to prevent a politically devastating divorce.

By the time Roosevelt entered the White House, Eleanor had turned lesbian. The press made veiled references to Eleanor's strange 'companion', the cigar-smoking, Bourbon-swilling AP reporter, Lorena Hickok, whose sexual proclivities were no secret. However, during the Depression and then the War, Roosevelt was seen as America's saviour. The press were happy to keep quiet about the Roosevelts' sex lives, just as they made no mention of the fact that the President was wheelchair-bound as the result of polio.

During the crucial days of World War II, Roosevelt and his mistress lived uneasily in one wing of the White House, while Eleanor and her lesbian lover occupied the other. Roosevelt hated his wife's sapphic liaison but there was nothing he could do about it.

One sex scandal did rock the Roosevelt White House, however. Under Secretary of State, Sumner Welles, Roosevelt's envoy to Hitler, Mussolini and then Churchill, was entrapped propositioning a Pullman porter. Roosevelt tried to hush up the affair, but J. Edgar Hoover leaked it, forcing Welles from office.

Roosevelt died in the arms of his lover at their retreat in Warm Springs, Georgia. She packed and fled before he was cold, leaving Roosevelt's reputation untarnished.

PRESIDENT Eisenhower's wartime affair with his army driver, Kay Summersby, was well known by the press. They were often photographed together in wartime Britain and on trips to North Africa, but when he returned to the USA to pursue his political career, he abandoned her.

She hinted at the affair in her 1948 book, *Eisenhower Was My Boss*. And when he ran for office in 1953, she threatened to spill the beans to *Look* magazine. The affair caused a lot of sniggering during the election, but it was only in her autobiography, *Past Forgetting: My Love Affair with Dwight D. Eisenhower* in 1972, that she revealed the full details of the affair.

JOHN F. Kennedy's prodigious sex life is now well known. He always sailed close to the wind. During World War II, Kennedy was kicked out of US Navy Intelligence when the FBI taped him in a hotel room with Danish beauty queen, Ingrid Arvad, a known Nazi sympathizer who, J. Edgar Hoover claimed, was a former mistress of Hitler. Kennedy was transferred to the Pacific where he became a war hero.

His behaviour was extraordinarily reckless. During the Cuban Missile Crisis, when the world hovered on the brink of nuclear war, JFK was in the cabinet room in the White House discussing whether to press the button when a pretty young secretary came in. Kennedy turned to his Secretary of Defense, Robert McNamara, and said: 'Bob, get me her name and her phone number. We may avert war tonight.'

As with Roosevelt, the press covered up for him. Plenty of hints were made about his affair with Marilyn Monroe and the others. A *Newsweek* reporter walked into Kennedy's hideaway in Palm Springs during the 1960 election to find actress Angie Dickinson relaxing on Kennedy's bed. Nothing was published.

Even more scandalous stories were hidden away. Kennedy, the first Catholic president, was a divorcee when he married Jackie. He had married Florida socialite Durie Malcolm in 1947. Kennedy also had daily reports of the Profumo scandal delivered to the Oval Office, marked for his eyes only. He had been involved with some prostitutes in London and was frightened that he might become embroiled.

LYNDON Johnson was even more blatant. He flaunted his infidelity in front of the press, even boasting that he had celebrated signing the equal rights legislation into law by having sex with a black girl in the Oval Office.

'I had more women by accident than Kennedy had on purpose,' he bragged memorably.

In fact, Johnson had only got into the White House because of sexual blackmail. As a senator in Washington, he had lived next door to FBI boss, J. Edgar Hoover, and had borrowed FBI files as his bedtime reading. He knew about Kennedy's wartime affair with Ingrid Arvad.

When Johnson lost the Democratic nomination to Kennedy at the 1960 convention in Los Angeles, Kennedy was not going to put him on the ticket as his running mate. Johnson went to see Kennedy and threatened not only to ruin his clean-living image but also to lose him the Jewish vote. Kennedy capitulated.

'Lyndon, I'm 43 years old,' Kennedy said. 'I am not going to die in office, so the vice-presidency doesn't mean a thing.'

Johnson said: 'I looked it up. One in four presidents dies in office. I'm a gambling man, and this is the only chance I've got.'

Alongside his general promiscuity, Johnson maintained a second family in Texas and he had regular sex sessions in the Oval Office with a female reporter from the *Washington Star*.

When Johnson stepped down, JFK's brother Robert Kennedy ran for the presidency. It was only after he was gunned down in a Los Angeles hotel during the primaries that it was revealed that he, too, had had an affair with Marilyn Monroe, after his brother had finished with her.

The Kennedy clan continued its scandalous saga, which had begun with paterfamilias Joe Kennedy, prohibition bootlegger and one-time lover of Gloria Swanson. With JFK and RFK dead, Edward Kennedy was next in line for the presidency, but his chances died in 1969.

On the night of 18 February 1969, he took off from a party on Chappaquiddick Island, off the coast of Massachusetts, with a young campaign worker, Mary Jo Kopechne. After missing a turning, he skidded off a narrow bridge into the water. He managed to get out of the car. Mary did not. He claimed to have dived repeatedly in an attempt to rescue her from the car, but the surging tidal waters made rescue impossible.

He ran back to the party, avoiding a house only 200 yards from the bridge. Without telling the other partygoers, he returned to the bridge with two friends, Joe Gargan and Paul Markham. They, too, dived on the car, fruitlessly.

Gargan and Markham then returned to the party while Kennedy swam across to Edgartown on the mainland. They assumed he had gone to get help. Instead, he went back to the hotel where he was staying and changed into dry clothes.

The following morning, he again failed to raise the alarm. After drinking a cup of coffee and chatting to other guests, Gargan and Markham came to get him and, together, they took the ferry back to the island.

By this time the tenant of the house near the bridge had called the police. Edgartown Police Chief Jim Arena arrived. Seeing the car in the water, he called for help. Police diver, John Farrar, turned up 25 minutes later. He found the body of Mary Jo Kopechne in the back seat of the car. She was uninjured and had survived, Farrar reckoned, in an air pocket for about an hour before drowning. Had he been called straightaway, Farrar said, she would have lived.

When Kennedy and his two friends arrived back on Chappaquiddick Island, they heard people talking about the discovery of the car. They turned right around and took the ferry back to Edgartown. Kennedy went straight to the police station and reported the accident. Chief Arena had already discovered that the car in the water was registered to Kennedy and was looking for him.

Kennedy told the police that he had not reported the accident earlier because he had been dazed. In court, he pleaded guilty to leaving the scene of an accident and failing to report an accident. He later admitted that he had delayed in the forlorn hope that 'the sense of guilt would somehow be lifted from my shoulders'.

Although Chappaquiddick was not the end of his political career, it was the end of his presidential hopes. When it was mooted that he would stand for the nomination against the desperately unpopular Jimmy Carter in 1980, the *New York Post*, freshly purchased by Rupert Murdoch, brought Chappaquiddick up relentlessly, pushing home the point that, if it were not for Ted Kennedy's presidential ambitions, 29-year-old Mary Jo Kopechne would still be alive.

In Washington, Kennedy's womanizing became legendary. He was once caught making love to a waitress in a restaurant. Bedsheets with his life-size portrait printed on them went on sale. His reckless behaviour came into the public spotlight again when his nephew, William Kennedy Smith, was accused of rape after his Uncle Ted had taken him out on a drinking spree.

Kennedy then had to sit through the conformation hearings of Clarence Thomas with a straight face. Anita Hill, a one-time legal employee of Thomas, charged Thomas with sexual harassment. During the 107-day hearing, which was televised, she claimed that he boasted of the size of his penis, accused her of putting a pubic hair on her Coke can and talking, at length, about a porn movie called *Long Dong Silver*. Thomas was confirmed as a Supreme Court Justice by the narrowest margin ever – 52 votes to 48.

In 1999, Kennedy also sat through the senatorial trial of President Clinton, without once crying out 'good on you Bill'. But then he was in distinguished company. The Senate's oldest member, 90-year-old Strom 'Sperm' Thurmond, had married a 22-year-old beauty queen at the age of 66. Three years later, she was carrying their first child. He claims to have a permanent erection. In the US Senate, the story is that Thurmond keeps a baseball bat in his office so that when he dies, the undertaker can beat his member down to close the coffin lid.

LYNDON Johnson's successor, Richard Nixon, was so deeply mired in the political sleaze of Watergate that his sexual misdemeanours were overlooked – except by his archenemy, J. Edgar Hoover. Before he became president, Nixon had been filmed by British Intelligence having sex with a young Chinese woman in Hong Kong. She was thought to be a Communist agent.

The pictures came into Hoover's hands, which explains why Nixon could never sack him – although he tried twice. Nixon's Chinese woman turned up in the USA for his inauguration. She settled in California, not far from Nixon's home in San Clemente.

President Jimmy Carter caused a scandal by not having sex. During the

1976 election campaign, he told *Playboy* magazine: 'I have looked on a lot of women with lust. I've committed adultery in my heart many times.'

Bill Clinton would probably not think that that counted.

Ronald Reagan lived the feckless life of a Hollywood movie star. While planning to marry the pregnant Nancy, he forced his attentions on 19-year-old Selene Walters, whom he picked up in a Hollywood night-club.

'They would call it date rape today,' Walters told the author Kitty Kelly.

Butter would not melt in his First Lady's mouth either. In the White House, Nancy Reagan masterminded the 'Just Say No' campaign. But *Spy* magazine said that when she was an actress, she gave the 'best head in Hollywood'.

During the 1988 election, it was alleged that George Bush had had a long-term affair with Jennifer Fitzgerald, an aide on his vice-presidential staff. The allegation came from US Ambassador, Louis Fields, who had arranged private accommodation for Bush and Fitzgerald on a trip in 1984. He claimed 'first-hand knowledge of the affair'.

In the 1988 election, the rules were changed, thanks to Democrat hopeful Gary Hart. He was a youthful candidate in the JFK mould. A young Republican voter summed up the situation, when she said: 'My heart is for Bush, but my bush is for Hart.'

Hart made a fateful mistake though. When he was accused of having an extramarital affair, he challenged the press to catch him out. And catch him they did. Reporters from the *Miami Herald* spotted 29-year-old jeans model, Donna Rice, creeping out to Hart's Washington town house one morning when Hart's wife Lee was away. Later they were pictured fooling around on a yacht aptly called *Monkey Business*. Hart abandoned his campaign.

Hart's legacy was that the media dropped their self-imposed restrictions on reporting on the private lives of presidents and presidential candidates, which had been in operation since Franklin Roosevelt's administration. If it had not been for Gary Hart, there would have been no Zippergate. No one would ever have heard of Monica Lewinsky, that stained dress or her novel way of enjoying a cigar.